Methods and Manners
of Cooking

METHODS AND MANNERS OF COOKING

The fundamentals of cooking

presented as an aid to

people who learn

to cook by

cooking

BRUCE H. AXLER

WITH DRAWINGS BY JEAN SIMPSON

FUNK & WAGNALLS   NEW YORK

Published by Funk & Wagnalls,
A *Division of* Reader's Digest Books, Inc.

Printed in the United States of America
DESIGNED BY VINCENT TORRE

Contents

Part 3

SPECIFICS OF PREPARATION

Part 4

APPENDICES

Methods and Manners
of Cooking

Introduction

I suppose that the genesis of this book stems from three rather simple observations:

First, it is impossible to achieve style or sophistication in cookery unless you are completely aware of what you are doing and also know food thoroughly.

Second, the "secret" of fine cooking lies in applying the lesson of one dish to the preparation of another.

Third, good recipes do not make good cooks.

Picasso painted somewhat like Raphael before he began to paint like Picasso. In cooking, as in art, mastery of techniques and a sound knowledge of the medium is clearly a necessary preliminary to developing any individual or creative effort.

Since this book is a summary of the revelations, discoveries, and common sense of cookery that would otherwise have to be won by years of trial and error, it is somewhat autobiographical; the results of my years of trial and error and my training as a professional chef are documented here. Although a summary format and a somewhat didactic style may not reveal it, the days on which I learned, for instance, what I know about egg whites, or broiling, or brown sauces, appear very large on my personal calendar.

I have attempted to present in this book the basic techniques of cooking and the major cooking elements in a manner that in certain ways parallels the learning experience of people who must learn to cook by cooking. Each chapter examines a single topic—beef, or broiling, or brown sauces, for example—so that the experience of an apprentice chef who must spend several months on the broiling station, the sauce station and in the butcher's shop is communicated in readable capsule

3

form. Someone who has learned these fundamentals has at least the background with which to begin to create fine foods.

The secret of fine cooking lies in applying the lessons learned from cooking one dish to the preparation of another. This is the only way to insure a continuing development on one's skills and adding to one's knowledge. The accomplished cook does not approach cooking dish by dish, but sees every complete operation, every foodstuff used, in a larger context. For instance, braising must be considered as it relates to roasting and stewing; making mayonnaise must be seen as related to making butter cakes before the cook can really cook well.

I hope something of this grand scheme has been revealed in *Methods and Manners of Cooking*, for one of the most thrilling moments in cooking comes when individual operations cease to be unrelated and take their place as part of a single integrated method. Accomplished cooks, aware of this larger context, reduce any preparation, no matter how complex or extraordinary, to a series of familiar procedures involving familiar ingredients.

The best of recipes presume a great deal of knowledge and experience on the part of the cook. It is said to be impossible to write a recipe without assuming that the ingredients and equipment available to the cook are exactly the same as those available to the author, that the conditions under which the recipe was tested and is being reproduced are the same, and that there is effective communication between the author and the reader. None of these assumptions can ever be absolutely true; often they may not be true at all.

There is little real understanding of the cooking terms and procedures by the novice cook, and often more experienced cooks are also confused. A perfectly legitimate author will instruct that egg whites be beaten stiff—how? Or that the chicken be sautéd—what does that really mean? Or the author will call for a cup of stock—where does stock come from?

Obviously no cookbook author can deal effectively with these problems individually or every recipe would run for pages, yet there is an obvious need for a way to supply the information required.

That is why each chapter of *Methods and Manners of Cooking* treats a specific operation, a basic preparation, or the characteristics of a category of food in a way that will complement any recipe book by stating once and for all, how to beat egg whites properly, sauté, make stock, and how to master every aspect of an integrated approach to cooking.

I hope that there is enough here to bring any home cook to the point where he can begin to surmount the technical problems of cooking—by

4

thoroughly mastering the fundamentals and transcending the medium so that he can eventually understand the system and order that all accomplished cooks must know; and, finally, to be able to create as he wills.

Once these skills are acquired, the cook can be a master-creator, savoring the joys of cooking and deserving the kudos of the fortunate guests for whom he has cooked. The home cook will find the drudgery of cooking evaporating in the creative excitement of the culinary artist.

PART

1

Basic Procedures

I

Broiling

Broiled preparations dominate the menus of most restaurants. Grilled steaks, chops, lobster, fish, and chicken seem to have more appeal than do the complicated sauce dishes whose places they have usurped. Perhaps because they are somewhat more digestible; perhaps because they take less time to prepare and are prepared to order; perhaps because they are less fattening.

Unfortunately the equipment sold for home broiling—the units utilizing infrared elements—will not produce a steak of restaurant quality. The broiler in the oven of a gas range, although sometimes seemingly designed for maximum inconvenience, still delivers the most satisfactory broiled meats.

As steaks are lightly garnished and often served without any sauce, the meat itself takes on paramount importance. The superior grades of meat, Prime and Choice, are better for broiling than lesser grades because their high percentage of internal (marble) fat keeps the meat flavorful.

Before the meat is cooked, any splinters should be removed, and the steak should be trimmed and wiped with a cloth. The fat should be scored in several places to prevent curling. Frozen meat should be defrosted under oil to prevent bleeding.

Just before cooking, the steak should be oiled with butter or olive oil, to insure the quick formation of crust and to speed cooking. Meat should not be salted as this tends to draw out the natural juices and create steam during cooking, which results in gray meat.

Most authorities recommend that the broiler of the oven be heated to 500°, the steak be seared on both sides by exposure to this heat at a distance of three inches, then the temperature be reduced to 350°, and the steak cooked to the desired doneness. Thin meats may be left close to the grill, but thicker cuts should be lowered. Cooking at relatively low temperatures after searing (which is for appearance, as it does not reduce shrinkage) prevents the burning of the fat surrounding the lean, the charring of the bone, and excessive curling because of a rapid contraction of connective tissue. Meats cooked at low temperatures are also more tender.

Steaks should be served immediately, although thicker cuts can be left to set if they are to be carved. A rise in internal temperature must be anticipated during the setting time (*see* Roasting).

This method results in the most satisfactory steak possible with home equipment, but unlike a professional steak the meat will not be scored by the red hot grate. It may well be grayed instead of being browned (by being steamed by its own vapor), it may taste slightly acrid because of being bathed, in the enclosed space of the broiler, in the acrolein produced by the fat burning during cooking.

Little can be done about this until the manufacturers of cooking equipment decide to improve the efficiency of their equipment as well as its appearance, and to vent broilers properly.

A thick steak is easier to cook than a thin one, and it is much better eating even if cut into slices, because the meat is cooked partially by its own heated juices in the container formed by the seared outside, and because the cook has a better chance of determining the degree of doneness. Meat can be cooked by the time method (*see* Roasting); by the use of an internal thermometer; by touch; or by cutting the meat and observing the color of the juice.

Steaks generally should be turned only once during cooking. A fork may be used in turning if the punctures are confined to the fat; if this is impossible, tongs or a spatula might well be used.

Punctures are much more of a problem when they have been deliberately made in an effort to tenderize meat with some commercial tenderizer. In broiling, most of the advantage gained in tenderizing is lost as the meat loses juice in cooking.

A well-broiled steak will be evenly browned, the fat will be golden, the steak should be puffy rather than shriveled. The flesh should be uniform throughout.

One can cook a steak *blue* (seared on the outside, cold on the inside), *rare* (bloody but with no blue parts), *medium* (pink without any blood), and *well done* (uniformly gray).

The white meats, fresh pork and veal, should not be broiled as they lack internal fat and are full of connective tissue that requires longer

Broiling

A

Unwashed steak treated with butter or oil; fat scored so it doesn't curl preliminary to broiling.

C

Pan-broiling in pan with ridges to keep meat from frying in fat.

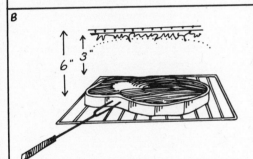

B

Steak seared for color close to flame, then lowered to cook, handled by fork in fat.

D

Greased fish in wire grill for easy turning in broiling.

cooking. When they are broiled, they should be breaded, the breading browned and the meat finished in the oven.

Lamb and mutton are excellent grills. In France, cuts from the tenderloin are available as well as chops.

Ham steaks, liver, kidneys, skewered preparations of meat and vegetables can be broiled, but nothing particularly commends broiling over other methods for these foods.

The term *pan-broiling* indicates the cooking of meat without fat in a heavy skillet by contact of the hot pan directly with the meat. This process, unless done in a pan with ridges along the bottom, usually deteriorates into a form of frying as some fat is rendered from the meat.

Grilling is used interchangeably with broiling. It does imply, however, the use of a metal grill to sandwich the meat being cooked, facilitating turning. Lobsters, fish, mixed grills are best cooked in specially designed grills.

Charcoal broiling has come full cycle since its original popularity. Modern charcoal cookers which are gas fired and use a pumice composition as coal are simply broilers that cook from beneath, without any advantage whatsoever. The very considerable disadvantage is having the fat spatter on the coals and burn, bathing the meat in acrid smoke.

The original charcoal broiler, which used genuine wood charcoal, had some advantage of flavoring the meat with a mild smoke, but it also had the overwhelming disadvantages of awkward fuel, an uncertain cooking temperature, and the undesirable products of decomposition of fuel bathing the meats.

While wood charcoal was bad enough, no case can be made for the charcoal that is a by-product of the coke furnace and adds genuine coal tar to the flavor profile of whatever is cooked. Most charcoal available today is made in a coke furnace.

▼▲

II

Roasting

We must recognize three distinct schools of roasting: French, English, and American. Each method was developed in an effort to make the process we call roasting (which is really baking) as much like the traditional roasting (on a spit) as possible. While spit roasting remains the ideal system, laying a fire, preparing the coals, using a spit and a screen is obviously impractical in most modern situations. We bake or oven-roast instead.

This creates several problems. The most considerable is that the air that surrounds the meat has a different water content and temperature from the air that surrounds a roast cooking on a spit.

Although the efforts of each school have been concerned with dealing with this difference in atmosphere, no one has really been able to duplicate spit roasting. The best that can be said is that, with sound oven-roasting techniques, the home cook can avoid stewing the roast or drying it out, which is a measure of progress.

While the best method for roasting is a combination of all three schools, it remains basically French. Three important procedures should be noted. The French place the roast on a rack so that it has no contact at all with its drippings. This keeps it from stewing in the bottom.

Unfortunately, many roasting pans do not have racks and a rack must be pirated from an old refrigerator, a barbecue, or made specially (at little cost) by a tinsmith. A V-shaped rack for roasting fowl breast down allows the naturally fatter dark-meat of fowl to baste the drier breast.

The French prepare a stock from either the carcasses of fowls or the bones of previous roasts to add to the degreased drippings for gravies. French chefs also lard with bacon where necessary (in lean cuts like

Roasting

A

Meat roasting on rack uncovered with internal thermometer deep in lean.

D

Meat thermometer inserted in thigh of fowl.

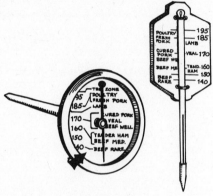

B

Types of thermometers for roasting; spike type (right) can be used for broiling steaks thicker than one inch.

E

Fowl roasting breast down in rack; dark meat bastes lean.

C

V-shaped rack for roasting fowl breast down.

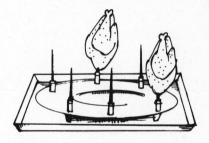

F

Oven spit for roasting small birds breast down.

tenderloin) and protect the breasts of fowl with buttered paper or sheets of fat.

The contribution of the English to roasting is basting and dredging. (Of course, the French also baste—the first three times with melted butter, from then on with the drippings.)

The English baste mutton and pork with a variety of bastings: herbs and red wine; cream and melted butter; yolks of eggs and orange juice; herbs and a liqueur.

Part of the basting process used to be called heeling. The heel or the bottom of a bottle of cognac or red wine was saved and poured over the meat for flavoring about thirty minutes before the roast was finished. Obviously, only the outside was flavored, but this is desirable, and the drippings from the heeling improved the pan juices.

The English also dredge or coat the meat with a paste mixture about half an hour before it is finished: flour and bread; dried herbs and bread; fennel seeds, cinnamon, sugar and flour; sugar, bread and salt. This has the effect of forming a crust which froths attractively when splashed with brown butter and passed under the broiler.

The American school stands as a reversal of some traditional methods. For example, both the English and the French sear or cook the meat at a high temperature to seal in the juices. The latest studies suggest that the loss of weight in cooking is higher with seared roasts than with unseared. My own opinion is that a large joint need not be seared, but small cuts should. The searing of smaller cuts insures that the appetizing crust which the larger pieces have time to develop will form. The object is not to reduce shrinkage so much as to increase flavor and eye appeal.

The Americans do not baste. To my thinking, one need not baste large pieces with a good fat layer like prime ribs, but should baste smaller cuts to prevent drying. If the fat side of large cuts is placed up, the meat bastes itself.

Another interesting conclusion of American food scientists is that long cooking at a low temperature is preferable to the traditional temperatures at 350°. This succeeds in reducing both loss by dripping and evaporation, but, if applied across the board, following this counsel would stretch cooking time beyond practicality. The temperatures recommended in other cookbooks can, however, be dropped 25° to 50°.

A low cooking temperature also insures that the fats rendered from cooking meat will not break down and produce elements that will ruin the pan juices and give the meat the flavor usually associated with burnt-out frying fat.

17

One fact to come out of American research which I can heartily endorse is that salting is not necessary, as the penetration of the salt is minimal. By not salting, one avoids the risk of oversalting the drippings.

In roasting, it is wise to start with a preheated oven and to have the roast at room temperature to shorten the cooking time. It is also wise to truss and tie all roasts to insure uniform roasting. For example, a whole tenderloin will cook unevenly—the tail cooks faster than the head—unless the tail section is folded and tied under the head to produce a symmetric roast.

The use of a meat thermometer is a fairly common practice in America. Cooking by thermometer is far superior to the minute per pound method because it allows for the age of the meat, its ripening, and the condition of the animal. Some judgment is still required of the cook, especially in dealing with rare meat, because the internal temperature of meat *rises* after the roast leaves the oven. Depending on the composition of the roast, its size, and the heat of the oven, the rise might be considerable enough to cook the rare meat medium. Another factor to be considered is the degree of ripening. Unripened meat requires about five degrees more cooking than the temperature recommended on the chart that comes with the thermometer.

The size and shape of the cut is also important. A large cut will take longer, but the minutes per pound necessary for its cooking will be fewer. A flat cut will cook faster than a blocky cut of exactly the same weight. It should be noted as well that the higher the percentage of fat, the quicker the cooking, because fat is a better conductor of heat than red meat.

One must know the meat, estimate by the minute per pound method the time to start roasting, and determine the doneness by the internal temperature, allowing for the rise after the meat leaves the oven.

▚▚

III

Frying

Frying is a difficult culinary procedure because the margin for error is small. In pan-frying, deep-frying and sautéing, there is a moment when an error in judgment, a second's carelessness, dooms the preparation. In the other cooking processes, an opportunity to rectify an error often exists: at worst, an overcooked roast or a watery stew can be eaten. Fried food, however, is either delicious and wholesome, or it is revolting and inedible.

Pan-frying is an abbreviated form of deep-frying. Its relative inexpensiveness is the only thing that commends it. The food is placed in a heavy pan in which fat has been heated. As it has been treated with some kind of breading, a crust is formed on one side, then the piece is turned over and crust formed on the other side. Pan-fried foods are ruined by burning the outside surfaces before cooking the inside, or by placing so many pieces in the fat that it is cooled by the meat and does not form a crust but dissolves the breading, which proceeds to burn, ruining the meat.

To pan-fry successfully, a sufficient volume of oil is necessary to seize all the pieces being cooked, as is a temperature low enough to allow them to cook through.

Deep-frying is much more satisfactory: the food is entirely submerged and cooks evenly. When properly prepared, blotted on brown paper, and served on a napkin, fried foods are not greasy. A leg of lamb, for example, cooked in a sufficient quantity of hot fat (ten or twelve gallons, which would make it a horribly expensive preparation) would be almost indistinguishable from a similar piece of meat treated traditionally. And it could be cooked in half the time.

The fat in deep-frying is kept from penetrating the food, either by coating the article being fried with some preparation which will form an impenetrable crust—batter, bread crumbs, bread crumbs and eggs (*see* Breading And Glazing)—or by maintaining a temperature sufficiently high so that a barrier of steam produced by the food will form between the fat and the piece being fried.

Of course, in deep-fat cookery, there will be some fat absorption. This is minimized, however, by proper cookery. It can also be minimized by reducing the surface exposed to the fat. A round croquette will absorb less fat than a rectangular one of the same weight. A pound of potatoes cut in half-inch sections will absorb less fat than a pound cut in quarter-inch sections.

A fritter is an excellent example of the first procedure. By coating a food that, because of its moistness, could not normally be cooked in hot fat, we protect it. Instead of exploding in the heat of the fat, the food cooks inside a shell of batter, which then expands with the force of the steam from the food. Artichoke bottoms, poached calves brains, wedges of Swiss or Camembert cheese, all the soft moist fruits, are prepared as fritters.

Breaded fish, the hypothetical leg of lamb, any moist or porous food is cooked by this principle.

French fried potatoes and any food which is put, uncoated, into a fryer and does not form a crust itself is properly cooked by maintaining a vapor barrier. The problem that presents itself in this kind of frying is that the items being fried can reduce the temperature of the fat below that required to keep the vapor around the food. The effect is immediate penetration of the food by the fat and soggy, greasy results.

One must either cook very small quantities or use several fat pots. That is, there must be an abundance of fat, a superabundance. Six parts fat to one part food is not too much. In some frites (French fried potatoes) shops in Belgium, there are as many as six pots. As the fat in one becomes cool, the potatoes are transferred to another pot. In the home, obviously, six pots are impractical. However, the problem can be approached from a different direction in any deep-fat frying. If potatoes are soaked in hot water and thus preliminarily heated (they must be patted dry), or another item is heated in a slow oven before being fried, necessarily the fat will not be cooled to the same degree.

Preblanching of some foods will accomplish the same end, not, however, without some undesirable changes in the product.

The home cook should have a standard French fryer: a black metal, straight-sided heavy pot with a matching basket and a deep-fry thermometer which attaches to the side (meter on the outside, bulb on the inside), or an electric deep-fryer with a thermostat.

Frying

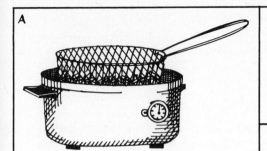

A — Proper deep fat fryer for use on stove, with basket and external thermometer.

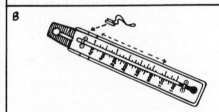

B — Deep fat thermometer that hooks on the inside of any heavy pot.

C — Wire skimmer for removing items from fat when frying is done without basket.

D — Nesting baskets for making potato baskets in deep fat.

E — Timbale maker, which is covered with batter and dipped.

F — Butter which has been frozen in fluted mold.

G — Molded butter heavily treated with breadcrumbs.

H — Breaded butter fried in deep fat until crumbs form solid shell.

I — Butter drained from inside crumb shell in warm place.

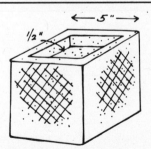

J — Croustade box cut from stale bread and deep fried, then hollowed.

A strainer for removing bits of crumbs and stray pieces of food is also useful.

Judging the temperature of the fat by the point at which it smokes is entirely unsatisfactory. First, because fat cooking is done below the smoking point in most instances, ideally at 25° below, and, secondly, the smoking point of fats varies considerably. It even varies within brands of the same fat. The lard of the five most important meat packers in America varies 90° between the lowest and the highest; none is closer than 10° to any other.

The procedure of putting a piece of bread into the fat and counting the seconds for it to brown, which is widely "recommended," does not take into account the condition of the fat or the staleness (moisture content of the bread). Naturally, if one fries a single item all the time in the same type of fat, a rule of thumb can be worked out, but for general frying a means of determining the temperature accurately is essential.

One can and should work out a table of frying for the particular items being fried in the particular fryer by experimenting with the volume of fat, the cooling power of the items being fried, and the temperature, to determine how long an article should cook. This must be done by the home cook with his equipment, because of the considerable number of variables.

The fat for deep-frying should have three qualities: a high smoking point, a pleasing taste, or tastelessness, and a low rate of decomposition.

Butter is eliminated because it burns at a very low temperature. Also unsatisfactory are cottonseed oil—which is the cheapest widely available vegetable oil but which leaves a ghastly taste—and cheap animal fats or drippings because they are quickly useless.

Of the animal fats, that from around the kidney of veal or beef, which is the richest and purest in the animal, is the most satisfactory. Most professional establishments use this or purified renderings from the fat which accumulates in the butcher shop. Lard, although more or less satisfactory, gives a greasy appearance to food. Among vegetable oils, soybean, corn, peanut, and coconut are widely used.

Peanut oil, which is preferred in France, and coconut oil are adequate for French fries, but have a smoking point dangerously close to the temperature needed to cook soufflé potatoes. As the smoking point becomes lower with usage, these oils are soon too tired to be used. Soybean and even corn oil or commercial compositions are preferable. Olive oil, which is expensive, has the highest smoking point of all, but does give a distinct taste.

A major factor in the decomposition of fat is foreign particles. The life of the fat can be prolonged by straining the liquid oils through a bouillon strainer lined with several layers of cheesecloth. The bottom layer of solid shortenings can be removed, and along with them the embedded particles, when the fat is cool.

The area exposed to the air while cooking is also a factor. If one is making do with a pot converted into a fryer, a deep pot is preferable to a wide shallow one. The fat should be covered when not in use.

Salt should not be used on the article being fried before it is immersed, because this causes loss of water from the food and disrupts the frying.

The home cook might well keep two different fats. One older and darker and more fatigued for fish, which will taint fat, and another cleaner batch for other preparations.

Fatty foods, such as red meats, bacon, or mackerel, which introduce factors of decomposition into the fat, should also be cooked in the fatigued fat. Of course, there are not too many occasions to prepare them in this manner.

The cook does not usually offer a hot sauce with a fried preparation, as the crispness of the food is the keystone of its attractiveness. Cold sauces on the order of tartar sauce are used. Another answer is to serve a garnish with a sauce, for example, a creamed vegetable or a macaroni. Or the food being fried can be preliminarily seasoned either by adding some ingredient to the breading or batter (*see* Breading And Glazing) or by marinating it for a time before cooking.

The *fritots*, for example, pieces of brain, fowl, head, feet, liver, giblets, are treated with lemon juice and herbs, then dipped into a batter and fried. They are served usually with tomato sauce.

Fish can be marinated in lemon juice alone, which will eventually effect a change similar to that which occurs during cooking. Or it can be marinated in milk or cream and seasoning.

Fruits for fritters can be soaked in a liqueur, especially if one is to be used in the batter.

Condiments may also be pounded into meat. Or, the pieces to be fried can be stuffed with some seasoned farce, then sealed with the batter or the breading.

Another rather effective method is to inject, with a hypodermic, a strained reduction of white wine with shallots, or seasoned cognac into the meat.

Fritters, of course, are not the only compound preparation cooked in deep fat. A preparation wrapped in a piece of calf's udder or a crêpe can be cooked by frying. The wrapping may be used as a pouch and then

24

treated with batter, or it can be rolled like a Chinese egg roll and the end secured with some egg white.

Deep fat is used for making a kind of croustade, which is an elegant case cut out of bread, browned in fat and filled with some preparation. Take a cube of day-old bread, about five by five inches, and trim it of crust. Fashion a cover by describing a square on one side, half an inch from the edges and half an inch down. Brown the cube, then pull out the cover, hollow the case, fill it with a preparation, and replace the cover. Cylindrical cases can be cut from bread with a glass and the sides of the cases fluted or otherwise adorned with a sharp knife.

One can also mold various shapes in butter and chill the butter thoroughly in the freezer. Coat the model with crumbs or bread it in any fashion, fry it in very hot fat and then allow the butter to melt out by placing the case on the open oven door. One can then fill these *cassolettes*.

Two nesting baskets are also standard professional deep-frying equipment. The larger is lined with a julienne of raw or partially cooked potatoes and the smaller placed inside it while the potatoes are fried so that a basket is formed.

A special mold designed for deep fat frying is used to make timbale cases in deep fat. These are available in a variety of sizes in restaurant equipment stores.

Rissoles are a preparation of minced fish, meat, or fowl mixed with some vegetable elements and bound, cold, with a thick cold sauce, most often a white or béchamel sauce. They are then wrapped in puff paste or unsweetened short paste in the shape of patties, turnovers, triangles, pockets, and are fried in deep fat.

On occasion, a variety of unusual items can be fried in deep fat: pastry goods—like doughnuts, popovers, bows—white and wild rice, frogs' legs. Items which float should be turned over, to cook both surfaces evenly.

There are two kinds of sautéing. Vegetables, croûtons, mushrooms, which are not expected to contribute to a sauce, can be sautéed in a thin black pan. They are added to a small quantity of hot fat and tossed about in the pan to treat all surfaces. This tossing motion, otherwise called flip-frying, is typical of French cuisine. The Chinese "stir-fry" in a specially designed pan for a similar effect. The food is moved around the pan with a chopstick or a specially designed miniature shovel. There are different degrees of sautéing. One can sweat the article in a small quantity of fat; that is, cook it slowly in fat. Or it can be sautéed until it

25

becomes lightly browned or merely takes color. It can be browned, or seared, or frizzled in very hot fat.

The fat used depends on the article. Butter is often used when it can be, otherwise vegetable oils, bacon fat, stock chicken fat, or the renderings from fowls are employed to give flavor as well as a cooking medium.

Sautés of chops, tournedos, noisettes of lamb, pieces of fowl, which add flavor to the sauce of a dish, are performed in a heavy pan to allow deglazing. This is perhaps the single most important process in cuisine and is used for literally thousands of dishes. The food is fried in a small quantity of fat. The thinner the piece the more rapidly it must be sautéed. When blood appears on the uncooked surface of the meat, it is turned toward the pan and the meat cooked until blood appears on the other side. Then the fat is poured off and the particles adhering to the pan are scraped into it and a liquor (wine or spirits) is added and swished around in the pan, which is then set to boil. An already prepared sauce or some thickening agent may be added, the consistency adjusted by reduction and the sauce finished.

Sautés are ruined if the flame is let into the pan. Burning fat leaves a residue that tastes somewhat as burning plastic smells. Choose a pan that more than covers the fire, so that, despite manipulation over a high flame, the fire does not find its way into the pan. On the other hand, the pan must not be too large or part of the fat will burn, eliminating the possibility of deglazing.

Another variation of the basic sautéing procedure is to brown an article in fat, then pour some of it off and sprinkle the fat or the article and the fat with enough flour to make a roux, which can be developed into a sauce by moistening with some liquid. This is the procedure for some stews (see Stewing).

Sautéing can also be used as a preliminary process for that category of preparation confusingly called in French sautés—confusing because these preparations are only partially sautéed and then completed by stewing or braising. They differ from real stews in that they are deglazed and moistened with an already thickened sauce, and differ from the genuine sauté (of tournedos, etc.), which is only heated in the sauce, not cooked in it.

As these preparations are restricted to veal, chicken, and lamb—the white meats—the word sautés implies a rather quickly made stew of these elements.

For example, one can sauté veal, deglaze it with white wine and add demiglacé; or deglaze with white wine and add brown stock with diced

26

Sautéing

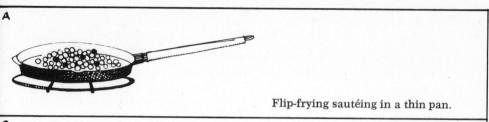

Flip-frying sautéing in a thin pan.

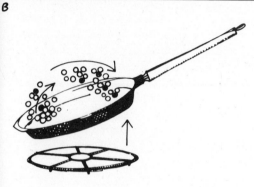

Flipping to sauté all pieces evenly.

Classic sautéing in heavy pan, treating both sides and cooking meat to desired doneness.

Deglazing heavy pan with spirits, scraping bottom of pan to pick up particles before developing (or adding) sauce and returning meat for finishing before going to table.

tomatoes; or sauté lamb in oil, deglaze it with white wine stewed with brown stock, tomato sauce, garlic and onion.

Chicken sautés are popular. Generally the chicken is cut up and the breasts removed from the pan before the thighs, which require longer cooking. The chicken may be finished in the sauce or in the oven and the sauce prepared afterwards. Chicken is usually sautéed white rather than browned for preparations which have a white sauce.

Another form of frying, or at least a cookery process which pretends to be a form of frying, called fatless frying, has occasioned some interest. Whether this is fatless cookery (in which case it could not properly be called frying) is debatable, since a certain amount of fat is rendered from the article being cooked. More important, the real usefulness of this process escapes me. Fats are an important food and an important flavoring agent. Good cooks, cooking properly, do not cause pans to stick; bad cooks are not protected from their negligence: the surface of these fatless frying pans reaches the threshold of decomposition at about the temperature where fats burn. As well, some foods seem to produce a certain amount of steam which remains between the coated pan and the frying food, with very unsatisfactory results.

▀▄

IV

Water Cooking

Boiling would seem the simplest culinary process, yet the cook very seldom boils food. We poach, we reduce, we simmer, we steam, we double-boil, but rarely cook in a boiling liquid.

Blanching, or the plunging of food in boiling salted water, is one of the few examples of true boiling. One blanches to harden the proteins of certain meats like brains, to remove the bitterness of vegetables like chicory, to facilitate the peeling of thin-skinned fruits like peaches. Parboiling is blanching sufficiently protracted to partially cook the food.

The cooking of green vegetables like peas is an extension of their blanching. Water is boiled in sufficiently large quantity to continue boiling even after the vegetables are added: the vegetables are added and cooked at a boil.

In boiling green vegetables, the lid is left off the pan. Since the water boils from the bottom of the pot, there is a circulation of water in the pan as the hottest water moves upward to be replaced by the cooler water above it. When the pan is covered, the upper surface is not cooled by air and the entire mass of water becomes very much hotter—too hot to maintain the color and palatability of green vegetables.

In cooking macaronis and noodles the cover is rather useful. The best way to avoid unevenly cooked or gummy pasta is to boil it for several minutes with a cover and then allow the pot to sit in a warm place until the cooking is complete. Then stop the cooking process by rinsing the preparation in cold water.

Some foods are started at a boil to coagulate some of the protein, thereby conserving a good part of the nutritive value. Boiled leg of mutton (mutton and lamb are more vulnerable than beef to water loss) is boiled for five minutes. On the other hand, when the object is to

Types of Water Cooking

A

Simple water cooking at a simmer; bottom of pot is hottest and cooks fastest, top of pot is cooled by room air.

B

Blanching using a wire basket with water at a slow rolling boil.

C

Simple steam in a vented pot with vegetables on rack to prevent contact with water.

D

Waterless cooking in a closed pot with less water than simple steaming.

E

Poaching fish in a fish poacher with rack and court-bouillon as liquid.

F

Pressure cooking with temperature of pot above boiling point of water.

G

Dry steaming: a foil-wrapped potato, and a parchment-wrapped filet of fish cooking in the oven by their own steam.

prepare a rich broth, the ingredients are always started in cold water to allow those soluble elements to dissolve.

After preliminary boiling, the temperature is reduced to a simmer, because the proteins in the food would harden excessively if cooked at a very high temperature. Other preparations are simmered for the same reason. Stock and soup are simmered because the evaporation of liquid is less marked and the flavor elements are conserved.

Poaching, like simmering, is done at a temperature below boiling. Poaching can, however, be done at a temperature below that of simmering. (In French, and in the strictest sense, poaching must be defined as synonymous with low simmering.) A more significant difference between them is that poaching implies the use of some specially prepared liquid such as stock, or court bouillon for fish.

In many instances, after poaching, the poaching liquid is reduced by rapid boiling to form the base of a sauce. Reduction is best accomplished in a shallow pan, first by boiling, and then by simmering. The shallowness of the pan aids in the evaporation of the liquid by minimizing the extent of the liquid above the boiling layer which tends to condense the steam as it passes through.

There are three types of cooking by steam: the suspending of a food in a sieve or some other device that permits the passage of the steam; the so-called waterless cookers; and the use of pressure in a specially designed pot.

In straight steaming, the pot is free-vented and no pressure builds. The food is cooked in an environment of steam, which also carries away some of the flavor and most of the soluble surface nutrients.

In waterless cookery, the pot is closed and the quantity of liquid used substantially reduced, thereby reducing the flavor loss. An extension of this process, dry-steaming, is often employed. For example, a potato wrapped in foil is dry-steamed—cooked by the heat of the steam produced within the wrapping. Clams wrapped in a parchment sack and boiled are dry-steamed as well. This procedure is superior to waterless cooking in that even in the best waterless cookers some of the food is cooked immersed.

In pressure cooking, which was all the vogue some years ago, a small quantity of liquid is used and the food cooked under pressure. This capitalizes on two distinct physical phenomena. The first is used in any steam cooking: steam when it condenses on food gives the food the heat that turned the original water into steam, so steam at 212° is far more effective in cooking food than water at the same temperature. The unique aspect of pressure cooking is a higher boiling point.

Unfortunately, while pressure steamers have a considerable professional use, home pressure cookers are extremely limited. They are effective in cooking tough meats because the fibers are mechanically softened by the pressure of the steam being forced into meat, but slow cooking is at least as effective and has the advantage of developing flavor. The pressure cooker is not particularly good for fruits or green vegetables.

When these pots are generally equipped with an adequate and accurate pressure gauge, a broader utility could be projected. But as many critical cooking times must be determined by the moment when the weight jiggles, and as a jiggle is a highly questionable unit of measurement, pressure cookers are not advised.

In discussing cooking in a liquid, there is an assumption that one is dealing with pure water at sea level. Of course, this is almost never the case. The most obvious problems is altitude; the boiling point drops about one degree for every 500 feet increase in elevation. Water in Denver (with an altitude of 5,280 feet), for example, boils at 201°F. Most of the recipes in classic cuisine were developed at below 2,000 feet. The cooking times must therefore be extended; a filet of sole needs a longer time to poach; a filet of beef a longer time to braise; and an artichoke a longer time to steam. Unfortunately, there is no simple formula for determining how much longer as the fashion in which different food reacts to the lower boiling point depends on its water content.

When a recipe fails, this should certainly be among the first things to consider. It should be reworked, increasing the cooking time 5 percent, then, if necessary, 10 percent and so on.

Substances dissolved in the water also complicate the cooking by raising the boiling point. A certain amount of consideration of the density of the cooking liquid is necessary, although all signs will indicate a gentle simmer, a nice gelatinous stock may be hot enough to harden the proteins in the food to the point of unpalatability.

34

▀▼

V

Braising

Braising is a misunderstood process. It has fallen from favor because of a confusion about method. Whatever the refinements, braising is the cooking of meat, moistened with liquid, in a closed pot. The traditional method demanded that all the ingredients that figure in the ultimate sauce be included as part of the braising. In effect, this meant that additional pieces of meat were added to the meat being braised to contribute to the sauce, then they were discarded. To avoid this waste, chefs of the last century added already prepared stock to the braising. Often the problem in the home has been how to braise without the expense of auxiliary meats and without already prepared stock.

There is a compromise method. As braising often involves a period of marination of four or five hours, the home cook can start a stock, and add this almost-stock and bone mixture to the meat as the braising liquid. The result is satisfactory although not quite up to either of the other methods, because the cooking time is insufficient fully to extract the flavor from the stock elements.

Braising even under these circumstances is worthwhile because the results are very professional and the cuts of meat involved are relatively inexpensive: the chuck, brisket, plate, and rump of beef; the shoulder and shanks of veal; older fowls; and any of the variety meats.

There are two types of braising, "black" and "white": the braising of beef and mutton, and the braising of veal and fowl.

The cooking of mutton and beef is the more complex. In France the first step is always the introduction of strips of bacon into the meat, *le piquage*. In America, where the meat is rich in fat and well marbled with internal fat, it is not necessary although desirable. Really proper larding is beyond the skills of most cooks, but the same result is attained simply by making slits with the grain of the meat and forcing bits of fat into them.

The second step is marinating. The meat is placed in a container just large enough to hold it. Sliced onion, sliced carrots, parsley stems, bay leaf, and thyme are added. The meat is then covered with red or white wine depending on the ultimate sauce. Usually, it is red wine.

At this point a stock can be started (*see* Brown and White Sauces). If a stock is available, all the better.

After five hours of marinating, during which the meat should be turned, it is removed and dried. The meat is then seared thoroughly in hot fat. This third step is extremely important for it insures that the meat will not lose all its juices to the braising liquid.

The fourth step is the preparation of the accompanying vegetables and the braising pan. Pieces of carrot and onion are browned. The marinade is reduced to a fourth of its volume. A pot with a tight fitting lid that approximates the size of the meat and vegetables is chosen. A layer of bacon is placed on the pot's bottom, then a layer of vegetables and some of the bones from the stock. The marinating liquid is strained into the pot, the meat settled in place and the pot filled almost to the top with the stock. For color, add a half cup of tomato purée. Another valuable addition is a boned and blanched veal foot to give a gloss and pleasing texture to the sauce.

In the fifth step the cooking is started with a boil to fix the surface protein (this is done on top of the stove), and it is continued after the pot is removed, covered, to an even moderate oven. The dish should cook about twenty to thirty minutes a pound, but a great deal depends on the age of the meat being braised, and the pot should be closely watched.

The sixth step in braising is taken after the cooking is two-thirds completed; the meat is removed from the liquid. The sauce is degreased, reduced, and thickened. The veal foot is often removed, cooled, and chopped into the strained sauce.

At this point, the finished sauce, the meat and aromatic spices— thyme, savory, sage, tarragon, chervil, according to the dish being prepared—are returned to a rinsed braising pot. Sometimes the final garnish is added to cook with the meat, especially if it is a root vegetable (most braising garnishes are) like carrots, turnips, potatoes, or onions, and pieces of slab bacon (lardons). Other garnishes like cauliflower, cabbage, artichoke bottoms, or spinach should be cooked separately.

At this stage the sauce should not cover the meat as the object is to

Larding, Barding, and Trussing

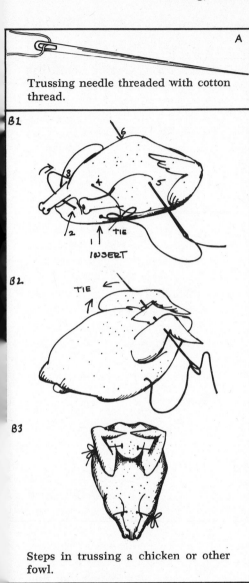

A

Trussing needle threaded with cotton thread.

B1

B2

B3

Steps in trussing a chicken or other fowl.

C

Trussed and larded fowl.

D

Fowl covered with a thin bard of bacon and tied.

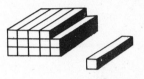

E

Lardons cut from chilled block of bacon.

F

Lardon inserted in larding needle is pulled through meat.

G

Dowel knife or boeuf à la mode needle.

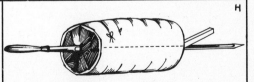

H

Cut of beef being prepared using dowel knife and lardon.

force some of its juices into the sauce; the meat should be basted, however, to prevent excessive drying.

Finally, the seasoning is corrected with salt and pepper, the garnishing is arranged around the meat, some sauce is poured over the dish and the entire preparation glazed under a hot broiler.

White braising of veal and fowl differs in three respects from the braising of dark meats. Veal and fowl are not marinated, white stock is used, and the meat is not browned, it is sweated.

The object of sweating is to force some of the juices into the braising liquid. It is accomplished by preparing the pot with a layer of bacon, raw diced carrots and onions, by adding the meat and cooking it covered for twenty minutes, taking care to avoid all browning. Then a glass or two of white wine is added. Again with the object of forcing some juices into the meat, the wine is reduced to almost complete evaporation. The meat is then moistened with the stock and a second reduction is performed, with the same goal. Finally, the remaining stock and bones are added to fill the pot two-thirds full. Then the preparation is brought to a boil, and the procedure from there on parallels that of dark meats.

Although the terms braising and pot roasting have often been used interchangeably, some distinction should be made. Pot roasting, as the term implies, is much closer to roasting than braising, as the quantity of liquid involved is less in pot roasting than in braising. In fact, a badly roasted meat, one that has been allowed to cook in liquid to form "gravy," is effectively a pot roast.

As a rule, very tough cuts of meat do not lend themselves to pot roasting as the cooking time is shorter and the full benefits of moist cooking cannot be expected. Pot roasting is reserved for dishes of relatively tender, flavorful beef which need not be completely braised.

A process related to braising—*poêlage*—has often been translated as pot roasting. This is essentially an error as *poêlage* refers to a specific type of braising, with a specific supplemental preparation: lean ham, diced bacon (without rind), and lean veal are cut in a dice and sweated in fresh butter with onions cut in slices and peeled seeded lemons. It is essential that the mixture does not brown. It is then simmered with good stock, and a *bouquet garni* of bay, clove, thyme, basil, mace, pepper, and garlic (in a cheesecloth) for two hours over a very slow fire. After this mixture is forced through a sieve, it is used to moisten and dress the large fowl traditionally prepared by *poêlage*. A white braise with the *poêlage* mixture as the moistening element follows.

▀▄

VI

Stewing

Stews by definition are preparations of meat, vegetables, and seasoning cooked by moist heat. The difference between braising and stewing as procedures concerns the size of the meat. Large cuts and whole fowl and variety meats are braised, while small cuts, disjointed fowl and cut up meat are stewed. As well, stewing is generally done on the top of the stove in an open pot while braising is definitely done in a closed pot. Stews are often one-dish courses, or even one-dish meals, while braises are definitely composed of a major element and garnish.

In French cuisine, the broad category of stews (ragoûts) is further divided. Stewing is a process. Each of the major types of stew indicated below is, in effect, a name given to a variation of the process. We have the ragoûts themselves, the civets, the sautés, the salmis, the daubes, the fricassées, the matelotes, the étuvées, and the salpicons.

Ragoûts are of two types. Brown ragoûts are prepared by searing and browning chunks of meat in hot fat until the meat is well colored. Some of the fat is then poured off and flour added to form a kind of roux around the meat. Some liquid—stock, consommé, or water—and appropriate seasonings are added. The preparation is cooked in an open or covered (but not sealed) pot until the meat is tender but not completely done. At this point the liquid is strained and colored with caramelized sugar (blackjack, or a commercial product) and the garnishing vegetables added. Finally, when the meat is tender and the vegetables fully cooked, the sauce is seasoned and the consistency adjusted.

The combinations of protein elements, vegetable elements, and seasoning are almost infinite. Navarin de mouton; mouton aux navets (turnips); mouton à l'oriental (with saffron, eggplant, tomatoes, and garlic); veau aux écrevisses (veal stewed and garnished with cooked crayfish, finished with crayfish butter); ragoût de poulets are all examples of this preparation.

The other kind of ragoût is called English-style stew in French (ragoût à l'anglaise). It differs from the brown ragoût in that the ingredients are not browned and the stew is not thickened either with flour or roux but by the potatoes which are among its elements. Irish lamb stew is in this category.

The *civets* are distinguished by being thickened with the blood of the major element or with pork blood for meats and chicken blood for fish, should the original blood by insufficient or unavailable. The blood can be kept from curdling by the addition of vinegar.

Cut the meat, and brown it with onions and shallots. Flame the preparation with cognac, then moisten it with red wine and brown stock. Most civets are then garnished with bacon cubes and tiny onions. Cook the mixture to reduce the sauce and to tenderize the meat. The speed of cooking and the intensity will depend on the type of meat. Just before the dish is finished, in the case of rabbit or hare, one adds the liver finely sieved. As the food is going to the table the blood is poured in and the thickening accomplished.

Civet de mouton (shoulder), civet de saumon, civet de boeuf (rumpsteak), are all practicable, but most civets are done with small furry game.

The *sautés* are prepared with tender portions of veal, lamb, and chicken cooked first in hot fat. The fat is poured off and the contents of the pan moistened with some liquid, usually stock or an already prepared sauce like curry, hongroise, cream, etc. Then the meat is stewed in the sauce.

In a sense sautés are not proper stews as they are initially cooked in hot fat, making them fried dishes as well. They bridge the two procedures, just as salmis bridge roasting and stewing.

Salmis, which are generally, but not necessarily, restricted to game birds, involve two cooking processes: roasting and stewing. First the birds are partially, or almost entirely, cooked (depending on how long the rest of the cooking takes). Game birds are disjointed and simmered in a sauce. Often, in grand class restaurants, the carving of ducks, prepared as salmis, or the disjointing of birds and their final cooking take place in front of the client.

To make a salmis, roast the bird, detach the breasts, legs and wings from the carcass. In the case of grouse types, remove the skins, as they will make the sauce bitter. Take the carcass, some chopped onion, carrots, and celery, and brown them in butter. Moisten the preparation with white wine (red is occasionally used), reduce the preparation until almost dry, cook with game stock and finish the sauce with a little demiglace sauce. Strain it, and stew the pieces of bird in the sauce. Serve the dish with a canapé spread with a purée of the bird's liver, heart, and intestines.

One makes salmis of quail, pheasant, duck, grouse. But the word *salmis* can be applied to a dish of lobster or langouste which is grilled then finished in a sauce (generally cream).

Daubes were originally prepared to be eaten cold. To that end they are prepared as braises to produce a sauce which will gel. The meat is marinated, browned, and placed in a pot that can be sealed. There is a special daube pot, but an ordinary tight casserole can be closed with a flour and water paste. Vegetables, bacon, stock, and the reduced strained marinade are added. Generally, daubes are served as is, so the vegetables are arranged with the meat in layers. The dish is cooked at least six hours to almost melt the meat. A pressure cooker accelerates the process; whether or not it improves the dish is moot. A veal foot can be added at the beginning then boned and chopped into the dish before serving, to give luster.

Daube Provençale, for example, is made with beef marinated in white wine with garlic, cognac, and oil. Cooked with chopped onions, bacon, mushrooms, coarsely chopped tomatoes, black olives, and dried orange rind.

One can cook fresh pork, turkey, duck, veal, or goose *en daube*.

The *fricassées* are white stews prepared without browning the meat. The meat is, however, seared by immersion in hot butter. Then flour is added to make a roux and the dish is moistened and cooked. It can be finished with cream, and buttered. *Blanquettes*, which like fricassées are made of white meats like veal and poultry, are not seared. They are given a characteristic taste by the addition of cloves to the cooking, and a thickening of egg yolks in cream with lemon juice.

Matelotes are fresh fish stews for the most part. Matelote panachée is moistened with white wine (à la marinière) or with red wine (à la meunière), seasoned, heated, and flamed with cognac. The dish is cooked according to the type of fish, then the sauce is strained, the fish put aside and the sauce reduced and thickened. The *meurette* of Bourgogne and the *pochouse* or *pauchouse* of Franche-Comté are regional matelotes thickened with beurre manié (butter worked with flour); other matelotes can be otherwise thickened. *Waterzoie* is a matelote of eel, carp, and pike.

Sometimes a fricassée made with a beurre manié is called a matelote even if it has chicken or veal as the major ingredient.

An *étuvée* is a stewed preparation much like a fricassée or a matelote, except that the ingredients are sweated in some fat to extract the juices, then are moistened and stewed.

Salpicons are stews of choice morsels, often as not entirely cooked before being assembled and little more than heated in some savory sauce. They are used to fill pastry shells, as hors d'oeuvre, as stuffings. Examples are foie gras and truffles "stewed" in madeira sauce, shrimp in béchamel sauce, tongue and truffles in demiglace.

A final classification of stews is rather less well defined than the others. These stews consist of meat that is already cooked and reheated in a sauce. The most notable examples are *salmagundis,* several different meats heated together; the *capilotade,* different pieces of fowl simmered in sauce; the *miroton,* slices of beef covered with a sauce and heated in the oven or broiler.

Many regional preparations in French cuisine would seem to be distinct types of stews; rather they indicate preparations that fall within other categories. For example a *carbonnade* is a brown ragoût moistened with beer, while a *navarin* is a brown ragoût of lamb; the famous *cassoullet* and the less famous *estouffat* must be called étuvées, while *estouffade* is a daube, because there is no technical variation in their preparation that can be otherwise applied.

VII

Thickening

The consistency of a sauce is an important element in its flavor. As the liquid from cooking, be it braising, poaching, stewing, sautéeing, or roasting, is usually too thin to be pleasing, the sauce is completed by reduction and thickening.

Reduction (*see* Water Cooking), or the simmering of a sauce until its volume is reduced, thickens the sauce to some extent and adds savoriness, mellowness, and subtlety to the taste. During reduction, the sauce also throws off impurities, becoming "brighter."

Except in the instance of a preparation having self-thickening properties, like pea soup, a supplemental thickener is needed. There are three major types of thickening: those which rely on the gelling power of a starch—roux, simple starch, mustard, bread crumbs or bread are in this category; those which rely on partial coagulation of protein, for example liaisons with egg yolks, cream, blood, the creamy parts of a lobster; and those based on the partial solidification of a fat, like butter, or even peanut butter.

Starches vary widely in their thickening power, clarity in the sauce, and the texture they contribute. Flour, the traditional thickening agent in American kitchens, is among the least desirable. It is inefficient: a vast amount of flour is required to thicken a small quantity of sauce, and it contributes a floury taste. The sole permitted use in French cuisine is in the thickening of gravies for roasted meats.

Make a loose paste of flour and water and strain it into the pan. Cook the mixture with the appropriate seasonings until the gravy is adequately thick and the floury taste is substantially gone.

Pastry flour having a high starch content is superior to bread flour for thickening purposes as the gluten in bread flour develops in the gravy.

Eight ounces of cake flour will thicken as well as ten ounces of bread flour.

Thickening with a cornstarch or arrowroot mixture in water is a fairly common practice in American kitchens, even among French chefs. In France it is rarely used. The sole exception that comes to mind is Sauce Bigarade, the traditional sauce for duck.

Both arrowroot and cornstarch produce sauce with a peculiar translucence. They are generally mixed with a small quantity of cold liquid, well agitated, then added to the hot sauce in an effort to avoid lumping.

Other starches—rice starch, popular in the Orient; potato starch, used in Teutonic cuisine; tapioca, used in the tropics; sago, used in candy making—all perform similarly.

The home cook must not cook the starch beyond the point where the preparation loses its starch taste. Prolonged cooking of a thickened preparation will break down the starch liaison. High temperatures and a high acid content of a sauce will have the same effect.

Potato granules intended for use as "instant potatoes" will thicken, although there are few opportunities to introduce this particular flavor.

Bread crumbs and bread were once quite in vogue for thickening. Their disadvantages are obvious; they are not pure starch and a good deal more is required. In cookery today, bread is used in making bread sauce for fowl and horseradish sauce for meat by boiling the bread in milk or cream and then straining and seasoning and enriching the resultant sauce.

Bread crumbs also figure in some dishes like Carbonnades à la Flamande. A piece of toasted bread is spread with mustard and placed on top of the cooking stew. It melts into the mixture to thicken the sauce.

Mustard, which is sometimes used in small liaisons where no great thickening is needed, contributes an attractive flavor and thickens because of the mustard flour used in its preparation. Steak Diane is prepared in some restaurants with a mustard liaison.

Roux, or flour fried in butter or oil, is a considerable improvement on flour. Roux is made by melting six parts of butter and adding five parts of flour to it. Cook the mixture, stirring constantly, until butter and flour fuse into a homogeneous white, blond, or brown mass. The darker the roux, the better is the thickening power. However, white sauces require a very white roux. Most stocks are thickened with roux to produce the mother sauces of French cuisine, which are, in turn, added to the products of the actual cooking. For example, roux is used to thicken a stock made from fish meat, bones, and heads. The stock is stored. When a fish dish is being prepared, some of the thickened stock is added to the poaching liquid.

Escoffier was the first to suggest that rather than making roux from flour, it could be made from a purer starch, like cornstarch or arrowroot. The procedure and the uses are the same; the same amount of pure starch roux is simply twice as effective.

Roux is an extremely controllable liaison. Two tablespoons of roux to a cup of liquid would result in a thin sauce or soup liaison while a medium thick liaison is accomplished with three tablespoons, and a thick sauce with four tablespoons. The roux is not as vulnerable to the reaction of the other ingredients in the preparation as other starch thickeners, since the starch has been partially developed by the fat.

A quantity of roux may be made ahead of time and stored with some success. However, it is extremely important that the roux be cooled very fast in cold flowing water, if it is to maintain good efficiency.

While butter is the most frequently used fat for roux making, any fat is effective; but the flavor it will impart to the sauce must be considered. Often roux which are to be stored are made of some hydrogenated fat which has already been stabilized and will not deteriorate as fast as butter. Goose fat or chicken fat can be used to make roux to be used for thickening fowl stocks and ordinary sauces.

Buerre manié is a convenient liaison for small quantities of sauce and for thickening the pan juice produced in sautéing. Softened butter is worked with an equal quantity of flour to form a smooth mixture. It is then rolled in small balls which are tossed as needed into the sauce until the liaison is made. The sauce is simmered for a few minutes to lose the flour taste, and the seasoning is adjusted.

Egg yolks are excellent binders and they contribute a distinct velvetiness to soups and sauces in which they are used. Unfortunately, the egg liaison is very delicate. It is usually added at the last minute and often on top of another liaison. For example, in blanquette de veau the sauce which is primarily thickened with beurre manié is further thickened by adding egg yolks beaten to a foam with a little cream and a few drops of lemon juice. After this liaison is made the preparation cannot be heated above 160° without risking curdling.

Cream alone is used to thicken sauce because in reduction it becomes thicker. A very effective liaison, which is more stable than a plain egg yolk thickening, can be made with three parts cream to one part egg yolk. Otherwise, heavy cream or acidulated cream which is already partially thickened (see Incidental Ingredients) is added to the cooking liquid or pan juices and reduced until a liaison is made.

46

Steak au Poivre is made in most Paris bistros with a cream liaison. Ground white peppercorns are forced into a sirloin steak or filet mignon. The steak is cooked in very hot butter, then the pan is deglazed with cognac and cream (crème fraîche) added.

Dry milk solids will also thicken although much less efficiently than cream.

Blood liaisons are more common in provincial cookery than in the classic cuisine primarily because the blood must be fresh. The general procedure is to drain the blood from the animal, say a hare for a civet de lièvre, and keep it from turning during the cooking of the dish by adding a few drops of vinegar. The notable blood liaison in formal cuisine is for pressed duck. The carcass of the bird is pressed to extract the blood which is used to thicken the cooking liquor produced by the breasts and thighs.

The roe and tomalley (liver) of lobsters and other crustaceans is a very effective liaison that need not be limited to those preparations which have a crustacean base. The creamy parts are reserved and forced through a fine sieve and then added to the preparation. Game sauces can be thickened with this liaison.

Most sauces made in the sauté pan after the meat has been cooked lend themselves to a treatment of beurre maníe and butter or cold butter alone. The basic procedure involves cooking the meat, pouring off the grease, deglazing the pan with wine or spirits, adding either water, stock, or cream, and then thickening the sauce with a lump of cold butter. For example, in making escalopes de veau à la Normande, the veal cutlets are cooked in butter, the pan is deglazed with apple brandy (Calvados), cream and mushrooms are added, and the sauce is then reduced and thickened with butter.

The butter in a butter liaison must be very cold, and quickly added away from the fire to make a good liaison. In binding vegetables with butter, after the vegetables have been sautéed, toss them in the pan with cold butter.

Often a butter liaison is used as the final touch on a dish, thickening by another liaison, especially a cream liaison.

Peanut butter will work almost as well as butter because it is quite solid at room temperature. In African cuisines it is widely used as a flavoring agent and liaison.

▀▄

VIII

Seasoning

Considering the immensity of the classic repertory, very few seasonings are used in the classic kitchen. The diversity of French cuisine lies more in the variety of the food products available in France: the fish from her seas, streams, and lakes; the mushrooms and game of her woods; her vines and her vegetables; and in the skill of her chefs.

Unfortunately, top-quality products are rare and costly and almost unavailable outside France. Consequently, more and more chefs, cooking traditionally, are turning to exotic seasonings to increase the possibilities of somewhat limited material. This is not entirely regrettable. The gourmets of the last century, foremost among them Brillat-Savarin, were looking forward to enjoying the integration of spices and foods of foreign countries with classic cookery techniques. It is essentially healthy for classic cuisine to continue to evolve. What must be condemned, however, is the indiscriminate use of spices—and always with a heavy hand—in a classical dish that can be perfectly executed. It is one thing to add a little dill to a sauce for salmon, and quite another to overwhelm a sole Dugléré with cumin or poppy seeds.

Home cooks are often guilty of this particular sin; the temptations of the spice rack are too strong, holding the never fulfilled promise of hiding bad cooking with strong seasoning. It is far better to cook well and develop the natural flavors of food, than to rely on doctoring poor cookery.

Spices should be purchased in extremely small quantities because their deterioration is rapid, another reason why collecting spices in racks is not to be encouraged. Spices should always be purchased from purveyors who continue to get fresh supplies. Spices should be stored in airtight containers. In purchasing spices, they should be sniffed for potency and carefully examined for the color deterioration which generally indicates weakening.

When the seasonings are crushed or broken for use, an effort should be made to keep the volatile oils from dissipating. For example, in making marinades, the spices should be crushed and crumbled *under* the surface of the liquid.

When possible, spices should be bought whole and then ground at home as needed, in a mortar and pestle. The deterioration of ground spices is much higher than that of whole spices.

Another procedure which maximizes the flavor in the spices is pan frying, actually toasting, in a heavy clean frying pan to make the oils more available.

Fresh green herbs can be bought in season when they are at their best and cheapest, chopped, squeezed dry in a towel, and frozen one layer thick on a flat pan. When they are frozen, they can be removed to a jar and kept in the freezer. Each chopped leaf will be separate. Blanching may be useful depending on the freezing facilities and on the anticipated storage time.

The basic stock of seasonings for cooking almost all classical dishes consists of the spices listed as follows. They should be purchased in quantities sufficient for a month.

SEASONING	USE
Basil (Basilic) Annual herb of the mint family. Bright green leaves up to 2 inches in length.	Used for almost all tomato sauce dishes; excellent addition to vegetables, soups, potatoes, asparagus, carrots, squash, poultry dishes.
Bay (Laurier) Leaf of the laurel tree. Shiny green fresh leaf, up to 3 inches long.	Almost the universal seasoning, used in making stocks, court bouillons; part of the ubiquitous bouquet garni.
Cayenne (Poivre de Cayenne) A ground orange-colored very hot red pepper.	A touch of powdered cayenne will add flavor interest to any white sauce, brown sauce, hollandaise sauce, mayonnaise, cold sauce, or egg dish.
Chervil (Cerfeuil) A lacy fernlike herb between parsley and tarragon. Sold whole.	Important herb in Béarnaise, cold sauces like Tartar sauce, sauce Verte, etc. Used in salads, stuffings, omelettes.

49

SEASONING	USE
Cinnamon (Cannelle) Dried bark, bought in sticks of a reddish brown. Also ground.	Used in baking, with fruits, with chocolate confections, and occasional sweet sauces for meats.
Cloves (Girofles) Dried, unopened bud of an evergreen tree, recognized by nail-like shape. Rich brown.	Most current use is in blanquette de veau to contribute to the "confectionary" taste. In whole form almost always introduced into the dish by forcing the clove like nails into a half onion. Also used in custards, pastries, picklings, and in some marinades.
Curry (Cari) A blend of spices containing allspice, black pepper, chili pepper, cayenne, ginger, cinnamon, cardamom, coriander, mustard seed, fenugreek, nutmeg, saffron, and turmeric. Exact blend varies with brand. Good personalized curry can be made by choosing a high quality brand and adding additional seasoning.	Several curry dishes exist in French cuisine for lobster, turbot, and lamb. Curry is helpful in very small quantities for white sauces which taste of flour. Often it is moderated by the addition of a fruit juice to the preparation: apple, orange, coconut.
Garlic (Ail) Garlic bulbs should be well-filled, heavy for their size. Three kinds are available; the strong white Creole, the small pink Italian with small kernels, and the large Tahitian. Use of powders and extracts is not counseled.	Used moderately, garlic is an ideal background flavor that is unnoticeable except by its good effect. Most of the "problem" with garlic can be resolved by cooking the garlic slowly in whatever cooking fat is being used for the dish and then withdrawing the garlic. When it is browned, or—worse—scorched, or allowed to remain too long in a sauce, it develops that characteristic objectionable taste. Used in stocks, pickling, marinades, brown sauces.

SEASONING   USE

Ginger (Gingembre)

The root of a tropical perennial, it is available whole, cracked, or ground. In whole form, it can be rubbed on food.

Some sauces for meat, pastry, fruit dishes; possibly in some roasts and stews. Requires cooking to release flavor.

Mustard (Moutarde)

Purchased as prepared mustard, powdered mustard, and whole mustard. Whole mustard can be ground and mixed with wine, water, or fruit juices. Prepared Dijon mustard is widely used.

Used in salad dressings, in preparing meats à la diable, in sauce piquante, in cold sauces like Cumberland, and sometimes as a liaison. Prepared mustard should be added to hot dishes at the last minute as prolonged cooking reduces its flavor.

Nutmeg (Muscade)

The seed of the nutmeg fruit which also yields mace. Nutmeg is bought whole and grated as needed.

Used in preparing some vegetables as hors d'oeuvre, like artichoke bottoms; for Quiche Lorraine. It has the virtue of relieving "flatness" in white sauces, especially in creamed vegetables.

Onions (Oignons)

Dry onions are of two principal varieties; the early Bermuda or Spanish onion which is sweet and mild; the late or northern (globe) which is more pungent. Dry onions should be bright, well-shaped with clean hard dry skins.

Onions are used constantly in cooking in the preparation of every course. They can be peeled by quick blanching. The smaller the dice, the less pungent the flavor in raw use.

Paprika (Piment doux)

A mild pepper. Hungarian is darker than Spanish. Color is an important consideration.

Used widely in decoration, for "browning" fish, potatoes, and for relieving white salad sauces. It adds a sweet spicy taste that gives richness to soups, gravies, and veal stews. Used in many dishes of Hungarian origin or pretensions (à la Hongroise).

Parsley (Persil)

Purchase fresh or dried (some-

Certainly the most widely used herb. A garnish, part of the

51

SEASONING

USE

times freeze dried). Two types: curly and broadleaf.

bouquet garni for stocks, in "herb" sauces, butter sauces, compound butters, etc.

Pepper (Poivre)
One should have white and black pepper. Whole is preferred, ground for use: the finer the grind—the more available the flavor—and the shorter the shelf life.

Absolutely universal uses.

Sage (Sauge)
The leaves of a member of the mint family. A sweet herb. Sage comes whole, rubbed, and ground. Rubbed sage is fluffy and supposedly has a superior flavor to ground.

The leaf form is useful in stuffings, especially those involving sausage meat. Powdered sage used sparingly improves weak brown sauces.

Salt (Sel)
Common salt is generally purchased in containers and is free running. Sea salt, which contains other salt compounds than sodium chloride is also available.

No taste is as personal as the use of salt in cooking. Season to taste is the only fair prescription in recipes. The cook fulfills his obligation if he adds only enough salt to bring out the flavor of the food, leaving the final seasoning to the diner. As a general rule, one might consider one teaspoon for every quart of sauce or soup; one tablespoon for the cooking of every pound of pasta; one half teaspoon per pound for cooking vegetables. Salting in roasting and broiling is not counseled.

Shallots (Echalotes)
A member of the onion family. It has a mild onion taste with overtones of garlic. Purchased in pints. Same standards as dried onions.

Part of the foundation of classic cuisine, shallots can be peeled, run through a food grinder and sautéed until tender in peanut oil without much loss of flavor. They are then used in sauces,

52

SEASONING	USE
	soups, sautés, dressings, etc., as needed.
Tarragon (Estragon) A member of the aster family, the long slender dark leaves have a faint taste of anise. Sold fresh and dried, whole.	Used in many cold sauces; in making tarragon vinegar; for herb sauces; compound butters and, of course, in sauce Béarnaise as the dominant herb.
Thyme (Thym) The leaves of a small bushlike plant. Sold whole and ground.	Along with bay, a spice for all sauces as part of the background taste. Used in making stocks, poaching fish, white sauce dishes, vegetable soups.

The kitchen stock of seasonings can be enlarged by several spices if they are used with some regularity. Used carefully, respectfully, and moderately, they will add considerably to the repertory.

One way of having a limited supply of a number of fresh seasonings is to buy crab boil or pickling spice that contains at least twenty whole spices. Certain ones are easily recognizable—fragments of bay, caraway, peppercorns, allspice, dill, celery seed—and can be picked out of the mixture.

Auxiliary Spices in French Cuisine

SEASONING	USE
Allspice (Toute-Epice or properly Poivre de la Jamaïque) The dried berries of an evergreen. Sold whole and ground.	With a taste of cloves, cinnamon, and nutmeg, allspice berries enhance the flavor of vegetable-based soups (pea, carrot) and can be used in the braising of large pieces of meat, in the preparation of stock for brown sauces (especially when the bones are not from old animals). Never use more than two berries to a quart.
Caraway (Carvi) Sold whole. Brown seeds curved and tapered, about 3/16-inch long.	Baked goods. Caraway figures in German, Swedish, and Balkan cuisines. Can be used quite

53

SEASONING	USE
	satisfactorily in the cooking of cabbage, broccoli, Brussels sprouts, and cauliflower.
Celery Seed (Graines de céleri) Tiny brown seeds. Available whole or ground, or ground with common salt.	Ground celery is used in fish sauces, in mayonnaise-based salad dressing. Useful in improving flavor of weak brown sauces for veal.
Dill (Aneth) Available fresh, dried, or as dill seed. The seed is small, oval-shaped and tan-colored.	Fresh dill is used in salads, with vegetables, with fish. Seeds can be added to cream soups, purées of vegetables (carrots, turnips, peas).
Fennel (Fenouil) Available either fresh or dried, or as fennel seed. The seed is long and oval; flavor resembles anise.	Gives a subtle licorice flavor that is pleasing in boiled fish, creamed spinach, cabbage, omelettes.
Monosodium Glutamate Available under its generic name and under several brand names. Seasoned or plain.	Monosodium Glutamate should be used extremely sparingly and never in more than one dish in a meal as it tends to fatigue the palate. A touch of MSG or one of the preparations containing it does develop some flavors.
Marjoram (Marjolaine) A gray-green herb sold whole and in powdered form.	Used with vegetables, lamb, mutton, and small birds.
Oregano (Origan) A herb much like sweet basil with light green leaves ⅝-inch long. Extremely popular since World War II.	Used like basil.
Rosemary (Romarin) A gray-green narrow pine-needle-like leaf. Sold fresh and dried.	Used with lamb, chicken, vegetables, citrus fruits. Very little is needed.
Saffron (Safran)	Used in bouillabaisse and saffron rice. It makes good background flavor in lamb and veal preparation, giving them an

54

SEASONING   USE

Oriental feeling which is not
undesirable. One or two
filaments heated in the cooking
oil before browning the meat
will be sufficient. Effective in
chicken-based soups.

▼▲

IX

Breading, Coating, and Glazing

By breading or flouring meat or fish, by dipping foods to be fried in a batter, by sprinkling bread crumbs or cheese on some sauce dish, the home cook adds new dimensions of color and texture to a dish. By sealing the juices in a crust, these processes also play an important role in the cooking of some foods.

Flouring is the basic process. Thin slices of meat, veal cutlets, calf's liver, are floured to give them a pleasing color. The meat is simply laid in seasoned flour. For fish or frogs' legs the food is dipped in milk and rolled in flour. Shaking the food in a plastic bag or paper sack with flour is also effective.

Crumbs of white bread, brown breads, or crackers are used for pieces like chops and chicken parts. The color is a good indicator of the flavor; dark crumbs are strong.

For frying, the food is dipped in beaten eggs mixed with water, and then rolled in the crumbs. If salad oil is used instead of water, the coating is more adhesive.

For broiling, the food is dipped in melted butter, then in bread crumbs.

Breading, English style (à l'Anglaise), involves using the yolks of eggs mixed with an equal volume of butter.

Milan-style breading (à la Milanaise) consists of four processes. The food is dipped in melted butter, then flour, then beaten eggs and finally in a mixture of half Parmesan cheese and half bread crumbs. The heavy breading makes it necessary to press the meat after breading to insure that it adheres.

Split baby turkey, beef ribs, game birds, can be treated à la diable by coating the food with good Dijon-style mustard, dipping it in beaten egg yolks, then rolling it in brown crumbs.

Cornflakes make excellent breading as they seem to adhere well, and remain crunchy despite treatment with sauces. Other baked goods are suitable as well: pork chops breaded with gingersnap crumbs are quite excellent. Food must be fried immediately after breading, before the crust gets soggy.

Batters are used in deep-frying. The basic batter is a mixture of flour (sifted), salt, oil or butter, and enough tepid water to mix it. This batter should be mixed rather than stirred to preserve its plasticity. It can be improved considerably if white of egg is beaten to a froth and added just before the batter is used.

For deep-frying vegetables egg yolk is added to the basic batter (the whites are not used).

For frying fruits (pineapple, apple rings) use some beer instead of water, or add brandy or any liqueur and beaten egg white just before using.

Another good fruit batter can be made by adding brandy and egg yolks to the basic batter and then beaten egg whites.

When batter is frequently used, it is worthwhile keeping a yeast batter working. To start it, add a packet of yeast dissolved in some warm water to the basic batter. When it begins to ferment add flour, a little oil, and enough water to restore its consistency.

Bread crumbs or a mixture of bread crumbs and grated Parmesan cheese are used for stuffed broiled vegetables or macaroni, creamed vegetables, and some sauce dishes to form a light crust which adds interest to the texture and improves the appearance. Butter and bread crumbs; bread crumbs sifted with paprika; bread crumbs mixed with parsley and garlic make useful gratin. Crushed cornflakes although sweet are quite effective.

The English use a series of similar preparations to dredge roasts a half hour before they are finished to make a crust (*see* Roasting).

Glazing of foods is another effort to improve the appearance. Boiled tiny onions and artfully shaped baby carrots are glazed with caramel, by heating some clarified butter or oil, adding sugar, and allowing it to caramelize, and then rolling the vegetables in the pan.

Large pieces are glazed by reducing the sauce (from braising or roasting) and coating the upper surface of the meat with the reduction, then passing the whole dish under the broiler. *Glace de viande* (*see* Brown Sauces) is similarly used.

Sometimes the basting liquid in roasting effects a glaze; for example, basting ham with pineapple syrup and crushed pineapple glazes as well as flavors the ham.

Brown sugar, cider and maple syrup, melted currant jelly, honey, mustard and brown sugar, applesauce, and orange marmalade are also among the possible glazes for ham.

Broiled meats can be glazed with plain butter or compound butter as both will give a pleasing shiny finish to the broiled meat (*see* Cold Sauces).

Butter heated until it browns and gives off a hazelnut aroma is a good glaze for meat or fish which has been previously cooked and is now being reheated.

In hors d'oeuvre preparations, a light covering of well-flavored clear gelatin will prevent excessive drying if it becomes necessary to prepare the hors d'oeuvre long before serving.

In desserts, gelatin serves as a coating for fruit tarts, to give them that glossy bakery appearance. Apricot preserves are also used to give a pleasant yellow glaze.

▚▞

X

Baking

Unlike other cookery processes, baking involves relatively pure substances in precise chemical relations with each other. Each of the ingredients, their proportions, their handling, and their treatment when combined, will be reflected in the product.

Cakes, pastries, and some breads contain sugar which sweetens, makes the baked product more tender, and gives color to the crust as the sugar is caramelized. Sugar also tends to aid in retaining moisture and makes the bakery product keep longer. Too much sugar, on the other hand, will mean a dark hard crust.

Other sweetening elements can be used. Honey, for example, can be substituted for as much as half the sugar called for, if one compensates for the moisture introduced by the honey, which is 25 percent water, and for the somewhat reduced acidity of the mixture (more cream of tartar, for instance, would be necessary).

Flour acts as a binder for the other ingredients in the mixture and gives form to the final product. Several types of flour are available (*see* Incidental Ingredients)—bread, cake, all-purpose, in many brands. The baking properties of any flour depend on the grain from which it is milled, the fineness to which it is ground, its aging, and the chemicals added to it by the miller. As far as the home cook is concerned, the ratio between the protein—the "gluten"—and the starch is the most important factor. A high gluten flour will make a tough elastic dough, good for bread, bad for pastry and cakes. In fact, it is the gluten with which the cook is constantly concerned. For example, if the water and flour are not well mixed in a pastry, too much water will come into contact with the gluten. Or if the pastry is stirred the gluten will be developed. Piecrusts are crumbly, dry, stringy, mealy all because of gluten development.

Milk is sometimes used in bakery goods, but some bakery products, especially cakes, are apparently "dry" because the eggs and shortening (when it has melted during cooking) contribute all the necessary liquid. Insufficient liquid will result in a tough cake.

Eggs are an extremely important ingredient. They effect the volume, texture, structure, grain, flavor, and color of a baked product. Egg yolks and egg whites, when separated, play different roles. In general, the eggs combine with the protein in the flour (whatever there is) to form the structure of baked goods as the essentially protein eggs firm during cooking.

Egg whites, in the bakery products which contain them, are, of course, a leavening agent. Whole eggs and yolks are tenderizers because of the relatively high fat content of the yolks.

Shortening, although it does not enter into all pastry goods, plays a tenderizer role where it is used in cakes. Butter and hydrogenated shortenings are used in cakes. Butter because of its flavor, hydrogenated shortenings because they lend themselves to the creaming method of mixing and encourage leavening action by holding a great deal of air. "Emulsified" hydrogenated shortenings, in common with egg yolks, have a similar leavening effect by emulsification.

Butter for pastries is not wholly satisfactory, as it is not 100 percent fat and introduces water into the preparation, which develops the gluten. In pastry use, butter should be washed by kneading it under cold running water to remove some of the liquid and some of the milk solids.

Lard although extremely popular as shortening is not standardized, and there is a risk of spoiling the preparation by introducing unknown qualities. It also seems to work out on the board, substantially altering the flour/shortening proportion. Other animal fats like bacon drippings and chicken fat are good, but they should only be used by an experienced pastry cook who has the feel for dough and can judge when there is sufficient fat mixed with the flour.

Chiffon cake, the only really unique pastry product of modern times, is shortened by vegetable oil.

Some measure of leavening is required for cakes and breads. Most breads are leavened by the action of the yeast, a live organism which produces carbon dioxide as part of its growth process.

In other baked goods some of the leavening comes from air captured in the batter, water vapor produced in cooking, from air beaten into egg whites, or from baking powders and baking sodas.

The classification of baking powders and baking soda depends on the type of acid used to neutralize the alkali produced. In baking soda, for example, sodium bicarbonate plus the acid gives a sodium salt, water,

and carbon dioxide. The speed of this reaction is described on the can as
fast acting, slow acting, or double acting (*see* Incidental Ingredients).
In general, it can be said that quick mixing (mix the dry ingredient first,
then all the dry ingredients with the liquid) and immediate baking in a
hot oven are necessary to obtain the best results from tartrate and
phosphate leavening agents.

Flavorings are not essential in the production of bakery goods, many
of which rely for their flavor on combinations of major ingredients.
Some flavorings are used: orange water, extracts, spices like vanilla,
ginger, cloves.

Accurate measurement of ingredients in baking is a must. Most
authors of baking recipes will carefully define the specifics of measurement. Almost all will consider that a cup of sifted flour refers to a cup of
flour which has been accumulated under the sifter and has been leveled
off, while shortening is measured in hard-packed cups. In most cases
medium-sized eggs are considered as average. Cups of liquid should be
measured *full* and completely emptied. Sugar should be spooned into a
cup then leveled off. The cook must resist the temptation to pack or tap
the cup as this will substantially change the measurement.

In any cake recipe by a reputable author, measurements must be
followed exactly below 2,000 feet. Although the rule is that above 2,000
feet one should reduce the leavening agents by 15 percent and after that
by 5 percent for every 500 feet, this is almost impossible to compute
when one is dealing in fractions of a teaspoon. The best course is to
convert whatever leavening agents are called for into sweet milk and
baking powder and reduce the quantities by an eighth of a teaspoon
(this is 12.5 percent of a teaspoon) and work from there.

Eggs should be increased by 2.5 percent after 2,500 feet. Practically,
this means the addition of one teaspoon of egg for every cup of eggs (48
teaspoons = a cup = 5 eggs) initially, and then by a like amount for
every 1,000 feet.

The mixing of ingredients in baking is of prime importance, as it
determines the sequence of chemical reactions.

Most mixing procedures as indicated in common cake recipes can be
reduced to three distinct types:

The sugar-batter method consists of creaming the fat and the sugar
until light and fluffy, adding the eggs and continuing mixing until
thoroughly combined, adding the mixed dry ingredients alternately with
the liquid, mixing the preparation thoroughly after each addition.

The dough-batter method involves creaming fat and flour, adding a
mixture made of sugar, salt, baking powder, and half the milk, and

61

mixing. Combine whole eggs, flavoring, and the remainder of the milk, and add the second mixture to the first.

The sponge cake method consists of beating the eggs and sugar until the mixture peaks. Adding the liquid (whatever there is), then the flour, and finally folding in egg whites.

In pastry preparations, especially in making pies, mixing operations are designed to minimize the development of the gluten by keeping the entire mixture cool—ice water is used, the marble slab is chilled, the dough is chilled—and by keeping the liquid out of contact with the gluten as much as possible—cutting the shortening into the flour with a pastry cutter, adding the water after chilling and just before rolling out.

In rolling pastry doughs, either sticky dough or short, nonsticky doughs, basically the same procedure is used. Soft doughs, however, must be floured on top and rolled on a floured board to facilitate the work, while short doughs can be rolled between sheets of wax paper to avoid incorporating more flour into the dough.

In either case, shape the dough as desired and roll with an even pressure from the center to the edge then in the opposite direction. Then roll diagonally to insure that every part is rolled evenly. (Sticky doughs require more force than short doughs.) The basic procedure is the same even when the dough is rolled out after resting a dough that requires several "turns," like puff paste.

If the dough begins to stick, or if it does not spread evenly from the center, loosen it with a knife. Do not turn over a pastry dough (except when it is between sheets of wax paper) or the flour picked up from the board will alter the proportions. Always use the same type of flour on the board and in the dough.

When using the dough, take care not to stretch it; rather use enough dough for the preparation and keep any trimmings for decoration or small baked goods.

Although baking must include consideration of all these other incidental operations, by the strictest definition the term is confined to the processes occurring in the oven.

While tremendous improvements have been made in professional ovens, manufacturers seem to have concentrated on making home ovens easier to clean. Many are still without reliable thermostats. But the real problem of home ovens is uneven heat. A really good professional oven does not vary four degrees from corner to corner. The only defense against this problem is small-batch cooking in the middle of the oven.

That is in the middle of the middle shelf, with a reliable oven thermometer perched next to the baking pan.

Consideration must also be given the material of the baking pans and their shape as they will effect both the cooking time and the heat reaching different parts of the baking.

If tin is the standard, baking times must be shortened for enamelware, lengthened for aluminum and further if the aluminum is bright and new, and shortened for glass. (*See* Kitchen Equipment.)

PART
2

Basic Preparations

▝▝

XI

Brown Sauce and the Small Brown Sauces

Brown sauce is the foundation of several score of sauces and, through them, is the basis for several hundred dishes. Among these dishes are the preparations most appreciated in restaurants, yet this side of French cuisine is almost totally avoided by the home cook or prepared with incredibly hedged recipes. The crux of the problem is that the preparation of *demiglace*, or perfected brown sauce, takes approximately twenty-four hours and some attention. The whole process need not be completed in one day; operations can be suspended after the making of brown stock and then again after the brown sauce is completed. The third and final step, the making of demiglace, takes only an hour and a half.

To make brown stock, one starts with four pounds of beef shin (both flesh and bone), four pounds of veal shin, one pound of coarsely chopped onions, one-half pound of chopped celery, and one-half pound of chopped carrots. Two cloves of garlic, one bay leaf, several stems of parsley, and a pinch of thyme are tied in a cheesecloth to be added to the stock.

The bones must be absolutely fresh; so must the meat. The least bit of taint will communicate itself to the stock.

Bone the shins. Reserve the meat, cut the bones into small pieces. Brown the bones (both veal and beef) in the oven until they are slightly caramelized but neither brown nor burnt. Remove the bones to a large heavy pot. Brown the vegetables in the fat rendered from the bones. Add them to the pot with the seasonings. Fill the pot with five quarts of water (*it must be cold*). Bring the water to a boil, skim, reduce the heat.

Simmer the stock slowly for ten hours, skimming and degreasing periodically.

Brown the meat from the beef shins in some of the stock fat. Remove the meat to another pot and strain the stock into the pot. Discard the bones. The preliminary cooking time (of the bones) may be shortened. The stock will be less savory but the "bony" taste, which some individuals do not like, will be reduced. Cook the meat to extract all its juices. Skim the stock while the meat is cooking. This takes two hours. Strain the stock through a fine strainer. There should be about four quarts. The first step has been completed. This strained stock can be kept for several days. If it is thickened it can be kept longer and used as the foundation for braisings and stews like daube Provençale, estouffade, carbonnades, etc.

Game stock is an ordinary brown stock made with the neck bones of deer, hare trimmings, and an old partridge or pheasant. Veal gravy is very adequate as a substitute for game stock. Often, roasted game birds are simply deglazed with cognac to retain the exact flavor of the bird.

The second step in the making of demiglace is the perfecting of brown stock to make brown sauce (Sauce Espagnole). Take three quarts of brown stock (reserving one quart) and heat it in a saucepan. Stir in one-half pound of prepared roux. Allow the mixture to boil, but place the pan so that one side bubbles while the other remains calm. A scum will form on the calm side. Remove it. Continue to simmer the stock until it begins to look less murky and somewhat lighter. This takes about six hours.

Add one pound of good ripe tomatoes, two cups of tomato purée, one chopped carrot, one chopped onion, one chopped piece of celery, all browned in butter. Cook for another two hours. At this point the volume should be about two quarts.

Strain it. Reduce the sauce to one-and-one-half quarts. This takes about two hours. Strain the sauce again. The second step has been completed.

The brown sauce should be thoroughly degreased. This can be accomplished by first cooling the sauce, stirring constantly in cold flowing water (in a pot in the sink), then refrigerating it and removing the grease when it has congealed, or by scrupulously cleaning the surface of the hot stock with an ice cube wrapped in a kitchen towel, then cooling the sauce and refrigerating it. The sauce should never be covered when hot. The brown sauce can be kept for several days. It can be used effectively in finishing the sautés mixed with the deglazing liquid.

68

Making Demiglaze

(Brown Stock, Espagnole Sauce, Demiglaze, Glaze)

Bone (but not meat) cooking with bouquet garni(A1).

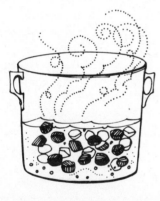

Bones removed from liquid, meat chopped fine and added; reduced to 4 qts. (after straining).

1 qt. of stock reserved.

Three qts. of stock cooked with tomatoes, carrots, tomato purée, onions and celery chopped fine; reduced to 2 qts.

Strained stock from (D) reduced to 1½ qts. Espagnole sauce.

Reduced sauce from (E) plus quart of reserved stock (C) reduced to 1½ qts. of demiglaze.

Demiglaze reduced to 1 pt. of meat glaze.

Brown sauce can also be frozen.

To make demiglace, take the one-and-one-half quarts of brown sauce and the stock reserved in step one. Combine them and simply reduce the mixture to one quart. During this reduction the stock should be skimmed, degreased, and strained once. This takes about two hours. The demiglace is finished. Tradition demands that it be buttered and a half cup of sherry be added. Unless it is going to be used immediately, don't butter it. Unless the sherry is really top drawer, don't add it.

Good demiglace has a strong, clean taste, good rich color, clarity, and a satisfactory consistency. The two errors most often made are inadequate degreasing and the introduction of either burnt bones, roux, or vegetables.

If demiglace is further reduced it becomes *glace de viande*, meat glaze, which has the consistency of rubber when cold. Small quantities of meat glaze can be used to enrich sauce made with brown stock and in stews and braisings that are weak.

Among the sauces that can be made with demiglace are:

Antin: Madeira sauce combined with chopped shallots reduced in white wine and garnished with truffles, cooked mushrooms, and fine herbs.

Bercy: Shallots reduced in white wine, plus demiglace, butter, and blanched beef marrow.

Bigarade: Reduced orange juice and lemon juice plus deglazing liquid from duck roasting pan, duck stock, demiglace garnished with zest or orange and lemon.

Bordelaise: Chopped shallots, thyme, bay leaf and white peppercorns, moistened with red wine, reduced three quarters plus demiglace, butter, beef marrow, and a few drops of lemon juice.

Bourgeoisie: Demiglace plus tarragon, vinegar and mustard.

Chasseur: Sliced mushrooms, chopped shallots sautéed in butter, reduced in white wine, plus demiglace, butter, and parsley.

Chateaubriand: Shallots, thyme, bay, reduced in white wine, strained, plus demiglace, butter, parsley, and tarragon. *Chartres* is like Chateaubriand but without shallots; *Colbert* is Chartres with lemon juice instead of white wine.

Diable: Chopped shallots, white peppercorns reduced in white wine and vinegar, plus demiglace, strained and finished with mustard and fine herbs.

Duxelles: Chopped onions and shallots sweated in butter, reduced in white wine plus demiglace and tomato sauce, chopped mushrooms,

71

chopped parsley. *Italienne* is Duxelles with the addition of chopped ham.

Lyonnaise: Chopped onions sweated in butter, reduced in half white wine and half vinegar, plus demiglace. *Hussarde* is Lyonnaise with the addition of raw ham, garlic, horseradish, and chopped parsley.

Madère: Demiglace strongly flavored with madeira wine. *Demidoff* is Madère with truffles; *Forestière* is Madère with mushrooms; *Périgourdine* is Demidoff with truffle essence.

Pauvre-homme: Demiglace with shallots, parsley, chives, and bread crumbs.

Piquante: Shallots reduced in half white wine, half vinegar plus demiglace with the addition of cayenne pepper, chopped pickles (or pickle relish), tarragon, and chervil.

Porto: Demiglace plus port.

Smitane: Reduction of wine vinegar, white wine, white peppercorns, and chopped onion sweated in butter, plus demiglace with sour cream added.

Zingara: Demiglace plus tomato purée, cayenne pepper, madeira, and garnished with julienne of mushrooms, truffles, ham, and beef tongue.

XII

Gravies

Although most of what passes for gravy tastes like coffee thickened with library paste, good gravies have an important place in fine cookery. Roasts, especially roasts of beef, generally have enough character to be simply garnished; a sauce of the juice exuded during cooking, or a sauce prepared to approximate it, suitably seasoned, is enough.

Ideally, the gravy for a roast would be made entirely of its own juices. However, two problems present themselves. The juice is not especially abundant if the roast is cooked properly, and the roast overcooks in the time it takes to prepare the gravy after the roast is taken from the oven.

Many cooks in an attempt to solve these problems, add water to the roast during the cooking, a considerable error as the roast is then converted into a stew. Actually the roast should be on a rack, and the drippings allowed to collect below while a basis for the gravies is being prepared. Then this base element can be combined with the natural juices from the pan and some of the fat.

This fat, incidentally, is as important as the juice. A beef gravy should not be confused with a consommé; it should have some fat to add savor to otherwise lean meats. If the drippings are not burnt in the roasting, some of them may be used; otherwise, bacon fat or clarified butter is added.

The most obvious vehicle for the natural juices produced by the roast is a broth made from the trimmings of similar roasts. In professional kitchens the bones of prime ribs are saved to make gravies. In the home, scraps of beef and beef bones can be roasted and then set to simmer for three or four hours, cleared of grease and strained.

If available, sauce Espagnole that is not dominated by a tomato taste can be used as a gravy base (*see* Brown Sauces).

When none of these methods is practicable, a base can be made from a commercial preparation: gravy bases, bouillon teas, canned bouillon or consommé. Unfortunately, when made strong enough to approximate good gravy stock, these products have a rather distinct taste, somewhere between licorice and tobacco juice. A liberal dose of monosodium glutamate seems to reduce this flavor, perhaps by fatiguing the taste buds.

A number of companies make products for professional use which seem to be better than those purchased in retail stores. Perhaps these will be made available. In purchasing any product (professional or consumer), it should be recalled that the label lists the ingredients in order of proportion. The first listed item has the largest percentage. A remarkable number of commercial gravies have more salt than anything else.

Only the color—the rich brown that is almost impossible to get without a little chicanery—really commends these gravy products. The most traditional method originated for coloring pot-au-feu is to *burn* some finely chopped Spanish onion and mix it with the gravy, then boil them together until the desired color is achieved. The color is great; the flavor is not now in vogue.

Equally traditionally, one can mix browned bread crumbs in the gravy, coloring and thickening it.

There are several commercial preparations that are adequate but seem to add a lot of incidental flavors.

Flour roasted in the oven will work.

The most common method is coloring with blackjack, or caramelized sugar. It can be purchased as "sugar color" or easily made by browning a pound of sugar in a heavy pot over a moderate heat and adding six cups of water and boiling it into a thick syrup, which can be stored in bottles. Or an old spoon may be heated red hot, a thick sugar and water mix dropped in, and the spoon used to stir the gravy.

Thickening gravy is a matter of taste. When it is thickened, the most practical method is to make a roux with some of the drippings and a little less than the same quantity of flour. The roux can be cooked white, blond, or brown (the taste of gravy will be slightly different) and then added to the gravy and the mixture stirred well. Figure on about a tablespoon of roux for a cup of gravy and boil them together for a few minutes.

There is absolutely nothing wrong with using cornstarch, arrowroot, potato starch or a roux made with any of these (*see* Thickening).

74

Having made a base, having colored it, and perhaps having thickened it, one can combine it with the natural juices of the roast.

The roast is removed and the roasting pan tilted so that the grease may be taken off with a ladle or a spoon. Then the prepared gravy is poured into the pan with the juice and sloshed around. The mixture can be heated so that the particles which adhere to the pan are freed. Then the gravy is strained. Care should be taken to observe that the pan has not been burnt somewhere in cooking. In that case, the natural juices are tasted, and if found good, added to the gravy base.

For roasted game birds, the drippings are degreased, the juice separated, and the pan washed with cognac. Then the juice and a gravy base, if desired, are combined with the washing liquid. Gravy for other roasts may be prepared similarly by washing with sherry, port, or cognac.

All sorts of seasoning can be imposed on a gravy. Salt, pepper, tomato, mushroom, or black walnut ketchup, bottled steak sauces, Worcestershire sauce, chili sauce, powdered horseradish, curry powder, garlic juices, mushroom essence, etc. Herbs, like parsley, chervil, and tarragon, may be added. Dried fruits, like peaches, apricots, raisins, and currants. Nuts like walnuts, almonds, filberts, and peanuts. Compound butters can be used instead of clarified butter or drippings.

Jellied gravy is the ideal accompaniment to cold meats. For this no fat is added. Most gravy will gel naturally; others may be gelled with gelatin or, preferably, by cooking a veal foot with the gravy base. For cold use, gravy is more highly seasoned than for hot.

XIII

▼▲▼▲▼▲▼▲▼▲▲■■■■■■▲▲▲▲▲▲▲▲▲▲▲▲▲▲▲▲▲▲▲▲▲■■■■■■▲▲▲

Tomato Sauce

The brown, the white, and the emulsion sauces all have varieties based on some tomato preparation: whole tomatoes, tomato sauce, purée, fondue, essence or extract. Tomatoes add savor, flavor, color, and brilliance to any sauce; to any braising; to any stew, and even to a deglaçage.

Fortunately for the home cook, tomato products are excellently prepared in almost all countries; Italian products, which are probably the best, are widely available.

Whole tomatoes are available in solid pack (no liquid is added), tomatoes with purée (purée added), and tomatoes with juice (juice added). The most economical brand among several might not be the cheapest, as the same size can will contain a different proportion of tomato and liquid. Several brands should be carefully examined (after being drained) to determine which one gives the most tomato for the money.

Tomato paste is also available in a variety of packs. Heavy is the thickest, then medium, then light. Light and medium are often (depending on the brands) closer than medium is to heavy.

Tomato purée is always less thick (contains less tomato solids) than paste. Light purée may contain as little as a third as much tomato as heavy. Brands will differ considerably. Good quality paste should have a good red tomato color, odor, flavor, and be free from specks of stem pieces and seeds.

Tomato sauce is not as well-controlled as paste and purée and may well have a concentration of tomatoes. In all the samples examined, it proved to be the least economical way of purchasing tomatoes with which to flavor.

Tomato juice is the thinnest preparation. It can be used effectively (and economically) in moistening small preparations; or in diluting cold sauces, as it does not have the characteristic cooked tomato taste peculiar to paste, purée, and sauce.

In purchasing tomatoes for home cooking the Italian plum meat varieties are best. The tomatoes should be just ripe for making sauces, preferably vine-ripened as these are much superior to those shipped to market green. When purchased, they can be ripened in the sun on a window sill. Tomatoes with white portions do not ripen. Bruised and overripe fruit is unsuitable for cooking. Before making sauces, remove stems, dark places, and green portions. If the tomatoes appear watery (some of the older varieties have this characteristic), cut them in half and squeeze out the seeds and the liquid surrounding them before use.

While there is more or less one way of making brown sauces, béchamel, and the other mother sauces, tomato sauce lends itself to several approaches.

For the standard French tomato sauce, assemble one fourth cup each of bacon or bacon waste, chopped carrots, chopped onions, flour, two and a half pounds of raw tomatoes, or one quart of canned tomatoes, two teaspoons sugar, one half cup of stock, and a half teaspoon of salt. Melt the pork, cook the vegetables in it, sprinkle the flour over the mixture and stir thoroughly to make a vegetable roux. Add the tomatoes and the stock, mix well and boil gently. Season with a clove of crushed garlic, bay leaf and thyme. The sauce is then simmered in a moderate oven for two hours. Strain.

The same ingredients can be used for a purée of tomatoes, except that the sauce is not thickened (no flour) and one half the stock is used.

Italian tomato sauce is much the same, except that no carrots are used, and the onions and pork are sweated in oil with garlic, sweet basil, and parsley.

Tomato sauce can be used cold and mixed with mayonnaise.

Whole cooked tomatoes can be run through a sieve and finished with oil like mayonnaise for a cold tomato sauce.

Fondue of tomatoes, which is used as a garnish, is made by blanching the tomatoes, peeling them, chopping them, and then cooking the pieces slowly in butter. Season with herbs, spices, and garlic.

XIV

◥◤

Cold Sauces

Cold sauces reflect English tastes much more than French. The beginning of this century saw French chefs inventing, and reworking, recipes to accommodate boiled fish, leftover joints, and Anglo-Saxon tastes. Two major classes of sauces evolved. The piquant, genuinely English sauces for example, Albert sauce and Cumberland sauce, and the compound butters.

Compound butters originally served to enrich sauces at the final moment of preparation. The butter served as a vehicle for some complementary and supplementary flavor.

When grills became the rage, compound butters were used to enhance the appearance of the broiled food and to add interest to the flavor.

Compound butters are also used as a base for canapés so that the moist garnish does not saturate the bread; for flavoring vegetables; for moistening sandwiches.

Basically, a compound butter consists of a base element, the butter, and seasoning passed through a sieve and worked to a homogeneous mass.

Anchovy butter, for example, is half butter, half pounded fillets of anchovies, seasoned with salt and pepper. Herbs, cheese, nuts, mustard, onion, shrimp, lobster roe, caviar, vegetable colorings, honey, hard-cooked eggs, liqueurs, tomato paste, watercress can all be compounded with butter.

A compound butter can be forced through a pastry bag into rosettes or stars, and frozen on a sheet of freezer paper, then gathered and stored in the freezer until they are needed. Small baking molds will also serve.

The chaud-froid sauces show very little English or American influence. They were originated to make cold stews more appetizing, by coating them with a gloss.

Today, their use is confined to coating buffet pieces (although gelled mayonnaise is used as often).

Béchamel sauce, Espagnole, or velouté tomato sauce can be made into a chaud-froid by the addition of gelatin. The quantity will be determined by the gelatin already present in the sauce. Chaud-froid should be made so that it is liquid enough to pour over a cold item, and will then gel and remain gelled at room temperature.

It can be colored with vegetable colorings.

Often it is put down as a first layer, then some attractive garnish fixed to it and the whole covered with clear gelatin.

The use of chaud-froid is really a matter of aesthetics as chaud-froids are often as tough as vinyl and as tasty.

▼▲▼▲▼▲▼▲▼▲▼▲▼▲▼▲▼▲ ▼▲▼▲▼▲ ▼▲▼▲▼▲▼▲▼▲▼▲▼▲▼▲▼▲▼▲▼▲▼▲▼▲▼▲▼▲

XV

White Sauces

There are four distinct white sauces in French cuisine: ordinary velouté, béchamel sauce, sauce bâtarde, and white wine sauce.

A family of sauces comprising the veloutés, the allemandes, and the
suprêmes is based on either veal or poultry white stock. Both these bases
are prepared from the same ingredients in different proportions so that
either the veal or poultry element dominates.

Unlike the brown sauces, which require at least twenty-four hours to
prepare, cooking time for sauce based on white stock never exceeds six
hours, making them relatively more practical for the home cook.

For one quart, start with two-and-one-half pounds of veal shins, one
carcass from a fowl or chicken or a few chicken heads and feet, a cup of
chopped carrots, an onion stuck with cloves, a half cup of chopped leek
white, seven or eight parsley stems, a quarter bay leaf and a pinch of
thyme.

Bone the veal and crack the bones with a cleaver. Sweat the vegetables in butter and then remove them from the pan. Add the meat to
the pan and allow it to cook in the juices derived from the vegetables.
Meantime, moisten the bones with a quart and one half of cold water
and set to simmer slowly.

Reduce the meat in the vegetable liquid until it is almost dry, then
add some of the water from the cooking bones. Repeat the reduction.
Add more liquid; repeat the reduction again.

After these three reductions, combine the meat, the bones, the vegetables, the seasoning, and the bone liquid and cook them slowly for four
hours, skimming constantly. Degrease the stock for a last time and
strain through cheesecloth in a fine strainer.

Poultry stock is made by adding an old fowl (in with the bones) to
this recipe.

If a better cut of veal is used along with the shin, the meat can be used for a blanquette, fricassée, or godiveau. The fowl can be used in making a galantine, soups, croquettes, etc.

These stocks will be more cloudy than beef stock and more gelatinous.

Veloutés are simply white stocks thickened with roux (*see* Thickening). Add the roux to the cold stock, bring it to a boil, cook on low heat, skimming constantly, for two hours.

Allemande sauce and its derivatives are built on velouté. To one quart of velouté add one quart of white stock and five or six mushrooms. Cook in a thick pan, stirring constantly to insure that the sauce does not stick. When it reaches the consistency of cream sauce (it will coat a spoon), remove the pot from the fire and add five egg yolks mixed with one half cup cream and the juice of one half lemon.

Return the pot to the fire and heat the sauce over a moderate flame. It should not be allowed to boil; in fact, the critical temperature is about 140° (indicated by a few bubbles breaking the surface of the sauce). Remove the sauce from the fire, strain it, and finish with nutmeg, salt and pepper. It is held warm until just ready for use and then buttered with two tablespoons of butter per quart.

The more traditional method of making this sauce is to combine all the ingredients except the cream and reduce them together, then cream and butter the sauce. Unfortunately, unless the sauce is absolutely greasefree, the eggs will curdle during the procedure.

Sauce suprême is made from one part poultry velouté and one part poultry stock with addition of mushrooms (eight medium mushrooms per quart), cooked and reduced by one third, then strained, creamed, and finally buttered by beating with butter. Sometimes egg yolks are added to sauce suprême (making it a poultry allemande), but this means sacrificing its whiteness for the velvetiness that the eggs contribute.

Veloutés

Aurora: Veal velouté colored with tomato purée.
Bretonne: Chopped onion moistened with white wine, reduced, poultry velouté added and finished with parsley.
Chivry: Veal velouté reduced with an infusion of herbs (tarragon, chives, chervil, etc.) in white wine.
Sauce au curry: Chicken velouté with curry powder.

Sauce à l'estragon: Reduction of tarragon in white wine until almost dry, chicken velouté, and finished with chopped fresh tarragon.

Sauce au fenouil: Reduction of fennel seeds in white wine, chicken velouté, finished with chopped fresh fennel.

Finnoise: Chicken velouté seasoned with paprika.

Gasconne: Veal velouté with anchovy butter and a reduction of herbs in white wine.

Ivoire: Veal velouté with meat glaze (or brown demiglaze).

Paprika: Chopped onions sweated in butter, paprika, moistened with white wine, reduced and mixed with veal velouté and creamed.

Polonaise: Veal velouté with sour cream, grated horseradish, and lemon juice. Taragon vinegar can be used instead of lemon juice. Can also be made with allemande.

Allemandes

Berchoux: Allemande heavily creamed with herb butter.

Milanese: Allemande with tomato purée and crushed tomatoes.

Mirabeau: Allemande with chopped garlic and herb butter.

Poulette: Allemande with mushroom essence (highly reduced mushroom stock, strained), lemon juice, and finished with chopped parsley.

Suprêmes

Albuféra: Suprême sauce with meat glaze and pimento butter.

Ambassadress: Suprême sauce with chicken purée, and finished with whipped cream instead of butter.

Arch-duc: Suprême with reduction of white wine or champagne.

Banquière: Suprême colored with tomato purée.

Cresson: Suprême with watercress purée and capers.

Impératice: Suprême with truffle essence (a commercial product), finished with whipped cream.

Printainia: Suprême with asparagus butter.

The American recipes that call for white sauce or cream sauce generally require béchamel either plain or creamed. Basic béchamel is made from milk and white roux in the proportion of one part roux to six parts milk (*see* Thickening).

The roux is prepared, the milk is scalded and kept hot, then poured over the hot roux. The mixture is stirred thoroughly and then stirred at intervals while the sauce cooks for half an hour. It is then strained.

Cold roux and cold milk can be combined with the same results, but the sauce must be simmered at least one hour.

The basic béchamel is adequate for some purposes—as the base for other sauces, certain vegetable preparations—but unsatisfactory because of its blandness if it dominates the dish. It can be improved by the addition of chopped onion, cayenne pepper, grated nutmeg, veal, veal stock, ham, mushroom peelings, mace, or even monosodium glutamate.

In actual practice the traditional recipe is compromised with the addition of chicken consommé, white stock, or fish stock for part of the milk.

Sauce Mornay: Sauce béchamel with the addition of grated cheese (either Parmesan, or Swiss and Parmesan) and enough liquid (either milk, cream, or stock) to restore its consistency.

Sauce Nantua: Sauce béchamel reduced with cream, buttered with crayfish butter, and garnished with crayfish tails. A more reasonable nantua can be made with shrimp instead of crayfish.

Cream Sauce is the most common variation of béchamel and the base of several other sauces itself. Add one part cream to four parts béchamel. Most compound butters can be added to cream sauce, and it can be garnished with whatever ingredient dominated the compound butter. It can also be blended with a purée of chicken, spinach, horseradish, sour cream, chopped onions, mushrooms, and garlic.

Sauce Bâtarde, also called butter sauce (*Sauce au Beurre*), is made by combining a quarter cup of flour with a quarter cup of butter to form a very light roux. To this roux, add two cups of boiling water and stir the mixture thoroughly. Remove from the heat and add three egg yolks mixed with four tablespoons of cream and one tablespoon of lemon juice. Heat but do not allow to boil (remove at the first bubbles). Finish the sauce with a quarter cup of melted butter beaten in slowly.

The sauce can be varied with the addition of mustard, herbs, horseradish, capers, grated lemon peel, commercial sauces like HP, A-1, Robert, or orange juice, chopped olives, or diced tomatoes.

White wine sauce is made from fish stock. For one quart of fish stock one needs a pound of whiting, a cup of chopped onions and three quarters of a cup of white wine. The fish is sweated in a buttered pan with the onions, then moistened with the wine, and the preparation reduced until almost dry. One quart of water is added, the mixture boiled, skimmed and simmered for 45 minutes.

83

Many cookbooks propose that the viscera, skins, fins of fish be saved for making fish stock. I don't believe that these articles make a contribution to fish stock as they introduce a variety of off flavors. Fish stock should be made from the meat of white-fleshed fish and its bones.

White wine sauce is developed as a velouté, generally by mixing the stock with an already prepared velouté; as a bâtarde sauce by substituting fish stock (fumet de poisson) for a portion of the water; or as a pseudo-hollandaise by reducing the fish stock to an essence (a viscous concentrate) and mounting the hollandaise on it.

Quite naturally white wine sauce is used for fish preparations. Without further preparation, it is combined with an equal quantity of hollandaise and unsweetened whipped cream to make a glaze.

Fish fumet itself can be combined with sauce allemande, béchamel, Mornay, cream sauce, hollandaise sauce, to form a parallel family of sauces to the white wine preparations.

Amiral: White wine sauce with chopped shallots, grated lemon peel, anchovy butter, and capers.

Alçide: White wine sauce with shallots and horseradish.

Aurore: White wine sauce (velouté) with tomato purée for color.

Bercy: White wine sauce (velouté) reduced with white wine, shallots sweated in butter, and chopped parsley.

Clovisse: (Clam): In making fish stock, mussels, clams, oysters, lobster, or shrimp can be added to give flavor to the stock.

Dieppe: White wine sauce (velouté) with shrimp butter.

François I: White wine sauce (any formula) with diced tomatoes and mushrooms.

Golfin: White wine sauce (any formula) with chopped pickles, diced tongue, and capers.

Grandville: White wine sauce with diced truffles, mushrooms, mushroom essence, and shrimp.

Havre: White wine sauce (any formula) garnished with mussels and shrimp.

Hongroise: White wine sauce (bâtarde), paprika, and sour cream.

Normande: White wine sauce (velouté) further improved with fish stock, oyster liquid, mushroom stock, and then bound with egg yolks. Normande sauce with lobster butter, lobster, and truffles is *Sauce Diplomate.* Addition of Rhine wine, mushrooms, and truffles to Sauce Normande is *Sauce Régence.*

Polignac: White wine sauce with cream and mushrooms.

84

Basic Preparations

Souchet: White wine sauce (velouté or bâtarde) with a julienne of carrots, leeks, and celery sweated in butter.

St. Malo: White wine sauce (any formula) with chopped shallots, mustard, and anchovies.

XVI

Emulsion Sauces

Hollandaise and *mayonnaise* can be made to professional standards in the home. Any decent cookbook has an adequate recipe for preparing them, but few discuss their variations and still fewer offer some method of preventing the sauces from breaking up or for reconstituting them after they break.

Emulsion sauces are delicate because they are an emulsion of oil in egg yolk (which is an emulsion itself). The egg yolk emulsion will break down if abused.

Of the two, hollandaise is the more difficult to work with. It is generally served hot and is less stable hot than cold, while mayonnaise is used cold. Secondly, hollandaise involves a suspension of egg yolk particles in melted butter, that is in itself less stable than mayonnaise, which is an emulsion of raw liquid egg yolk in oil.

I believe that hollandaise should be stabilized when one is dealing with more than a pint, when the sauce is not to be served immediately, and when the sauce is either to be served hot or poured over a very hot food.

The addition of simple starch insures the consistency of hollandaise. For a sauce of considerable stability, cook one ounce of flour and one ounce of butter in a saucepan to form a white homogeneous roux (a matter of a few seconds), add a cup and a half of hot water, and remove from the heat.

Add the water roux mixture slowly to the usual reduction of vinegar and peppercorns (or whatever seasoning and acidulating ingredients the recipe requires), then add six raw egg yolks stirring slowly and evenly. Then incorporate as much warm melted butter as the mixture will hold. Strain. This blend will keep just to the point of boiling.

A more delicate but less stable sauce can be prepared by the addition of a light paste of arrowroot and water to the egg yolks of any normal recipe. Large quantities are best stabilized with cornstarch and water or even béchamel sauce to one-third the volume of hollandaise desired.

Of course, unstabilized, unadulterated hollandaise tastes best. It should not be made in large quantities, however, because of the problem of stabilization, and because of the considerable risk of contamination. If a large quantity is made it must be used immediately. Some authors feel it can be kept in the refrigerator, but if it is possible to keep it in the refrigerator without breaking (it will break when the oil solidifies), then the refrigerator is not cold enough to keep it free from contamination. Although the public health aspects of cookery are not of endless fascination to me, hollandaise that is left out and not used immediately is extremely dangerous.

When making unstabilized hollandaise in small quantities, following certain rules insures a good chance of success.

This is a gentle process. While both hollandaise and mayonnaise can be made in the blender (with almost a hundred percent chance of success), the blender abuses the yolks and the sauce does not taste good.

Stirring, while constant, should not be overly vigorous as the eggs will become grainy. The heating of the egg yolks should be done slowly, over simmering water if done in a double boiler, over a very low flame if done on the stove.

The butter should be added slowly, and should not be too hot. A piece of cold butter standing by can save a hollandaise which looks as if it is going.

This same piece of butter is also useful in stopping the cooking process when the eggs are removed from the stove, by bringing them to a temperature where they will not continue to cook.

If the butter was too hot, or the process too quick, the hollandaise will break. To recover a small quantity of either hollandaise or mayonnaise that has not broken too badly, begin again with one egg yolk; then add the broken sauce drop by drop as though it were oil or butter. For a major separation, place a small ice cube in the bottom of a chilled clean bowl and slowly add the sauce while stirring vigorously, evenly, and constantly. When the ice has melted, start again with another cube in another bowl. Finally combine the contents of several bowls in a single one, drop by drop.

The acute problem of stability limits the variations of hollandaise. In any case, except with highly stabilized hollandaise the ingredients must not be added hot.

Béarnaise (meats, fish): Build a hollandaise on an almost dry reduction of shallots, tarragon, peppercorns, and vinegar. Strain and finish with fresh chopped tarragon and chervil.

Bavaroise (meats, fish): Béarnaise with horseradish.

Choron (meats, fish): Béarnaise with tomato purée or ketchup.

Foyot or *Valois* (grills, fish): Béarnaise with meat glaze (glace de viande).

Maltaise (grilled fish): Hollandaise with juice and outside peel of blood oranges.

Mousseline (poached fish as glaze): Hollandaise beaten with a small quantity of water to incorporate air and finished with either whipped cream or egg white beaten stiff.

Moutarde (vegetables, fish): Hollandaise with mustard.

Noisette (vegetables, lamb): Béarnaise with mint instead of tarragon.

Mayonnaise generally does not need the stabilization of hollandaise. It can, however, be stabilized like hollandaise, or by the addition of gelatin dissolved in water and whipped in.

Mayonnaise is made with oil rather than butter fat. It is important that the oil and the egg yolks be at room temperature before starting, and that the yolks be well whipped before adding the oil.

Whole eggs can be used for mayonnaise, but the result is less satisfactory.

Mayonnaise will accept almost any purée of meat or vegetables.

Chantilly (garnish for cold dishes): Sauce mousseline made with mayonnaise rather than hollandaise.

Génoise (cold meats, fish): Purée of herbs, pistachio nuts, and almonds in mayonnaise.

Rémoulade (seafoods, vegetables): Mayonnaise with mustard, chopped pickles, chervil, tarragon, and Worcestershire sauce.

Suédoise (cold meats): Applesauce and horseradish in mayonnaise.

There are a number of emulsion sauces, other than mayonnaise and hollandaise, that are based on emulsifiers other than egg yolks. As egg yolks make an especially good emulsion, these sauces absorb less oil but are otherwise prepared just like mayonnaise.

Aioli (meat, fish stews): Cloves of garlic are pounded in a mortar with boiled potatoes to a smooth paste; then the mayonnaise is built on top.

Echalotade (meats, fish, stews): Aioli made with shallots instead of garlic.

Gribiche (fish, cold vegetables, meats): Instead of with raw egg yolks, one starts with hard-cooked egg yolks pounded in a mortar, to which oil is added as for mayonnaise. Finished with mustard, chopped pickles, capers, chervil, parsley, and tarragon.

Tartare (fish, eggs, vegetables): Starts like Gribiche; finished with chopped onions and chives.

Verte (fish, eggs): Instead of with raw egg yolks, one starts with the white of bread and a purée of blanched greens, like spinach, watercress, sorrel, tarragon, chervil, pounded in a mortar to which oil is added as for mayonnaise; seasoned with garlic and saffron.

▼▲

XVII

Sweet Sauces

Sweet sauces are used for ice cream dishes, hot and cold puddings, cakes, soufflés, rice, pancakes, omelettes, fruit compotes, custards, fritters, pastry, and, very rarely, for meat dishes. Of the several types of sweet sauce, vanilla cream (English sauce or sauce Anglaise), sabayon, thickened syrups, fruit jams or fruit purées, only those with fruit have any use for garnishing meat. In formal French cuisine, game is occasionally accompanied by a dollop of currant sauce. Otherwise, the combination of salt-sweet or sour-sweet so popular with Americans and with Teutonic peoples does not occur. Sweet sauces are reserved for desserts.

Sugar is, of course, basic to any sweet sauce. It may be brown sugar, honey, or maple sugar, but most often it is white (beet or cane) sugar. White sugar is available in various degrees of fineness, designated by X's (the more X's, the finer the sugar).

Before being used, white sugar can be flavored by pounding the sugar with a relatively small quantity of spice, ten or twenty to one by weight, in a mortar and passing the mixture through a very fine strainer or two strainers imposed on each other.

Vanilla is the most common addition. However, anise, cloves, cinnamon, and ginger are equally suitable. Another method, more frequently used, is to enclose the spice with sugar for a period of time so as to let the perfume saturate the sugar, and then remove the spice.

English sauce is the basic sauce in this category. One combines one-half cup of sugar with six egg yolks and beats them well. To this mixture add two cups of scalded milk (to which any flavoring desired can be added), and whisk the mixture vigorously in a double boiler, or in a steel bowl in a pot filled with boiling water, until the mixture thickens. Do not allow the sauce itself to boil.

A caramel sauce may be similarly made if the sugar is burnt to caramel first, then reground in a blender or mortar when cold. Praline sauce is merely English sauce with crushed pralines. Peanuts, liqueurs, spirits, flavorings, or coloring can be added as desired to this sauce.

English sauce can be made with cream in the same proportions, and used either hot or cold.

Sauce sabayon, which is treated as a separate type, closely resembles English sauce except that the liquid involved is usually wine: Madeira, Port, Malaga, Marsala, Chablis, Sauternes. Sometimes it is made with a liqueur combined with milk. About half to three-fourth the quantity of liquid should be used for the same quantities of egg and sugar used in English sauces. Sabayon is thicker. It is important as well that the sabayon be whisked to increase its volume while it is stiffening.

For a light sabayon, an egg white beaten stiff may be combined with it after it has thickened.

Sabayon, when used cold, may also be mixed with whipped cream. It is thick enough, incidentally, to be used hot or cold as a dessert itself.

Simple syrup is ordinary sugar boiled with water to about 15° (*see* Frozen Desserts). For desserts it is slightly thickened with arrowroot or cornstarch, strained, and then mixed with some flavoring element.

Fruit sauces are made of puréed cooked fruits or puréed dried fruits, suitably sweetened, sieved, and thickened. Greengages, apples, cherries, plums, apricots, prunes, raisins, pears, loganberries, and currants are well suited to this treatment.

Jams, preserves, and conserves usually eliminate several steps. They are diluted with some liqueur or brandy, or boiled with a prepared syrup.

When a fruit sauce is used for meat, it must be highly seasoned, usually with cloves, ginger, or cinnamon, and acidulated with vinegar or lemon juice so as not to contrast too sharply with the meat. The berry sauces, which are naturally tart, can be diluted with red or white wine to the same end. Adding a small quantity of butter will make them more suitable for meats.

XVIII

██

Forcemeats
(Stuffings)

Forcemeats, preparations of ground, pounded, sieved, or chopped meats, are an important auxiliary to cooking. They are used in filling pâtés, galantines, terrines; in stuffing fish, breast of veal, fowls, meats; or alone as quenelles or patties for entrées, garnishes, or mousses.

All forcemeats are made of a base element, seasoning, and a binder element. The fundamental difference between stuffings is the nature of the base element, how it is prepared (cut, chopped, sieved, or pounded), the different seasoning that can be employed, and the holding power of the binder element.

The exact nature of the stuffing is determined by the role it is to play in the dish. Often a stuffing is merely filler, a means of supplementing the protein entrée with a starch. At other times the stuffing moistens or dehydrates the preparation and flavors it. Sometimes the stuffing is not really needed, and the forcemeat is only cooked inside the main dish because of convention or convenience.

In American and English cookery, the stuffing is almost always a filler, and the binder element is made very strong with bread and eggs. These filler stuffings are almost always characterized by a lack of flavor and integrity of texture, being nothing more than a mash of stale bread. They are almost always dehydrating, acting as the perfect blotter for cooking juices, which are summarily lost. This is especially true in cooking stuffed birds. The small amount of liquid in the breasts passes to the stuffing, making the breasts especially dry and improving the stuffing very little. It is wise to reverse the process, first by making the

92

stuffing moist; second by cooking the bird in a V-shaped rack, breast down.

American chefs generally soak the bread (white bread without crust, or bread crumbs) in milk, squeeze it to extract the liquid, and dry it over a slow fire. The mixture is then cooled, mixed with butter, raw egg yolks and seasonings.

English chefs proceed similarly, but use a white stock instead of milk, and beef suet instead of butter.

For a fowl stuffing, the chopped sautéed liver of the bird is added to the cold binder. The mixture can be improved with thyme, bay, sausage meat, grated lemon peel, walnuts, filberts, roasted chestnuts, bacon, chopped ham, garlic, onions, currants, pistachios, oysters, celery, and apples in any combination.

The mixture may be forced through a sieve, pounded in a mortar, or merely mixed thoroughly before being used. Many English puddings— bachelor pudding, steamed apple pudding, apricot pudding, even Christmas pudding—are used for stuffing (*see* Puddings).

It is desirable in making standard cookbook stuffings to loosen the entire mixture by cutting down on the binder element.

In French cuisine there are several farinaceous binders (panades) in addition to bread: flour, frangipane, rice, and potato panade. Although often quite dense, they are generally more moist than English and American stuffings, because of a high fat content.

Flour panade is made by heating one cup of water with four tablespoons of butter. When the liquid boils, add ten tablespoons of flour, one by one, stirring constantly and cooking until a paste forms, so thick that it does not stick to a wooden spoon.

All the panades are used similarly. Two parts of meat (veal, chicken, game, fish) require one part of panade and one part butter. The raw meat is cut, stripped of skin, nerves, and connective tissues, and either pounded in a mortar, or put through a meat grinder several times and then pounded. Then the panade and the butter are blended in the same way. The mixtures are combined and one egg yolk and two tablespoons of beaten whole eggs are added and blended in. The preparation is strained and mixed again.

Seasonings and complementary garnishes are added to the cold stuffing.

Pounding, grinding or blending the meat and the fat until they are fine particles is the essential operation in the preparation of delicate forcemeats. The finely ground particles combine with the liquid to form a relatively stable emulsion like an emulsion sauce (*see* Emulsion

93

Sauces) until the proteins are cooked. If the particles are not fine enough, or if the entire mixture is too hot, the mixture does not come together properly.

Mousseline, or fine foremeat, which can be used in any forcemeat role is bound with cream and egg white. When this mixture is poached in a mold, it becomes a "mousse." The delicacy of this preparation can be approached and a degree of stability gained by making the forcemeat à la crème but with panade as well.

Quenelles—poached portions of forcemeats—are made from any of these forcemeat recipes with butter and panade, with bread panade, with frangipane, with panade and cream. The forcemeats themselves are used for any stuffing purposes.

Quenelles are also made from a special forcemeat called godiveau. It is made by pounding the base element (rabbit, game, chicken, fish) with very brittle beef-kidney fat.

The molding and poaching of quenelles can be made a complicated and difficult process or can be done with slightly less elegant results and a lot less work and bother.

Professionals who do hundreds of quenelles mold them between two spoons. They take some forcemeat in one spoon and impose the other on top of it to mold the quenelle. Because the second spoon has been heated in water and is moist and hot, one can slide it around the forcemeat and plop the quenelle into a buttered saucepan. After the quenelles are formed, boiling salted water is poured over them and they are poached.

Unfortunately it is not as easy as it sounds. Quenelles can be made more simply by forcing them from pastry bags, or rolling slices of forcemeat (cut from a forcemeat sausage) between the fingers. A little flour on one's hands helps.

Godiveau quenelles are cooked on a buttered or greased piece of brown paper in the oven. When they are covered with a film of fat, they are done.

Among the common main course quenelle dishes are chicken quenelles mixed with onion purée, with sauce bâtarde (à la bretonne): crayfish forcemeat, with cream sauce finished with crayfish butter (à la cardinale); pike with sauce nantua; chicken with madeira sauce; chicken with sauce allemande.

Other French forcemeats are made with blood as a binding agent and a flavor element. While the blood of the animal being stuffed (hare, rabbit, chicken, goose) is desirable, pork blood serves as well and is generally more available. The blood need not be more than a small fraction (25 percent) of the total mass to hold it well.

94

Duxelles are another rather important French forcemeat. Good white mushrooms are finely chopped and squeezed in a cloth to expel the water. They are then sweated in butter with chopped shallots and onions, until quite dry. The mixture is used for filling vegetables, for pâtés, and for coating a fillet of beef in Boeuf Wellington.

A great many stuffing preparations have been neglected by formal cuisine. For example, the livers of fish, the roe, milt, and tomalley make excellent stuffings for fish preparations. Crab meat and lobster meat, loosely bound or merely seasoned and not bound at all, are equally suitable.

Sausage meat and chopped sausage contribute both texture and flavor to otherwise bland dishes. A dish as dull as meat loaf can be made acceptable if skinned garlic sausage is laid down so that every slice has a center of sausage meat.

Other starches (*see* Starch Cookery) are excellent binders in traditional stuffing instead of bread crumbs or panades. Wild rice, bulgur, sweet potato, potato, hominy, even oatmeal when well-seasoned, make fine different stuffings.

Other vegetables, especially those like eggplant, oyster plant, which hold their texture, can be used either as a supporting element in the stuffing or as the major element with a minimum of binder.

The home cook might well reconsider what items are to be stuffed. Fowl, chicken breasts, boned fowl (galantines and ballontines), crown roasts of lamb, and tiny rolls of tender meat (paupiettes) are currently treated with a stuffing; small furry game, bone cuts (shoulder, leg, breast, and hams) also become attractive with a stuffing that serves to blot the juices they exude during cooking.

Chops and steaks can be split and filled. Any rolled or thin cut can be rolled around a stuffing. Flank steak, which is not really suitable for broiling but has a well-developed flavor, can be stuffed, rolled, and braised with good results.

Chicken and turkey legs, while second-class meats, can become a delicacy when carefully boned, denerved, stuffed, and moist-cooked.

PART
3

Specifics of Preparation

XIX

▀▀

Hors d'Oeuvres

An hors d'oeuvres course often figures in modern meals. As it usually can be prepared well before the meal, and sometimes can be purchased already prepared, the hors d'oeuvre helps eliminate some of the pressure on the home cook at mealtimes.

The hors d'oeuvre can generally be eaten when soup isn't. Classicists tend to serve hors d'oeuvres at lunch and soup at dinner.

Caviar remains a universally accepted hors d'oeuvre. It is available in a variety of forms: the most preferred is the Beluga Malossol, large, very lightly salted grains. Other caviar, Ocietrova, Sevruga, conserved and pressed caviars, are less expensive.

Other roe products, red caviar from salmon, dyed whitefish or lump-fish roes; bourtarge, tuna caviar; and tarama, codfish roe, should be considered on their merits, not as substitute caviar.

Shellfish, especially oysters (*see* Mollusks), are another well-accepted hors d'oeuvre. Most fish stores will open shellfish at a very slight premium, but only oysters really present any problems, as clams can be opened easily. Hold the clam in the left hand, pointed end nestled in the palm. Place a clam knife in the groove at the edge of the shell, between the fingers of the left hand and the shell, and close the fingers of the left hand. Cut the clam's muscles and free the clam from the shell. Little-necks and cherrystones are generally used raw as hors d'oeuvre.

Oysters demand another sort of knife and a large cloth. The oyster is gripped in the cloth in the left hand and the knife (a short, stiff-bladed knife with a rounded end) is forced inside the hinge (the place on the oysters from which the rings radiate). Twist the knife back and forth until it penetrates and cuts the muscles. Discard the flat shell (most oystermen in America discard the deep shell, losing most of the liquid). Release the oyster from the shell.

99

All shellfish must be very cold to be easily opened.

Many hors d'oeuvre preparations are available commercially. Smoked trout, eels, herring, whitefish, and sturgeon for example, are widely used.

Smoked salmon is available freshly smoked and in cans. While fresh smoked salmon is preferred, it is not well-preserved by smoking and must be refrigerated both at the point of sale and in the home. Nova Scotia and Columbia River salmon are the best North American types. Scotch salmon, flown daily to the New York markets, is the world's best.

Herring (Scotch-cured) is often served as an appetizer, usually in sour cream. Other varieties: Matjes, Scotch-cured, with a developed milt or roe: Holland herring, more thoroughly cured than Scotch: Bismarck, a pickled herring: rollmop, herring around a pickle, also finds admirers.

Other herring products are available in cans and can be used as hors d'oeuvres. Mussels, shrimp, oysters, culps, cockles, eels, salmon, sardines, anchovies, and tuna are also canned. The best canned salmon is chinook, followed by sockeye, coho, humpback, and chum. Center cuts are most attractive.

Sardines are of five major types: sea herring, sild, domestic pilchard, imported pilchard, brisling. The best sardines are imported (French are preferred) packed in olive oil. Domestic sardines are generally coarser, less expensive, and packed in cheap oils or in a sauce.

Anchovies for hors d'oeuvre use should be imported, packed in olive oil, or salted and packed (skins on) in kegs. The domestic product is very inferior. Canned anchovies are used as they come from the can; the salted preparation should be skinned before use, just like a small fish fillet.

Fancy albacore (labeled white meat) is the first-class tuna, followed by yellowfin, bluefin, skipjack (labeled light meat). The best tuna is packed in olive oil, and several excellent imported brands are also available. Although bonita and yellowtail are packed in similar cans, they are a different fish and inferior.

Sausages of various types have traditionally served as hors d'oeuvres: salami, garlic sausage, mortedella, zampino, andouille are among the favored types.

Pickled meats, veal tongues, smoked beef, smoked goose, beef jowl, and the various hams, prosciutto, Westphalian, Bayonne, York, and Virginia are quite suitable, as well.

Some vegetable preparations are also commercially available; eggplants, stuffed vine leaves, stuffed peppers, marinated mushrooms, cauliflowers, pickled pumpkin, pickled watermelon, marinated asparagus, cocktail onions and tomatoes, palm hearts, and pimientos.

In most cases, commercial preparations are completely prepared and need only be garnished with pickles, capers, pomegranate seeds, hard-cooked eggs, onion rings, radishes, parsley, or herbs.

Next in importance as cold hors d'oeuvres are the fresh vegetable dishes. Some can be eaten raw, but they are more often cooked in water or simply blanched and then dressed: artichokes, button onions, grated cabbage, boiled potatoes, boiled beets, lentils, and white beans.

The composed salads (*see* Salads) especially Niçoise, Italienne, Jardinière, Grecque, and Russe are quite acceptable appetizers.

Stuffed eggs (*see* Eggs) prepared with purées of fish, foie gras, chopped small salads, and mayonnaises are also popular.

Canapés have become particularly important with the rise of the cocktail. Basically, the canapé is a thin toast without a crust, cut in triangles, squares, or circles, about one and one half inches across, covered with a compound butter, then some foodstuff: salami, goose liver, lobster, anchovies, shrimp, stewed vegetables, chicken liver purée, caviar, crayfish purée, beef tongue, oysters, smoked goose, tuna, mushrooms. Canapés can be served on a folded napkin.

Galantines, goose liver en bloc, terrines, which allow the cook some exercise of skill, are among the more sophisticated cold hors d'oeuvres. Preparations of goose liver in aspic, in a mousse, chilled in a jelly-lined mold are as well eminently suitable.

Thin pancakes can be filled with salad mixtures, like shrimp, lobster, mussels, or a composed salad, and covered with a cold sauce.

The "American relishes," a variety of hors d'oeuvre which is seldom seen abroad, consists either of spiced apples, crab apples, pickles, watermelon rinds, pumpkin, and the like, strongly perfumed with cinnamon; or raw vegetables like celery hearts, fennel roots, white and red radishes, baby asparagus, carrot sticks, and green onions.

A great many preparations which have other roles in the meal can be served as hot hors d'oeuvres.

Pastry preparations garnished with highly seasoned but delicate stews of food of a convenient size are the largest category of hot hors d'oeuvres: Allumettes (in puff pastry), barquettes, bouchées, croûtes, tartelettes (in almost any dough), filled brioche (in brioche dough), filled choux (in chou paste), blinis, ravioli, rissoles, croustades (in almost any dough), filled with mushroom purée; foie gras and truffles in madeira sauce; oysters and mushrooms in sauce Normande; veal sweetbreads and mushrooms in a white wine sauce; beef tongue and raisins in a piquant sauce; lobster in Newburg sauce; mussels in Poulette sauce, etc.

The various fritters, croquettes, fondants, subric treatments applied to traditional hot hors d'oeuvre foods, shellfish, variety meats, vegetables with character, are another important group.

Small soufflés of cheese, ham, spinach, lobster, salmon, could be classed as hot hors d'oeuvres.

Brochettes of various meats and vegetables cooked or grilled, or breaded (and called atteraux) and deep-fried; scallop shells filled with any of the small stew preparations suitable to other hors d'oeuvres, covered with a sauce; duchesse potatoes, hollowed and filled; croustades, or hollowed crusts, that are deep-fried and filled; filled crêpes, either rolled and sauced, or breaded and fried; deep-fried ravioli; all belong to this category.

Egg preparations: hot stuffed eggs, molded eggs, poached eggs, egg au miroir, if appropriately garnished, make admirable first courses.

Fresh fruit and fruit salads are the American contribution to cold hors d'oeuvres and that funny little course, the savory, is the English contribution to the hot: Angels on Horseback, oysters wrapped in bacon, skewered and grilled; Scotch woodcock, slices of bread with anchovies, cheese, and scrambled eggs; bread pudding with cheese, Welsh rabbit and its variations.

XX

▼▼

Soups

Soups are divided into three major classes: the classical soups of French cuisine, home-style regional soups, and fruit soups.

The soups of classic cuisine can be further divided into consommés, purées, veloutés, and crèmes. Consommés are clear broths made from fish, beef, chicken, or game. Often as not some sort of garnish is added: fried bread (croûtons), finely cut vegetables, rice, shredded crêpes, hard-cooked eggs forced through a strainer, macaronis of various sorts, dumplings (quenelles), custards (royales), tapioca, or finely cut meats. The possible combinations of consommés and garnishes have been rather well explored; four hundred named varieties exist.

Consommés are begun like beef stock or chicken stock (*see* Brown Sauces and White Sauces); then the consommé must be clarified. This is their essential difference from broths.

The consommé to be clarified is first boiled for a few minutes with only one side of the pot on the fire so that the scum gathers on the other tranquil side. This also gives an opportunity to remove any grease present on the surface of the stock.

For a quart of stock, beat three egg whites with a half cup of ice and one cup of the stock, until the mixture is cool. Then slowly pour in the rest of the stock, and immediately transfer the entire mixture back to the pot. Make sure the eggs are dispersed throughout the mixture. Return the stock to simmer. A mass of eggs will form and rise to the surface as the whites reach their coagulation point. Do not break up the mass but let it rise. When the egg whites are floating, allow the pot to cook about five minutes. Then strain the stock through a cheesecloth in a Swiss bouillon strainer. Do not force the mixture through the cheesecloth but let it drain naturally. Stop pouring well above any sediment that remains in the bottom of the pot.

Purées have more interest to the home cook. Some fresh vegetables and a little beef or chicken consommé mean excellent soups made naturally without additional thickening. Simply cook the vegetables to a pulp with a little consommé and seasoning. Sieve, bring to consistency with consommé, and finish with butter and salt and pepper. Celery, cauliflower, lentils, peas, potatoes and leeks, beans are traditional, but artichokes and sweet potatoes, chestnuts, green beans are excellent; watercress, sorrel, herbs, salsify, and lettuce mixed with potato purée for body are very successful. Garnishing can be a finely cut vegetable that figures in the soup or croûtons.

Purées are not restricted to vegetables. Bisques are essentially purées of shellfish. The fish is cooked with onions, carrots, and celery in butter. Fish stock or chicken stock is added. Rice is added to provide some thickening element. The soup is cooked, strained, and garnished with bits of the principal ingredient.

Originally, the word bisque referred to any meat-based purée soup. The first bisque mentioned in ancient cuisine was Bisque of Pigeonneux (a bisque of pigeons). The same operation for fish bisque can be applied to any other food product: rabbit, pigeons, small game.

Veloutés are purées to which a thickened stock, a velouté, (see White Sauces) has been added. Add the already prepared purée of chicken, vegetables, whatever, to a velouté in the proportion of one part purée to two parts velouté and bring the soup to consistency with consommé. Then sieve the soup and bind it with three egg yolks and one quarter cup of cream for every four cups of soup. Just before serving, butter the velouté.

Crèmes are much like veloutés. There exist several notable differences. Although they are prepared in the same manner (the proportions are the same), béchamel sauce (see White Sauces) is used instead of velouté. The soup is brought to consistency with milk instead of consommé. The crèmes are not bound with eggs; they are not buttered but finished with cream.

When diluting either crèmes or veloutés with milk or cream, pour a small quantity of the soup into the dairy product rather than the other way around. Most of the vegetable-based soups are slightly acid, and the smaller volume of dairy product will curdle if it encounters all the acidity at once.

One cannot overemphasize the importance of soup in the diet of almost all rural people. The evening meal for many individuals is exclusively soup. Not the refined subtle infusions of French cuisine but robust, hearty vegetable and meat soups that sometimes border on stews.

Clarifying Stock for Consommé

A

Egg whites mixed with some cool stock, broken ice in pan.

B

Mixture of egg whites, stock, and ice added to body of cool stock.

C

Stock heated slowly until raft of coagulated egg whites forms.

D

Stock poured through double layer of cheesecloth in strainer without forcing raft through.

The use of these preparations is rather limited; they are hardly the preface to a gourmet meal. Rather they are often a meal in themselves. These soups are extremely easy to prepare; in fact, the only real problem is that the vegetable elements cook before the meat. The obvious solution is either to cook separate vegetables to flavor the soup and then introduce attractively cut vegetables for their ideal cooking time, or add the vegetables at their ideal cooking time and sacrifice some small amount of flavor.

Many of the regions of France have a local soup. However, not all of these provincial creations can meet sophisticated standards. Soupe à l'ail and the cabbage soup of Landeudoc, for example, are losers. Other regional soups, excellent in France, cannot be prepared outside of her borders. Bouillabaisse, the most famous regional soup, cannot be made without the fish of the Mediterranean: le rouqier, la firelle, le saint-pierre, la boudroie, la murène and, of course, la rascasse.

Pot-au-feu and petite marmite, although not exactly the same, are similar enough to be treated as a single preparation. Although almost every region in France, and perhaps every French housewife, has its own recipes, they all include meat (usually beef—the rump, breast, tail, shin, chuck), a chicken (sometimes stuffed, sometimes a game bird or duck), carrots, turnips, celery, white of leek, and an onion studded with cloves. Cook the meat in water until almost done, degreasing and skimming constantly. Then add the vegetables and cook them. Cook a cabbage and add it to the finished soup. The dish is always served in the pot in which it has been cooked, almost always with a slice of bread, sometimes spread with the marrow of a bone cooked with the soup. One can vary the basic recipe by adding veal shins, goose, garlic, white beans, ham sausage, bacon, mouton, in various combinations.

A potée is a pot-au-feu with the emphasis on pork. Generally the meat portions are served separately.

There is a romantic myth about an endless pot-au-feu in which ingredients are constantly added and from which choice morsels are regularly taken. A surprising number of excellent authors hold this notion.

Nobody who had attempted this would mention the idea again. After cooking for a few days, the pot-au-feu develops an incredibly foul taste as the bones, originally put in it, begin to dissolve. If the stock were completely strained every twenty-four hours, the development of this off-flavor might be delayed, but there is absolutely no purpose in doing it as most of the value of the ingredients is in the liquid after seventeen hours.

Many soups, which are generally eaten hot, are excellent chilled: consommés, bisques, creams, are almost all quite good cold. They should be more highly seasoned cold than hot, and garnitures like custards and croûtons avoided.

Beef consommé, consommé cooked with celery, garnished with bits of raw celery; madrilène, chicken consommé with raw tomatoes and red peppers; beef broth with mushroom essence; beef with pimentos; beef with leaf tarragon, are especially good cold.

Cream of chicken, with port wine, with sherry; cream of tomatoes; cream of mushrooms, and, of course, the ubiquitous vichyssoise, a cold cream of leeks and potatoes, are among the cold crèmes.

Fruit soups are also served hot or cold. The basic formulation involves crushing either fresh fruit or boiled dried fruit, mixing it with sugar and boiling liquid (usually wine), rubbing the entire mixture through a sieve, diluting the resulting purée with cold wine, and garnishing the soup with pieces of the fruit element.

Fruit soups are thickened with cornstarch or powdered agar-agar for gel. (One-half teaspoon of agar-agar is used where one tablespoon of cornstarch would be.)

These soups are usually seasoned with cinnamon, lemon juice, grated lemon rind.

XXI

▀▄

Eggs

An egg is a useful element in cuisine: as a thickening agent for sauces, soups and custards; as a means of leavening in soufflés and cakes; as a stabilizer in mayonnaise and hollandaise; as an adhesive in breading; and as a clarifying agent for soups.

An egg is also the basis for 1,500 egg dishes.

Fresh eggs of good quality are of course more valuable as a food and in cooking than inferior eggs. A good fresh egg when opened on a saucer will cover a small area and not spread over the plate. The white immediately surrounding the yolk will be firm and high, the remaining white will be proportionately small and very clear. The white may, however, vary in viscosity, depending on the season; summer eggs are more watery than spring eggs.

The yolk will be round and high, without blood spot or developing germ. It may vary in color from light yellow to deep orange, depending on the season and the diet of the hen.

The color and the size—the two characteristics apparent in the store—have nothing to do with the quality of the egg. Brown eggs or speckled eggs are as good as white. Large eggs, although more attractive for table use, are often not a good buy in comparison with smaller eggs, which deliver more egg for the money.

For example, if the grades are the same, medium eggs are a good buy when prices are about 12 percent below the large. Small eggs are worth buying when they are 25 percent below the large.

One can, however, inspect the eggs in the store to avoid obviously inferior eggs. Shake the egg. An egg that rattles is not fresh. Tap the egg. The size of the air cell increases as the eggs get older. An egg that sounds metallic is of inferior quality.

Dirty eggs, irregular eggs, broken eggs, all should be avoided. Shiny eggs are almost always not fresh, although they still may be quite good. Sometimes the shininess (a newly laid egg has velvety dullness, or "bloom") is due to oil preservation; other times the egg has been polished to remove minor flaws.

One should also purchase eggs in a store where they are refrigerated or at least kept in a cool place, as they must be in the home, for eggs deteriorate rapidly in heat. Eggs should be stored pointed end down.

In cuisine, the yolk and the white are used separately, often as not, because they have different properties. (To separate eggs: first chill the eggs, as cold eggs separate more easily than warm ones. Break the shell at the equator by striking it against a sharp edge. Turn the yolk from one half shell to the other, each time gathering the strings of white with the edge of the shell and letting them fall into a cup. While it is not important if some white is introduced into the yolks, great care must be taken not to allow any yellow into the white. Therefore, when separating a large number of eggs, work with two or three at a time in a small cup and then pour off the whites into a larger vessel.)

The yolk is used in binding sauces—for example, Beurre Blanc and the veloutés most importantly—and for making custards.

The fact that an egg yolk is itself a very stable emulsion allows it to absorb large quantities of oil to make the emulsion sauces, mayonnaise and hollandaise.

Egg yolks are used as adhesives in most kinds of breading (à l'Anglaise, à la Milanaise, etc.).

When egg yolks are introduced into preparations, the dish must not be allowed to boil, or, as in the case of custard, heated too hot or too fast. Heat above 160° will cause the eggs to curdle, to scramble in the sauce or soup, with absolutely disastrous results.

Beaten egg whites figure in a number of preparations: cakes, mousses, snow islands, soufflés, and batters. To whip them satisfactorily, certain peculiarities should be taken into consideration.

Spring and fall eggs beat to a larger volume than midsummer eggs. When a recipe calls for beaten eggs, use large midsummer eggs and medium spring and fall eggs to compensate for this difference.

Thin whites mount better than thick whites. Their foam is less fluffy, however, making them better for cold preparations, while thick whites, which lose less of their volume when cooked, are better for hot ones.

Egg whites at room temperature whip more easily, quickly and to a larger volume than eggs just out of the refrigerator. It's even asserted that slightly warmed eggs are yet more effective.

Eggs several days old whip better than newly laid eggs.

Beating Egg Whites

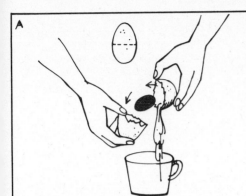

A Separating egg whites and yolks by dividing the egg along the middle and pouring the yolk from one half of the shell to the other.

C Lifting the egg whites preliminary to whipping. Cream of tartar but *no* salt added at this point.

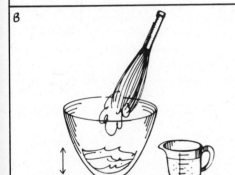

B Whites have started to mount but are still fluid. Sugar can be added at this point.

D Whites beaten stiff but not dry. For maximum stability they are not beaten to full volume.

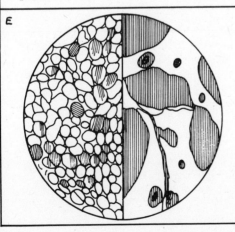

E Left side: properly beaten egg whites seen with hand glass. Right side: over-beaten whites, which have initially more volume but will not hold.

The white should be drawn up out of the bowl prior to being whipped, by dipping the whip in and out of the eggs.

Bowls with small rounded bottoms and sloping sides are preferable to bowls with large flat bottoms.

A fine balloon with large widespread wire whip made especially for egg whites is the most effective beater, better than an all-purpose whip, and much better than a rotary egg beater.

Stainless steel bowls are excellent; aluminum is not, as it reacts with the whites. Copper is the traditional vessel and is preferred because of its slight acidity. The bowl must be absolutely grease free in any case. The smallest quantity of fat, even a few drops of egg yolk, will destroy the whipping value of egg whites. Milk and cream cannot be added to the whites to be whipped for this reason.

Acid, generally cream of tartar, will aid stiffening. Add one eighth of a teaspoon for every three whites.

Sugar added to the egg whites while they are being whipped increases the time required to attain maximum volume; therefore, it should be added after whipping (except where necessary to preparation). However, when the whites seem in danger of falling, sugar can be added in a fine snow over the entire surface; it may very well save the whites. Add between one and two tablespoons per white.

Egg whites should not be beaten dry as this will decrease their efficiency. They are ready when the whites flow slowly if the bowl is turned, form peaks or tails on the whip which stand up straight, and have a shiny, smooth look with small regular cells.

For many cooks, a hot soufflé is the most frequent operation involving egg whites. Although there are several formulas for soufflés, most recipes involve a béchamel sauce made either with a flour roux or a roux made from some simple starch like potato flour, arrowroot or cornstarch.

When this sauce is prepared, four egg yolks (beaten fluffy) per cup of sauce, are added one by one away from the fire. When the soufflé involves a purée of some substance rather than a flavoring agent, the sauce is prepared to the normal thickness and up to ¾ of a cup of purée is added. For every four egg yolks, add five egg whites beaten stiff. Pour the mixture into a buttered soufflé dish or mold and cook for 25 or 30 minutes in a moderate oven.

Although a soufflé should be served immediately, it can be kept for up to half an hour by placing it under a thick pot in a warm place.

Egg whites have considerable use as a lightener in the hot mousses of ham, poultry, game, fish and the lighter mousseline preparations (*see*

113

Forcemeats). Many cooks add beaten whites to the whipped cream in whipped cream mousse to give it firmness and stability.

Angel food cake (without fat and without egg yolks), sponge cake (without fat but with egg yolks), white cake (with fat, without egg yolks), and "chocolate cake" (gâteau au chocolat) (with fat and egg yolks), also illustrate the different effects of beaten egg whites.

Eggs are cooked in seven ways and elaborated to at least fifteen hundred egg dishes. They are hard-cooked, soft-cooked, poached, fried, "shirred" (en cocotte), scrambled, or made into omelettes. They are combined with cockscombs, truffles, sweetbreads, snails, mussels, carrots, sorrel, crayfish, macaroni, and almost everything else.

Hard-Cooked Eggs

Method no. 1: Place the eggs in boiling water, allow the eggs to stand in a warm place in the pan for one hour.

Method no. 2: Add the eggs to simmering water; cook for six minutes and remove to a warm place for forty-five.

Method no. 3: Simmer over direct heat for 25 minutes.

The white of a hard-cooked egg should be firmly coagulated, yet tender. The yolk should be dry and mealy, not waxy. In hard-cooking eggs, one should allow eight ounces of water for each egg. After cooking, the eggs should be plunged into cold water. This makes peeling easier and avoids the formation of the green ring between the yolk and the white, which is perfectly healthful but not very attractive.

If a cracked egg is being cooked, vinegar added to the water prevents it from leaking. Eggs should be at room temperature before being cooked. If they are not, to prevent their cracking when plunged into hot water, pierce the round end with a needle to allow the air within the egg to escape.

Hard-cooked eggs, whether used hot or cold, are generally halved the long way. The yolks are removed and combined with other ingredients: vegetable purées, for example, mushrooms, asparagus, green peas, chopped meat or meat purées, rice, foie gras, onions, cheese, ham, herbs. The yolk is then returned to the egg. For hot dishes the egg is covered with a garnish—chopped meats, anchovies, diced lobster, mushrooms, chopped artichoke bottoms (all prepared in advance)—and coated with a sauce (chasseur, béchamel, curry, Mornay, crème), sprinkled with bread crumbs, grated cheese, or additional garnish to form a gratin, and passed under the broiler.

Cold egg dishes are much the same. The stuffing is cold; so is the garnish. The sauces tend to the mayonnaise-based sauces like Remoulade, Verte, Tartare.

In any treatment of hard-cooked eggs, overloading the eggs with sauce and garnish must be avoided, as should introducing ingredients which will color and make the white unattractive—for example, beets, pimentos, and certain pickles.

Soft-Cooked Eggs

Method no. 1: Allow one pint of boiling water for each egg. Add the egg to the water. Turn off the fire, cover the pan, allow the egg to remain in the water for four to six minutes, depending on size and desired doneness.

Method no. 2: Add the eggs to simmering water, cook for five to six minutes.

Method no. 3: Plunge the egg into boiling water, cook for two and one-half minutes to three and one-half minutes.

Method no. 4: Place the egg in cold water, bring the water to a boil, boil the egg one-half minute.

Soft-cooked eggs for children or the ill should be coddled rather than boiled, for greater digestibility. That is, they should be cooked in water just below simmering for eight minutes.

(One can flavor eggs in the shell before boiling them by washing them thoroughly and then enclosing them in a jar with truffles, saffron, or tarragon. Seal the jar and let it stay twelve hours before cooking the eggs. The odors will penetrate the porous shells of the eggs.)

Mollet Eggs

Soft-cooked eggs which have been cooked medium soft (five to six minutes in boiling water) and then peeled carefully under cold water are mollet eggs. Most often they are dressed on an oval croûton, slightly hollowed and covered with a sauce (diable, crème with horseradish, Mornay).

Mollet eggs can also be molded under the running faucet into fruit shapes (peas, apples, peaches) and decorated with bits of parsley, cloves, and vegetable colors.

115

Poached Eggs

For the most part eggs are poached in water. They can, however, be poached in cream, milk, red wine, broth, fruit juices, and almost any other liquid. The French Canadians poach eggs in maple syrup.

Fresh eggs poach best. When poaching eggs in water, salt and vinegar may be added. Two teaspoons of vinegar and one teaspoon of salt for each eight ounces of water will result in a classic poached egg.

The pan for poaching should contain enough water to accommodate all the eggs being poached. It should be placed on the heat so there is one small boiling point. It is not necessary to have the water boiling, but neither should the water be too cold as this will cause the egg to spread too wide.

More vinegar will result in a tighter more ball-like egg, which is not entirely undesirable. Too much salt will cause puckering and the egg white will be more opaque and less shiny than eggs poached in moderately salted or unsalted water.

When poaching in milk, it is wise to use a double boiler to eliminate the risk of scorching.

To poach an egg, break it into a small dish, then pour it into the boiling spot in the pan to set the outside. Either move the egg or turn the pan to remove the egg from the boiling spot and break another egg into it. Cook each egg three minutes. Cool it under the tap and keep it warm for use.

A properly poached egg will be round, the white will cover the yolk, the yolk will be liquid or semiliquid and the white will be coagulated but not jellylike.

To do a large number of eggs at once, when it is desirable to have them equally done and done at the same time, break the eggs into a bowl partially filled with vinegar. Then pour the contents of the bowl into a large pot filled with boiling water. The addition of the cold eggs and vinegar will cool the water to a desirable temperature and the vinegar will insure that the eggs are quickly set.

Poached eggs are served over toast, which can be grilled or fried in butter. They can be trimmed in any shape—rounds, squares, ovals. Tartlets, puff pastry shells are excellent. Poached eggs go well with meat cakes or croquettes.

They can also be served on various macaronis in sauce, braised endives, stewed tomatoes, macaroni croquettes, rice cakes, purées of vegetables.

They can be served in artichoke bottoms, halved broiled tomatoes, large squash halves, hollowed potatoes partially filled with a vegetable or meat purée, a chicken forcemeat, or stewed vegetable.

They can be garnished with diced meat, finely cut pieces of fowl, mushrooms, truffles, chopped green and red pepper, asparagus tips, anchovy fillets, slices of eggplant.

Almost any sauce can be used with poached eggs: a tomato sauce, demiglace, cream sauce, suprême, madeira.

Eggs that are poached in a liquid other than water should be given a sauce in basic accord with the poaching liquid: red wine sauce for red wine, cream sauce for cream, etc.

Molded Eggs (Eggs Moulés)

Molded eggs are prepared by buttering a small mold (*à darioles*), decorating the inside wall with truffles, pimentos, bits of meat, greens, herbs, a forcemeat, or a purée. An egg is then carefully broken into each mold keeping the yolk intact, and the white is salted. The molds are placed in a pan with enough water to cover the bottom half of the molds, then the molds are placed in a moderate oven for seven to ten minutes.

To remove the eggs from the molds, let them cool a minute or two, then turn them out.

Molded eggs are treated in large part like poached eggs, only their garnishes are simpler because the egg itself is garnished. Usually they are dressed on a toast or a bed of salad, with a sauce.

The egg to be molded can also be beaten like an omelette and mixed with a vegetable purée like spinach, then poached.

Molded eggs should have a firm white and a liquid yolk; the garnish should be attractive, even, and small.

Eggs en cocotte or en cassoulette

The real cocotte for eggs *en cocotte* is a small earthenware or silvered metal pot on three legs with a tiny handle. It holds two or three eggs. Lacking this, any small casserole, ramekin, or crock of an appropriate size and shape will do. This pot is buttered, heated, and a small amount of some preparation added: ham, creamed chicken, bacon, tiny shrimp, mushrooms, stewed tomatoes, chicken livers, tomato purée. The eggs (one, two, or three) are broken in and the whites slightly salted. When the three-legged pot is available it is placed in the oven. If one is using molds or flat-bottomed casseroles, the vessels are placed in water up to the halfway point and poached either in the oven or on top of the stove. Generally eggs cooked in cocottes are served in them with sauce in accord with the preparation at the bottom.

The eggs should not be cooked in a very hot oven, first because this tends to toughen the eggs, second because the pots break.

A touch of sherry or cognac in the bottom will steam up through the preparation during cooking.

Fried Eggs (Oeufs frits)

The English and the Americans eat an egg called fried, which in French would be *poêlé*. It is made by heating some butter in a pan and adding the eggs when the butter is warm but neither frothy nor brown. The eggs are then cooked on the side of the stove. Sometimes these eggs are "blinded" by placing a cover over them during the cooking. Because the cooking period is too long, this preparation is relatively indigestible. It is served with fried ham, bacon, or sausages.

In France, fried eggs are cooked in a small frying pan at least half full of very hot oil. The egg is broken into the oil, the white feathered around the yolk with a spoon. After the egg is cooked, it is drained and trimmed. This is probably the least desirable way to cook eggs. The whites are always tough, the eggs tend to be greasy. Most of the garnitures for fried eggs reflect their somewhat coarse nature: fried onion rings, fried sweet potatoes, salt cod.

Eggs can also be broken into a deep fryer and cooked.

Scrambled Eggs (Oeufs brouillés)

Method no. 1: Beat the whites and yolks of three eggs together until they are well blended but not excessively whitened. Add a tablespoon of cream, and salt, pepper, and a little butter. In the top of a double boiler, cook the eggs over barely simmering water, stirring constantly. Keep the water at a temperature low enough to stretch the time of preparation to twenty minutes. Just before serving, add a little more butter.

Method no. 2: Separate the egg whites from the yolks. Beat them separately but do not make a considerable effort to stiffen the whites. Recombine them, reserving one egg yolk for every six eggs. Add a little butter and a little cream. Heat some butter in a thick-bottomed pan, taking care the butter neither froths nor browns. It is important that the pan be thick-bottomed to prevent the eggs from scorching. Cook the eggs relatively briskly, stirring constantly until they are fluffy but still moist. Remove them from the pan and stir in one raw yolk.

Almost any ingredient can be mixed with scrambled eggs: mushrooms, artichokes, diced cooked bacon, chicken liver, celery, asparagus, broccoli, tongue, herbs, peppers, watercress.

Purées of shrimp, meats, pâté de foie gras can be mixed in small quantities with the eggs being cooked.

The ratio of whites to yolks can be varied for different textures.

Instead of cream, water or consommé can be used.

In making scrambled eggs, the most common error is overheating the pan. Again the question of toughening the eggs, this time compounded by the risk of browning them and thereby giving them a bitter taste.

Omelettes

Good omelettes require a good omelette pan. It should be thick so as not to scorch the eggs, with a good handle, preferably insulated, round sides to facilitate turning the omelette and an absolutely smooth inner surface.

An omelette pan is never used for anything else nor is it washed. Water captured by the pores of the metal is the cause of most sticking. The omelette pan should be cured initially by heating it with good quality oil until the oil is smoking. Then remove the oil, throw a handful of salt into the pan and rub it with a perfectly dry towel. Any water that was adhering to the pan is forced out by the oil, absorbed by the salt, and eliminated by the toweling. Should the pan be accidentally washed, it must be cured again. After each use, it can be wiped with a dry cloth. Care should be taken not to scratch the pan.

There are three basic formulas for an omelette mixture; one can beat three eggs until they are merely blended; one can beat the yolks and the whites separately to stiffen the whites a little to make a light omelette called mousseline; or one can substitute cream for a portion of the egg whites. In any case, the egg must account for more than 60 percent of the final preparation for it to be an omelette.

To produce the perfect omelette in either of its two accepted forms—cigar-shaped, pointed at both ends, or a perfect circle, folded once, unbrowned, symmetrical, high, fluffy, light—demands some dexterity. However, omelette making is not brain surgery; three or four omelettes carefully made are generally enough practice.

Heat a tablespoon of butter in an omelette pan. When the butter just begins to foam, pour in the egg mixture. The butter should be hot enough to set the omelette but not so hot as to toughen that part of the omelette in contact with it. Once set, the omelette is slid to pour some uncooked egg off the top into contact with the pan. When this is set, the pan should be moved by sharp jerks of the wrist to spin the omelette around. This insures even distribution of the egg and prevents sticking. After the omelette has been spun, the pan is lifted from the stove and held at an angle, the handle high to slide the omelette up the far wall. For a cigar-shaped omelette, the egg should be slid one third up the wall, for semicircular omelettes, one half. At this point the fully prepared garnish is introduced. Then the handle of the pan is rapped sharply at the end farthest from the pan with a fork. This should cause the omelette to fold over the garnish. The semicircular omelette is then slid from the pan and finished in a moderate oven.

The pointed omelette, a more showy presentation, still requires finishing. It can be finished by heating it in the broiler to dry the top, then folded; it can be covered with the same effect, or it can be folded completely and finished in a moderate oven.

In any case, the folding is accomplished by sliding the folded side of the omelette which is at the far end of the pan to the near end. Then slide the unfolded side down toward the plate and at the same time turn the folded side over it. The folded side, in other words, falls on top of the unfolded. The omelette is then straightened to the proper form with a clean towel or napkin.

The French or rolled omelette differs slightly from the standard omelette. This is the omelette made in restaurants at the table by a captain. While its presentation is often not as perfect as a well-made standard omelette, the beauty is in the execution, and moistness.

A heavy-bottomed omelette pan somewhat wider than the ordinary omelette pan is necessary. There are a number of special pans of cast aluminum designed for this purpose on the market.

Three eggs for the omelette are mixed with four teaspoons of water and a few drops of pepper sauce and a pinch of salt. The eggs are beaten with a fork until thoroughly mixed. A tablespoon of butter is melted in the pan placed over a medium flame. When the butter is

Making a Cigar-shaped Omelette

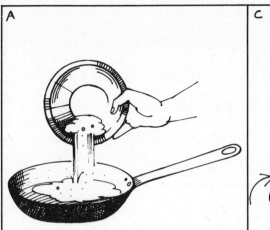

A

Lightly beaten egg poured into pan in which butter has begun to foam slightly.

C

Omelette with filling in center folded over by quick movement which causes third of omelette to clump wall and fall over filling.

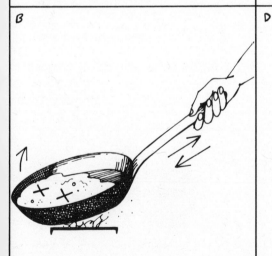

B

Pan moved back and forth over flame to pour egg off top of forming omelette.

D

Omelette turned in pan so folded portion is near handle, turned on unfolded part into plate.

melted and beginning to froth, the heat is lowered (very little heat is needed to coagulate a whole egg), the eggs are poured in and the pan rocked with the left hand while a fork in the right hand stirs the eggs. After about thirty seconds of this procedure, the mass of eggs will be filled with little ridges of cooked egg. At this point allow the mixture to set for a moment. Then tilt the pan forward and begin to roll the egg forward with the edge of the fork. The entire process revolves upon knowing how long to stir and how long to allow the egg to set. A filling can be rolled into the egg, or can be added to the mixture before cooking. And a slight slit may well be cut in the top of the already rolled and cooked omelette and some garnish added.

These omelettes are soft, long and narrow.

Omelettes admit a true wealth of garnitures: tomatoes, mushrooms, chicken livers, eggplant, veal kidney, morilles, sausage, truffles, shrimp, herbs, sweet potatoes, snails, brains, caviar, cheese, foie gras, cockscombs, macaroni in sauce, oysters, carrots, watercress, etc.

The garniture should be fully prepared before being added to the omelette; it should never be prepared in the omelette pan.

▝▜

XXII

Fish

Fish appears as a course in formal dinners and as a meatless main dish in many others. It is tasty, nutritious, inexpensive, and varied, over 250 species are available. It accepts myriad treatments, garnitures, and sauces. It can be canned, salted, dried, smoked, and frozen without serious deterioration.

Fresh fish must be absolutely fresh. When purchasing fish, choose those with bright clear skin, bright coloring, scales which are firmly affixed to the body. Clear, round, glossy eyes, red gills, firm plastic flesh; fresh odor in the gill slits and on the exterior are also signs of freshness. There should be little or no slime and a stiff body (still in rigor mortis).

A few fish, for example the California Dover sole, called "slimy sole" have superficial slime that is perfectly natural. Quick blanching will remove it.

Frozen fish is available in most varieties all year. A number of European fish are being imported. For the most part, frozen fish is treated as fresh fish, except that fish destined for poaching need not be defrosted, and already breaded fish or preformed croquettes must not be. Once fish is defrosted it should be used immediately.

Most fish is purchased in fish stores, which will prepare it for cooking: eviscerated with the entrails removed; dressed, with the viscera, head, and tail removed; in sections, in fillets (skin, head, tail, bones, and viscera removed), and steaks.

Although it is sometimes asserted that turbot and salmon improve with a few days' "aging," the best that can be said is that the flavor changes as some internal fat melts and is absorbed by the tissue, making it "richer" or, depending on one's taste, more oily.

The fat content of fish indicates the cooking process which lends itself. Lean fish are best poached, or baked, while fat fish can be broiled. Cooking times are relatively short in comparison to meat because fish has very little connective tissue. For this reason, heat need not be as intense.

Fish can be cooked by every cooking process: poaching, deep frying, sautéing, braising, grilling, and roasting.

In water cooking (*see* Water Cooking for explanation of boiling, poaching) large fish are placed on a fish poacher (a long covered pot with a removable drainer), covered with lightly salted water, and the water brought to a boil.

Or they are started in a cold court bouillon and brought to a boil. Slices of a large fish are slipped into boiling court bouillon and the heat reduced. Fish cooked au bleu are boiled. Lobsters are simmered. Turbot, salmon, and other fibrous fish are started in cold liquid and brought to a boil, and then poached over a very slow fire. Fillet of sole, similar preparations of fish, and for that matter any small delicate pieces, are best added to a large quantity of poaching liquid at exactly the desired temperature. When an item is started in cold liquid, it should be brought to the cooking temperature as quickly as possible. Fish is not *cooked* in boiling liquid.

Crimped fish, that is, fish that has been gashed on each side when alive, is also plunged into boiling water regardless of its size, to prevent the juices from escaping.

Very fragile fish may be wrapped in a cheesecloth, for poaching.

While salted water may be used for cooking many fish (bass, mullet, snapper), other cooking media brings out the character in others.

Barbel, turbot, and the fish treated similarly, are poached in water to which a tenth part of milk has been added.

Salmon and trout are cooked in a broth (court bouillon) of two cups of wine, one cup of carrots, one cup of oinions, two bay leaves, a good pinch of thyme and some parsley roots for an hour and then used hot or cold.

For carp and eels, one cup of carrots, one cup of onions are sweated in butter, moistened with a quarter cup of vinegar and reduced to dry. Then a cup of white wine and three cups of fish stock or water are added and the mixture cooked for an hour and strained.

For cooking carp or trout and for the basis of matelotes (*see* Stews), combine one quart of red wine with two cups of water, add two carrots, two chopped onions, a large pinch of thyme, two bay leaves, a crushed clove of garlic, and boil for forty minutes.

125

For cooking fish au bleu, mix two parts water with one part vinegar and lightly salt the mixture. Plunge the fish (just killed, emptied but not scaled) into the boiling court bouillon. The fish turns bluish if it has not been handled too much and the outer covering remains intact. This is suitable only for small fish. It is scaled at the table.

Poaching can also be accomplished in a 350° oven in a covered saucepan.

Fish cooked in water is done when the flesh has turned from transparent to opaque. It works out to be about ten minutes a pound at 190°.

One fries fish after soaking it in salted and peppered milk or cream and rolling it in flour. The piece being fried must necessarily not be too large or the outside will burn before the inside cooks. The fish is plunged into very hot oil (375°F—only oils are suitable because only they can be heated sufficiently hot) and allowed to cook until it comes to the surface. Fish for frying can also be treated à l'anglaise (dipped in egg yolk and rolled in bread crumbs).

Large fish (sterlet, carp, pike) can be braised like any white meat (see Braising). They are moistened with either red wine or white wine and fish stock or water.

Fish is broiled in a fish grill so that it can be easily turned. Large fish are cut in slices or filleted, medium fish are split from the back or stomach, and small fish are grilled whole. Prior to grilling they may be sprinkled with flour, or with a flour-paprika mixture. In any case, the fish should be brushed with either clarified butter or good olive oil.

Delicate fish are best sautéed in butter. Slices or fillets are sprinkled in flour and then browned on one side, turned, and browned on the other. The flesh side should be cooked first as the muscles in the skin side contract and curl the fish. Fillets of sole, because of their delicacy, are generally excepted from this rule. As butter burns at a relatively low temperature, melted butter may be used only for small pieces which cook quickly. Medium-sized pieces are cooked in clarified butter, and large pieces in a mixture of butter and oil.

Water-cooked fish is simply garnished with a boiled potato and melted butter or one of the Bâtarde sauces.

Fish poached in one of the court bouillons can be served with a sauce made from a reduction of the court bouillon developed like a white wine sauce or with a white wine sauce (see Sauces).

Fried fish is served with a cold sauce like tartare.

Braised fish is served with a sauce made of the braising liquid.

126

Sautéed fish is sprinkled with a few drops of lemon juice and a generous pinch of blanched parsley. The cooking fat is poured from the pan and a piece of butter browned in it. Still foaming, the butter is poured over the fish. This treatment is called à la meunière.

Other sauces, not necessarily fish-based, make attractive fish dishes: Bordelaise, Bourgignonne, Chasseur, Provençale, Italienne, Aurore, Bercy, Cardinal, Curry, Hollandaise, Hongroise, and Nantua.

While it is a rather dangerous business to suggest a French equivalent for fish found in America, it is even more dangerous to attempt an English equivalent for French fish, as many fish which are landed in England now have English names as well as French but share them with other species landed in America.

This whole procedure is saved from being a rather confusing academic exercise by the value of knowing the exact equivalents when they occur. Those fish for which a season is indicated are readily available in principal American markets.

Angler (Baudroie)　　　　　　　　　　　　Seven to twelve pounds
A saltwater fish whose flesh is soft. Generally bought as cleaned tails as this is the only edible part. It can be fried, sautéed, grilled.

Barbel (Barbeau)　　　　　　　　　　　　　Two to four pounds
A freshwater fish. Steamed in red wine, then the stock thickened with beurre manié; or steamed in white wine sauce seasoned with mustard; deep-fried; with horseradish sauce; braised with mushrooms and mussels; stuffed and steamed in fish stock.

Black Bass　　　　　　　　　　In season two to four pounds
This freshwater game fish although an excellent food is, like other fish of its type, protected under the game laws. Two varieties, the big mouth and the small mouth, are available. This fish is usually floured and sautéed.

Bluefish　　　　　　　　All year; normal size, one to six pounds
A saltwater fish from the Atlantic coast. Sweet, dark, delicate flesh, broiled, baked, pan-fried as a rule. It requires generous seasoning.

Bonito (Bonite)
(*see* Tuna)

Bream (Brème)　　　　　　　　　　　　　　About six pounds
Freshwater fish. Cooked in beer with onions, bay leaves, thickened with beurre manié; cooked in fish stock with mirepoix and sage; then thickened with beurre manié, finished with a little cream; baked with chopped mushrooms, bread crumbs, and shallots.

127

Brille (Barbue)   Five to six pounds
   Saltwater fish resembling turbot. Cooked in court bouillon, with
sauce Normande; poached in champagne with shallots; steamed in
white wine; *au beurre noir;* cooked au gratin by being coated with a
duxelle mixture and passed under the broiler; à la bonne femme;
with American sauce; Mornay sauce; à la Portugaise; à la Provençale.

Buffalo fish   February–August; three pounds up
   A fresh water medium fat firm-fleshed fish, often smoked. Can be
baked, deep-fried, or treated like whitefish.

Carp (carpe)   Cold months; two to eight pounds
   A freshwater fish that often grows immense. Most often it is quite
muddy and must be carefully cleaned, soaked in salted water and
vinegar. The spleen behind the head must be removed. Often carp is
baked, or poached, although it can be braised with great success. It
may also be broiled.

Catfish   All year; from one pound up
   A fatty freshwater fish, with a firm, flaky flesh and a delicate flavor.
Preferred are the channel cats. Traditionally, in America, catfish are
fried, but they may be braised or cooked like carp.

Char (Omble Chevalier)   Two to four pounds
   A very delicate fish, that is simply cooked to preserve its fine natural
taste. Can be lightly sautéed with plenty of butter.

Chub (Chevesne)   All year; two to eight pounds
   A delicate fatty freshwater fish that is smoked and sold, often as not,
as "whitefish."

Cod (Cabillaud, Morue)   All year; one to ten pounds
   Saltwater. Fried in butter, Bercy; poached with tomato sauce; baked
in butter; marinated in lemon juice, with curry powder; fried in
butter; as quenelles, with herb sauce.

Conger Eel (Congre)   Eight to twenty pounds
   A large eel, with few bones and fine flesh, that is prepared like eel or
stuffed after parts of the backbone have been removed.

Croaker   March–October; one to four pounds
   A saltwater fish that is inexpensive and generally good. It can be
cooked like trout.

Cusk   All year; one to ten pounds
   A soft saltwater fish, with very white flesh and a fine flavor. Is
generally baked.

Dab (Limande)   Two to three ounces
   Treated like sole.

Dace (Vandoise)   Two to twenty ounces
   A fish that in some ways resembles a chub, it is prepared like trout or
   perch.
Denie (Denté)   Four ounces to one pound
   A saltwater fish which may be prepared like bream.
Dog Fish (*see* Rockfish)
Drum   Winter; one to forty pounds
   A name given to a number of close species which are well known as
   channel bass, redfish, red bass. They are all cooked like bass.
Dwarf Dragon (Petite Vive)   Eight ounces to one pound
   A saltwater fish used in bouillabaisse.
Eel (Anguille)   All year; one to five pounds
   Eels are skinned (alive) prior to preparation, after which they may be
   boiled, fried, stewed, jellied, baked, stuffed, deep-fried.
Elvers   One hundred fifty to a pound
   The young eel, which resembles a slug, is generally deep-fried.
Flounder   Some varieties; three ounces to ten pounds
   While flounder is sold as English sole (which it is not), real sole is
   available imported. A great many subvarieties of quite different characteristics are sold as flounder. The dab, the gray sole, yellowtail,
   winter flounder, lemon sole. The gray sole is the best and closest to
   the European species. The fluke is as well a flat fish, summer
   flounder, and an excellent fish. Any of these fishes can be prepared
   like sole or turbot.
Fluke
   (*see* Flounder above)
Grayling (Omble)   One to two pounds
   A freshwater fish cooked like trout.
Gudgeon (Goujon)   One to two ounces
   A narrow freshwater fish, with a delicate flesh and few bones. They
   can be prepared like perch or trout; when small, like smelts, often
   deep-fried.
Gurnard (Grondin)   Three to four ounces
   A spiny saltwater fish, particularly ugly, with a firm, good flesh and
   few bones. Sometimes a little muddy. Grilled, fried, or perhaps best
   baked.
Haddock (Aigrefin)   All year; one to seven pounds
   A mild codlike fish, with good flavor and wide availability. Great
   quantities are smoked as finnan haddie. It is a relatively fine fish and
   is generally moist-cooked.

129

The smoked "finnan-haddie" is poached in milk, or in milk and sherry if the smoky taste is too strong.

Hake (Merlus)   All year; two to five pounds
A fish of the cod family, with lean, soft, rather mushy flesh. Prepared like cod.

Halibut (Flétan)   April–October; five to seventy pounds
A very excellent fish, relatively high in fat, that can be treated as turbot, which it somewhat resembles. Western halibut from the Pacific, oddly enough, is superior to Atlantic halibut.

Herring (Hareng)   Winter; two ounces to five ounces
While most of this saltwater fish is processed, it can be enjoyed fresh. It can be baked, broiled, or the fillets can be deep-fried or rolled and broiled.

Herring, Lake   One to two pounds
This freshwater fish is a type of whitefish, and it is often smoked.

Huck (Huch)   One to five pounds
Freshwater fish that is prepared like salmon.

King Mackerel (Able de Mer)   November–March; one to four pounds
A saltwater fish, with a flavor and flesh much like the Spanish mackerel.

King Whiting   One to three pounds
A saltwater fish with a lean delicate flesh. Broiled, fried, sometimes poached.

Lamprey (Lamproie)   One to five pounds
Both fresh and salt, cooked like eel.

Ling (Lingue)   All year; five to twenty pounds
A saltwater fish close to cod.

Mackerel (Macquereau)   January–April; five to twenty pounds
Generally refers to Boston mackerel, which is treated in the same fashion as the Spanish mackerel.

Marena (Marène)   One to three pounds
A rare European freshwater fish, cooked like trout.

Mostele (Mostèle)   One to four pounds
A rare European freshwater fish cooked like trout.

Mullet (Mulet or Muge)   September–December; eight
                                                           ounces to three pounds
A moderately fatty fish that is widely used. Often it tastes of mud, and, like many inshore fishes, of petroleum products. Prepared in all fashions, poached, grilled, baked, etc.

Ocean Perch   All year; eight ounces to two pounds
A saltwater fish with a firm sweet mild taste. The lean flesh lends itself to baking, broiling with plenty of butter, or frying.

130

Perch (Perche)   All year; six ounces to one pound
Freshwater perch are treated like trout. Their delicate flesh is excellent sautéed or broiled.

Pike (Brochet)   April–October; eight ounces to four pounds
A dry freshwater fish. Only the meat, which flakes readily, is generally used, often in mousse, in quenelles, etc. Skinned, larded, baked with butter, poached with white wine sauces; baked with sour cream; broiled in brown butter; marinated in white wine, oil and fine herbs, grilled.

Pike Perch (Sandre)   All year; one to ten pounds
A freshwater fish quite close to the pike and prepared in much the same way. There are several varieties, but from the gastronomic point of view, they are treated similarly.

Plaice (Plie)   Four ounces up
Flounder family. Cooked like sole. Baked with grated cheese and bread crumbs; with brown butter, or with hollandaise; grilled.

Pollock (Lieu Jaune)   November–January; three to thirty-five pounds
A saltwater fish related to the cod, haddock, hake, and cusk. Lean, sometimes mushy. Prepared like cod.

Pompano   January–April; twelve ounces to one and one half pounds
A saltwater fish of great worth, with a firm, flaky flesh and moderate fattiness. Because of the demand other fish are often substituted for it, and one must beware that fish purchased is an unqualified pompano, not a great pompano or Mexican pompano, and that the purveyor is honest. Pompano is fried, baked, boiled, cooked in a paper, poached.

Redfish (Bergolette) (*See* Drum)

Red Mullet (Rouget Barber)   One to eight pounds
(It has no gall bladder and is not gutted.) With crabmeat in white wine sauce; broiled with melted butter; fried with butter sauce, or marinated in oil, lemon juice, and chopped fennel; poached in oil and white wine, garnished with diced tomatoes, garlic and saffron rice.

Red Snapper   April–July; one to twenty pounds
While the red snapper is among the most excellent of fish caught in southern American waters, with an extremely fine flavor, it is too often masqueraded as *Rouget* in American-French restaurants, this is an injustice to both fish. The juicy, mild-tasting snapper has virtues of its own. It can be cooked like any lean fish.

Roach (Gardon)   One pound
A small freshwater fish with a compact flesh that is pinkish after cooking. It is generally sautéed, broiled, or deep-fried.

Rockfish (Sébaste)   One to two pounds
An ugly small saltwater fish with pointed fins that resembles the *rascasse* of bouillabaisse fame. These fish are good eating, poached, grilled, in fish soups.

Salmon (Saumon)   April–October; three to thirty pounds
Five major varieties are available: Chinook, Sockeye, Coho, Humpback, and Chum. Color is the major consideration in grading. The bulk of salmon is canned. Fresh salmon, when available, is often poached or grilled. With Maltaise sauce; cold with mayonnaise sauces; slices poached in white wine; with cucumbers; whole fish braised in champagne; with hollandaise sauce.

Salmon Trout (Truite Saumonée) (*See* Trout)

Sand Smelt (Prêtre) (*See* Smelt)

Scup (Pagre)   April–October; one to twenty pounds
Called the porgy, silver bass, this small, tender, sweet fish is most often fried.

Sea Bass (Bar)   All year; one on up
A saltwater fish with tasty, white meat. The leaner varieties are poached, baked, broiled with fennel; cold with mayonnaise; with tomato sauces.

Sea Bream (Dorade Commune)   Four ounces to two pounds
A fish that is close (in culinary terms) to the bass and the porgy. The flesh is especially delicate. They are poached; served cold; grilled; fried (when small), in butter; deep-fried.

Shad (Alose)   March–May; three to five pounds
A saltwater fish of great worth. Prized in season for its roe, which is generally broiled or sautéed. The fish can be filleted and the meat poached; broiled; breaded and fried; baked and used with fish sauces.

Sheepshead (Freshwater)   April–June; eight ounces
                                                to one and one half pounds
A freshwater fish, close to the Drum. Bony, with white flesh. A relatively coarse fish. Broiled or baked.

Sheepshead (Saltwater)   April–November
                                          Twelve ounces to three pounds
Unlike the freshwater sheepshead, the salt variety has a flaky, delicate, sweet flesh and can be treated like sea bass.

Spot (Lafayette)   Four ounces
A lean fish with sweet flesh, resembling that of the gudgeon.

Sterlet (Sterlet)   Sixteen to twenty pounds
The smallest member of the sturgeon family, which may be the most

readily available here. It can be poached, in white wine; filleted and grilled; the fillets poached and served with hollandaise sauce; served with horseradish.

Skate (Raie)   Ten pounds up
A flat fish that is rarely seen. It has a strong odor, which largely disappears in cooking. The fish should be thoroughly washed, then poached before further preparation. After poaching, and skinning, it can be further treated by browning in butter; deep-frying; with caper sauce; au gratin.

Smelt (Esperan)   February–June; one to two ounces
A small fish found in lakes and streams and in salt water. An excellent firm fish with a very mild taste. (Unfortunately stale smelts taste oily and they have gained this reputation.) They are fried; split and broiled; baked in a sauce; poached and treated à la grecque; stuffed and baked; sautéed.

Sole (Sole)   All year; one to two pounds
A flat fish found on all European coasts. Poached, all sauces, grilled, all compound butters; garnished with asparagus tips, mussels, shrimps, lobster, button onions, crèpes, truffles, tomatoes, chopped ham, etc.

Spanish Mackerel (Macquereau)   One to three pounds
A fat-fleshed fish of fine flavor (when fresh) and firm, textured flesh somewhat lighter than the common mackerel. Poached, with white sauces; baked, with herb and vegetable garnitures; grilled with compound butters; deep-fried; cold with a mayonnaise sauce.

Sturgeon (Esturgeon)   Two to three thousand pounds
Although sturgeon is delicious fresh, it is most often available smoked. Fresh, it can be treated like veal with veal garnitures as the flesh is sufficiently dense to resemble meat. Cooked by moist processes, it is especially excellent.

Striped Bass (Bar)   All year; three to six pounds
A firm-fleshed lean fish, with a good flavor, found in both rivers and the sea. Excellent poached, grilled, fried, cooked in a sauce (it keeps its texture well).

Swordfish (Espadon)   June–October; 100 to 200 pounds
A saltwater fish, very lean, very firm with white flesh, and a rich flavor. The meat is cut in steaks, which are poached, grilled, sautéed, etc.

Tench (Tanch)   One to two pounds
A fish of the carp family, which often tastes of mud. Cooked like carp.

Trout (Truite)   May–December; one pound to ten
The names refer to a number of different varieties of fish—the brook trout, brown trout, rainbow, golden—all of which are prized for their excellent rich flesh. To best appreciate them, they should be treated simply, cooked *au bleu,* floured, and sautéed, baked, etc. Otherwise, they can be treated as salmon; grilled, poached in white wine; braised; cold with sauces.

Tuna (Thon)   May–November; five to twenty-five pounds
Most of the production of tuna and similar fish goes into processing. Fresh tuna, has a strong oily taste that can be reduced by marination and slow moist cookery. It is often prepared like veal and accepts the same garnitures.

Turbot (Turbot)   Eight ounces to ten pounds
Turbot, a member of the flatfish family, is often available frozen, or, in the case of large fish, defrosted cuts are available. The creamy white gelatinous flesh is highly prized; however, frozen turbot is hardly as attractive as fresh. It is most often poached, served with white wine sauces.

Whitebait (Blanchaille)   One hundred fifty to the pound
The young of herring, they are generally floured, deep-fried until crisp.

Whitefish (Laveret)   All year; one to six pounds
A fresh water fish of the salmon family that is more often than not smoked. The flesh is white, rich, and delicate. Fresh, the whitefish can be treated like salmon or trout.

Whiting (Merlan)   Eight ounces to three pounds
A lean fish, often fried. In classical cuisine the whiting often contributes to fish stocks and to soufflé and mousse bases.

Wolf Fish (Loup Marin)   Spring; four to eight pounds
A saltwater fish of modest quality. Often fillets and pieces of the fish are poached and served in a sauce. Otherwise it is treated like sole.

XXIII

▰▰▰

Mollusks, Crustaceans, and Reptiles

Mollusks

The mollusks, crustaceans, and reptiles constitute a tremendous resource in cuisine. They are almost all among the foods people most enjoy: oysters, lobster, shrimp, frogs' legs, terrapin, etc.

Oysters (Huitres)

Of the shellfish, the oyster is the most prized. The particular variety of oyster is more a consideration when they are intended to be eaten raw; for cooking purposes, the common oyster of the area or the best buy is suitable: Mattituck, Blue Point, Gardiner's Island, Oyster Bay, Peconic, Lynnhaven, Seawaphaka, Bay Salts, Seapure, Robbins Island, and Greenport in Long Island; Cape Cod in New England; Chincoteague in Virginia; Chesapeake in Maryland; Coon in Florida; Cove and Virginia in Chesapeake Bay; Olympia and Japanese (Pacific) from the West Coast.

Oysters' shells should be firmly closed. The oyster itself should be firm, full, plump, well shaped and alive. It should react when touched. No odor should be apparent. When oysters are purchased shucked, the liquid should be clear, and should represent only a very small part of the total weight of the purchase.

They can be used as an hors d'oeuvre, a fish course, or a light main dish. When they are poached they are cooked in their own juice until the

135

edges curl, then returned to their shells and garnished: with American sauce, with grated cheese and bread crumbs, with snail butter, with hollandaise sauce, with white wine sauces, with Newburg sauce, and sauce suprême.

They can be treated à la Villeroy (*see* Variety Meats), breaded and deep-fried, sautéed, or wrapped in bacon and grilled. Oysters are suitable for vol-au-vent and other pastry shell dishes when combined with a sauce, usually white, and other ingredients like poached mushrooms, truffles, diced ham, crayfish tails, etc.

Scallops (Petoncles)

Scallops are of two types, bay or shallow water scallops, and deep sea scallops. Fresh scallops (generally only the muscle that closes the shell is sold) should be cream white, perhaps with a slight pink tinge. The deep sea scallops are much larger than the bay and are often halved for sale. Cape scallop refers to a very small bay scallop.

Scallops, no matter how they are to be finished, should first be poached to reduce shrinkage and add to the flavor of the meat. One can simmer them in cream sauce, any of the white wine sauces, Mornay sauce, Newburg sauce, or créole sauce. They can be grilled, or breaded and sautéed, or treated with a batter and deep-fried. The larger scallops (scallops are larger in France than in America) can be sautéed without bread crumbs and then pan deglazed with white wine, with sherry, with port, or with cognac, and a sauce developed.

They are also treated au gratin, curried, or used cold in a salad.

Only 10 percent of the scallop (the muscle) is marketed in America, while in Europe the entire scallop is sold. If a whole scallop is encountered, the dark sack should be removed as well as any stomach residue. The beard, the mantle, and the red portions can be trimmed, and the scallop used.

Abalone, a shellfish found in the Pacific, resembles scallops although it is considerably larger (like scallops, only the muscles are marketed). Abalone can be pounded into steaks and grilled or fried.

Mussels (Moules)

Mussels present a bargain in shellfish because of their abundance and the reluctance of most people to take on the task of cleaning them. First of all, the mussels should be cleaned when they are gathered. When purchased in the fish market they should be at least partially cleaned. Then they can be washed in two or three waters and placed in water to which a teaspoon of epsom salts per quart has been added. They are left for a day to purge themselves, washed again in several waters, and placed in water to which a half cup of cornmeal per quart of water has been added, and left to feed for a day. Finally, they are washed again and the shell scrubbed free of barnacles. The larger varieties can be eaten raw like oysters if one is assured they have been gathered in clean waters.

Generally, they are placed in very little liquid and steamed open. This liquid, be it wine, stock, cream, milk, can then form the basis of a cream sauce, a white wine sauce, a hollandaise sauce, etc. All reddish or black-ish mussels are discarded immediately, as should be any mussel that resists opening after the others have opened. One *beards* mussels before serving them by removing the black portions and the trailing material.

Mussels are also prepared with any fish sauce like oysters, poached and fried; prepared à la Villeroy; filled with some fragant stuffing and the shells closed, skewered, and grilled.

Clams (Lucines)

There are two main sorts of clams, the soft shelled and the hard shelled, though a number of different regional names indicating size exist. Clams should be purchased live with tightly closed shells. They are washed in several changes of cold water before use. For cooking purposes they can be immersed in boiling water or left in a moderate oven until they open.

The clam does not really have a French counterpart, although some effort has been made to introduce the littleneck into French coastal waters. The clovisse or palourde is about as close as France comes to the hard-shell clam. Clams are eaten raw like oysters, made into fritters, soups, or poached and the liquid developed by the same treatment used for mussels.

They can be stewed in milk or cream and seasoned with butter and paprika; deep-fried; steamed in a stock with thyme and bay.

The long or soft-shell clams are steamed and eaten with clarified butter and clam broth.

137

Sea Urchin (Oursin)

The sea urchin, which is a delicacy in Europe and extremely expensive (50 cents each during holiday seasons), is ignored here. It is eaten raw, or boiled and eaten with toast like a soft-cooked egg. (Only the yellow is eaten; the other material is dumped out.) The flesh can also be removed when raw and puréed and used in mayonnaise or fish sauce to give it a pleasing sea salty taste.

Squid (Calmar)

Squid and cuttlefish also belong to the mollusks. The ink sac (found by slitting the top), the beck, and the eyes are removed. It is advisable to beat the animal with the aid of a knife or a meat tenderizer, then let it soak in cold running water for a couple of hours before using it.

They are cut into pieces and deep-fried; made into croquettes; parboiled in salt water and treated à la provençale or with white wine sauce.

Octopus (Poulpe-Marin)

Octopus, a mollusk with a soft saclike body and a large head with eight arms, is prepared similarly to squid (which has ten arms). It should be well pounded, the beck and eyes removed. Often it is cut up and deep-fried.

Goose Barnacle (Barnache)

This barnacle can be steamed like a soft-shell clam. It has a delicate flavor. Only the neck is eaten.

Snail (Escargots)

Snails are the sole terrestrial mollusks used in cuisine. The finest of the several varieties is found in the vineyards of Burgundy, France, called, understandably enough, the *bourgogne*. The other edible variety is the *petit gris,* which is small and gray, while the bourgogne is striped in white and brown. Bourgogne snails are prepared and sold in cans all over the world.

The best snails, however, are those which are alive but have gone into hibernation (bouchés). While these are among those canned, this particular phase is not a requisite to their commercial preparation, and snails in other stages of their life cycle are included as well.

When one is fortunate enough to have live but hibernating snails with which to work, wash them thoroughly in three waters, and brush the shell under running water to remove the dirt. Lift off the flat seal which the snail has secreted to seal himself in. Put them in a vessel with a quarter cup of vinegar, a tablespoon of flour, and a teaspoon of salt per quart of water. Allow them to purify themselves for two days. Actually they are already purged, as they eat nothing for several days before going into the dormant state, and this additional purging is only insurance.

Wash them again. Put the snails in cold water and slowly bring them to a boil. All snails and all snail-like mollusks should be cooked slowly, rather than plunged into boiling water, as their reaction to violent treatment is to retreat into the shell, making them difficult to remove. It is also believed that the shock toughens them. Take care to remove the scum. Boil eight minutes. Drain and wash. Cook the snails in a white wine court bouillon (*see* Fish) for three and a half hours. Drain again. Remove them from their shells and reserve the shells for service. It is not necessary to remove the black portion (it is widely suggested to do so) as it is completely healthful and flavorful.

Most snails are prepared with a compound butter made with garlic, shallots, salt, pepper, parsley, and some of the poaching liquid. They are reinserted into the shells with some of the butter and heated in a special platter before being served. When heated, they are ready when the butter is just melted. It serves no purpose to frizzle them in the butter, and the garlic becomes bitter with overcooking. The lovers of snails in the Burgundy region do not use a holding device but take the snail shell with their fingers and, using the fork, pop the snail, into their mouths, followed by a bit of bread dipped in the butter.

Smaller snails which are unsuitable for the shell game are packed in cans and represent a tremendous bargain. They are sautéed in snail butter and served on toast, or combined with melted butter and melted marrow, or chopped shallots reduced in white wine. They can be fried in batter, or cooled after being poached and used as an hors d'oeuvre with vinaigrette. Snails are very good in omelettes or with scrambled eggs.

139

Conchs and whelks, which are varieties of sea snail, are not widely used in cuisine. When they are prepared, they are seldom cooked in the shell like ordinary snails. Rather, they are suspended by a hook through the foot, until the snail fatigues, then the foot section is trimmed from the shell, the extremities removed and the snail poached. It can be used like land snails.

Crustaceans

Most crustaceans are best parboiled in a fragrant court bouillon and then finished by some other process. This serves two purposes: the court bouillon flavors the meat when it does not have a tremendous amount of character, and the partial cooking reduces the time spent in dry (and drying) heat. Plain salt water as the cooking liquid would tend to whiten and toughen the meat.

Crayfish (Écrivisses)

Crayfish are abundant in American streams and rivers, inexpensive (less than a dollar a pound in New York), but almost unavailable very far from the place where they are gathered. Those that reach the major markets are generally in deplorable condition because of poor handling, or when frozen may have been congealed in a sea of mud containing miscellaneous pieces, stones, and weeds.

Contrarily, the frozen langoustines or Norwegian lobsters, which come from the Scandinavian seas and are in the same size range, are beautifully packed. Unfortunately, the taste of crayfish is especially distinctive, and parading a langoustine as a crayfish for an initiated diner is impossible.

The crayfish in France has considerable usage. It is used as a garnish on many dressed pieces, the tails are used to flavor meat and fowl stews, crayfish butter is widely used to finish fish sauces—Nantua, for example.

Langoustine and crayfish are in any case prepared similarly. They are poached in a court bouillon often highly spiced with "crab boil," a mixture of red peppers, bay, thyme, dill. They are served with melted butter.

The tails, removed from the shells by snipping off the end and forcing out the tail, can be made into croquettes, simmered in cream, marinated in lemon juice and oil, and deep-fried in a batter, made into a mousse or a soufflé, used as garnish for rice, "in aspic," or baked in pie.

Crayfish and langoustine are quite excellent in salads, as an hors d'oeuvre, or in mayonnaise sauce.

Crabs (Crabes)

The crabs, which range from the tiny oyster crab found in oyster shells to the giant Alaskan king crab, all have a basically similar sweetish taste. Most crabs marketed are either the Dungeness Crab of the Pacific or the Blue Crab of the Atlantic and Gulf coasts. Domestic crabs are far superior to imported (largely Japanese) varieties. Except for the larger varieties which can well be eaten from the shell with melted butter, the picked meat is generally employed in cookery. It is available frozen, canned, "fresh" flash pasteurized.

Grades are rather important. Jumbo Lump is all large lump and white, Lump is all lump but smaller chunks than Jumbo, Mixed is at least 50 percent lump, Flake is white broken pieces and small lumps. Claw meat is from the claws and brownish. Usually it is the lowest-priced crabmeat, but recently has been aggressively marketed as a "gourmet" meat.

In buying live crabs, the first requisite is that they be alive. Secondly, they should be heavy for their size. Medium-sized crabs are the best buy and perhaps are tenderer than the largest.

The meat is tossed in butter with chopped shallots and bound with Mornay sauce, with Bordelaise, with Newburg sauce, curry, or white wine sauce.

The meat can be mixed with an assortment of garnishes: pimentos, chopped ham, green peppers, fried bacon, mushrooms, parsley, garlic, and tomatoes.

The soft-shell crab, or the crab in its molting stage, is all edible meat with the exception of the breathing apparatus (the devil) found on both sides. Soft-shells are grilled, treated with batter and fried, or deep-fried à l'anglaise.

Lobster (Homard)

The lobster is the most appreciated food in this category. The langouste or spiny lobster is somewhat similar. The most apparent difference is that the langouste lacks heavy pincer claws and its shell is spiny rather than smooth. Often only the tails are sent to market.

While much of the spiny lobster used is imported from Cuba, Australia, and South Africa, the Laguna lobster from Pacific American waters is often available frozen, and sometimes available live in large markets.

Genuine lobsters are best purchased live. Excessive storage (in the refrigerator) is not recommended as they live on their own substance and rapidly become wasted.

Lobsters are grilled after being three-quarters poached in a court bouillon. The lobster is split either through the back or through the belly down the medial line and the halves broken apart but not entirely separated. It is basted with melted butter, sometimes seasoned with lemon juice, salt, pepper and MSG, paprika, herbs, the ingredients of any compound butter, and then glazed in the broiler.

The grilled lobster may also be stuffed, especially in the season when the meat is scant, by filling the chest section with a farce of crabmeat, parsley, and bread crumbs, bound with butter, quenelles mixture, a fish mousse or meat picked from another lobster.

The lobster may also be completely cooked and eaten boiled, in which case it should be cooked in beer, in highly seasoned sea water, or in a fragrant court bouillon.

Steaming is, as well, a very satisfactory way to cook lobster, especially if one owns a proper rack and the lobster can be placed backside up.

Everything in the lobster is edible, except the small sac near the head section and the blackish intestinal tract running the length of the lobster.

The meat from a cooked lobster or commercially prepared lobster meat—in the case of commercial meat, it is important to deal with an absolutely reputable purveyor who has cooked only live lobsters, otherwise the meat may be unhygienic and is certainly tasteless and stringy —can be treated with any number of sauces, cold as well as hot. With mayonnaise, chives, and chopped fennel; in aspic; as a mousse; or in a soufflé. The slices of the tail (both langouste and homard) can be sautéed in butter and deglazed with white wine, with cream, with sherry, with port, etc.

The genuine lobster (homard) is very often cut up in the shell and sautéed, then finished with a sauce. The live lobster is cut into pieces: three from the tail, two from each claw, two from the body, and all the little legs. The head is discarded and the soft parts are reserved. The meat, still in the shell, is sautéed in butter with a very fine mirepoix.

142

When the shells are well reddened, giving a color to the sauce and a pleasing light "bromide" taste, the preparation is moistened and then simmered until the lobster is cooked.

At this point, the meat is withdrawn and the shells are discarded or pounded in a mortar, moistened with some lobster stock (from a prior poaching), and cooked to extract some more coloring and flavor. The liquid in which the meat was cooked is strained, mixed with the liquid from the shells, reduced and strained again. The soft parts are mixed with flour or a beurre manié or left alone; they are then added to thicken the sauce and the lobster meat returned. The preparation may be finished by the addition of egg yolks to make a further liaison, by another sauce, a compound butter, a seasoning, or a garniture.

The exact nature of the dish depends on the liquid added as a moistening, the finishing, and the garniture. The moistening may be done with lobster stock, with white wine, with curry or tomato sauce, with fish velouté with sherry, with champagne. The finishing can be cream, sherry, port, cognac, pastis. The garnitures are myriad: rice, peppers, olives, vegetables, mushrooms.

Scampi (Caramote)

When purchased, scampi, or caramote, are generally frozen or raw, without their heads. After parboiling they are used either shelled or unshelled. They can be sautéed in oil with shallots, garlic and tomatoes, deglazed—after being sautéed in butter—with cognac, pastis, with white wine, with fish stock, with cream, etc. The tails can be simmered in cream sauce, seasoned with dill, or paprika, in sauce Mornay, in tomato sauce.

The large scampi can also be split and grilled after being glazed with melted butter.

Shrimp and prawns are available fresh, canned, frozen, unshelled or with the shell, dehydrated and dried. They are used as a garnish for soups, sauces, and other fish preparations.

The terms prawn and shrimp are used interchangeably in the marketplace, although the names do refer to different (but very close) species. In England the word shrimp is used to mean shrimp of the type found in San Francisco Bay, while *prawn* refers to the common shrimp. In ordinary parlance, prawns are larger and somewhat tougher than shrimp.

This type of crustacean is almost always overcooked. In general, the crustaceans should be added to boiling water, and should be cooked when the water has returned to a boil. A good deal, however, depends on the species and the quantities involved.

The tails can be used as a cold hors d'oeuvre, for which they should be cooked in a very fragrant court bouillon or in a good beer.

For hot dishes, after being poached, the tails are tossed in butter bound with creôle sauce, Mornay sauce, white wine sauce, sauce provençale, etc.

Reptiles

Except for an occasional can of rattlesnake meat or an alligator tail, the reptiles are represented in cuisine by turtles, terrapins, and frogs.

Turtle (Tortue)

The upper and lower shells of the turtle are prepared in cans for the confection of turtle soup. The meat is simmered in a seasoned broth made of both beef and chicken consommé with the spice compound called turtle spice.

The use of these rather strong seasonings was originally occasioned by the large quantities of spoiled turtle meat from Africa that first reached Europe. Nowadays, when preservation is not a problem, and strong spices are not necessary to compensate for its absence, more subtle seasonings may be used. Turtle meat can be developed much like veal.

The fins, when they are obtainable (usually from the Caribbean Islands or Nicaragua), are blanched, the outer skin removed, and the leg poached and then braised in madeira sauce. The flesh under the upper shell is also appreciated. It is larded with pork or with calf's udder, marinated for three days in white wine, with bay, thyme, garlic, red pepper, and then poached like a white meat.

The green snapping turtle which is available in both northern and southern inland waters is extensively used for making soup. To prepare for cooking, lay the turtle on its back, wait until the head comes out, slit the throat and bleed the turtle. Detach the flat shell from the top by passing a sharp knife around the edges, remove the meat from both shells. Cut the shells in inch square pieces. Chop off the head and fins, blanch and scrub off the scales. Pick the white meat from bones and bits of shell. The meat may be used for stews, or even steaks if the turtle is large enough. It can be treated like veal. Carefully remove the liver and entrails and discard them. Put the remaining material—bones, head, fins, shell pieces—in a saucepan with turtle spices (thyme, marjoram, basil, bay, cloves, pepper). Simmer until the pieces are tender. Strain, cut the shell in convenient pieces, reduce the cooking liquid, then mix it with equal amounts of beef stock and reduce by half. In the meantime, pick the bones, head and fins for meat. Return the meat to the stock, reseason and use.

Terrapin (Terrapène)

The terrapin, which runs between five and nine pounds, is a relative of the large seagoing turtle and is found in the tidal creeks of the Middle Atlantic states. The most prized is the diamond back of the Chesapeake Bay region. Unlike the turtle, which is captured for its shell, only the meat of terrapin is used in cookery. Sometimes they are available in major markets like the Fulton Fish Market. It is important that the animal be alive and in good condition when purchased. The tip of the head, the nose, should not be cracked or broken. The bottom of the feet should not be rubbed off, the eyes should be bright and the skin in good condition.

Put the living terrapin in several waters and allow it to swim around for an hour in clean water. Then wash it again. Blanch and remove the skin of the head and the feet. Cook the terrapin in a court bouillon for about an hour. It should not take any longer to cook a six- or seven-pound animal; the flesh of the feet will feel soft to the touch when it is done. If after an hour it is not soft to the touch, the terrapin is of poor quality and will not make particularly good eating.

Allow it to cool after poaching. Then break open the bottom shell, reserving the top shell as a serving vessel. Trim the nails and cut the legs into pieces at the joints. Discard the head, the tail, the heart, the entrails, the white muscles, and the gall of liver. Cut the remaining meat into convenient pieces and poach it with slices of the liver and any eggs found in the turtle for about twenty minutes. Cool the meat in the poaching liquid. It is now ready to be used.

It can be simmered in brown butter with some of the poaching liquid and seasoned with lots of salt and pepper and turtle herbs. It can be reduced in cream flavored with sherry, or prepared like a fricassée (*see* Stews).

145

Frogs (Grenouilles)

Cultivated bullfrogs, with fine white meat, small sweet grass frogs, and dark-meated common frogs are available along with a number of imported (Japanese) varieties.

The several varieties of frog used in cookery are prepared in the same fashion. Only the thighs are used. They are prepared in the home by snipping the nails from the feet and threading one leg in the muscle of the other. They can be poached and finished in some white wine or tomato sauce; or they can be sautéed in butter and garnished with chopped parsley, garlic, and garlic tomatoes; with creôle sauce; with the white wine sauce; or Nantua sauce.

They can be made into an interesting broth, about as exciting as chicken consommé.

The larger American types have thighs the size of a chicken drumstick and can be treated like them for some amusing effects.

▜▚

XXIV

Beef

A basic knowledge of beef is invaluable for the home cook. While other meats are supported by sauces and garnishes, beef is often eaten simply prepared; the characteristics of the meat itself are of paramount importance.

In America, beef is purchased either in small butcher shops or in large supermarkets. Quality in the butcher shops is often higher, so are prices. As well, the supermarkets tend to choose sides of beef which are apparently more economical. An individual who is purchasing "club" steaks for four individuals will find smaller (not necessarily thinner) steaks in a supermarket; the cost per portion will be less as well as the cost per pound.

Since most supermarkets maintain butcher shops that cut to order, service is equal to all but the most exclusive butcher shops.

The most considerable difference, other than price, is the availability of really high quality cuts of expensive meat in the butcher shops. A supermarket will rarely have a full tenderloin because the sides of beef they purchase are too small to produce a satisfactory cut. Nor will they have prime meat or even choice with a rich fat covering, because a thrifty shopper would reject it. Often the meat is *Good* grade because this presents a very high proportion of lean to fat. Likewise, the meat in the supermarket is not aged, as the appearance would not suit most housewives and beef during aging may lose up to 10 percent of its weight and the housewife would not be willing to pay the increased price.

The meat in butcher shops, especially the better ones, is aged. While the cost per pound might be more because of this, if there were no other differences in the price make-up, the cost per pound of meat on the dinner table would be the same because unaged meat loses just about as much moisture in cooking and carving as it would have lost in aging.

Butcher shops also carry Prime meat and Choice, rich in fat. While Prime meat is demonstrably superior to ordinary Choice, whether the premium price is justified is largely a matter of taste. In no way is Prime, at a 30 percent premium, 30 percent better than Choice.

The individual buyer must know what he wants. Even in countries where government grading is done, even where it is mandatory (only inspection for disease is mandatory in the United States), the government graders classify meat in very broad categories. They judge the whole animal, not individual cuts, which may differ substantially in quality. (Quality beef comes from young animals, either steers [unsexed bulls] or heifers. The two sexes are virtually indistinguishable in most meat cuts.)

The ideal piece of beef will be thick (each cut will appear plump rather than long and lean) with smooth white creamy fat uniformly covering the pieces. The lean will be very firm, smooth, velvety to the touch, filled with a webbing of white fat. This webbing, called marbling, is extremely important. Some meat with a rich fat covering will lack internal marble because of fast feeding. The marble is the last fat laid down, and requires a long session in feeding pens after the animals are taken off the range.

The bones will be soft, red, and terminate in soft white pearly cartilages. The quality of the cartilage indicates the age of the animal. The meat should be cherry red. Although this is not an indication of quality, it is the preferred color. Actually anything from rose pink to purple red is acceptable.

The beef classified in America as Prime is closest to the ideal. Other beef is measured and downgraded by consideration of all these qualities in sum; that is, old beef must have more marbling than young beef to be classified as Choice.

The quantity of Prime beef on the market depends on the cost of feed over the two years necessary to produce the steer or heifer. After spending the first six months of their lives on the Western range, the cattle destined for Prime are brought to Midwestern farms to be finished with grain feed for eighteen months. If grain is costly it may be of economic advantage to the rancher to keep them on the range until they weigh more, and market them as Choice. Grass-fed cattle with yellow fat are usually marketed in the fall and are not as satisfactory as the grain-fed. Freezers, in other words, should not be stocked in the fall, but rather in April and May, when most meat on the market is grain-fed. Some cattle are fed beets, which give them a very deep red color and an unsatisfactory texture.

Choice, which represents the largest proportion of the meat in markets, is a compromise between economy and gastronomy, the animal is grain-fed for a shorter period of time (with less fat and consequently less marbling).

Good grade, which is substantially, but not dramatically, different from Choice, is even a better buy. Other grades should not be considered.

Most of the beef one sees in the average neighborhood butcher shop in France would be classified *Good* in America. French breeds do not have the shape American graders desire and the majority of animals are not specially finished to qualify as Prime or Choice. There is also a good deal of meat from dairy and draught animals which would not reach the market in the U.S.A. Luxury butcher shops in Europe do have excellent beef, although it seldom has the marbling of Prime American, if for no other reason than that Europeans and Canadians do not consider internal marble particularly desirable.

Even the high quality beef, fresh from the abattoir, has a particular metallic, astringent taste to it. It is "green." Some aging is put on most beef. However, the systematic aging, which allows the natural enzymes in the meat to tenderize it up to 25 percent and improve the flavor immensely, is seldom done for average butcher shops and supermarkets. First, because a great deal of capital is required to stock beef for several weeks, and the modest shrinkage, when multiplied by thousands of pounds, would represent a large loss if it could not be passed on to the consumer. Unfortunately, meat aged in a protective wrapping, as is done for restaurants to minimize this loss—enzymes are indifferent to oxygen—has an appearance that would not be attractive to the consumer.

Some new methods have been developed. A process using relatively high temperatures—enzymatic action doubles with every increase of 8° in temperature between freezing and 140°—and ultraviolet lights, to solve the problems of bacterial and mold growth which increases logarithmically with higher temperatures, is used with some success by a supermarket chain. It does not produce results equal to low temperature aging. Some experimentation has been done with antibiotics to inhibit bacterial action while allowing the enzymes to work.

At this moment, little meat available is sufficiently aged. Most meat is tougher and less flavorful than it could be. The home cook's reaction has been an effort at supplemental tenderizing with papaya-based tenderizers, which may work effectively on thin pieces but are completely ineffective for larger cuts because of a lack of penetration. "Puncturing with a fork," as advised in the directions, increases the juice loss tremendously.

The home cook might undertake aging himself, provided that a sufficiently large cut can be bought to minimize trim loss. A "shell," the section from which restaurant sirloin, club, and delmonico steaks come, can be aged in the average refrigerator. Choose a first-quality piece of Choice beef with a good fat layer and let it ripen, loosely wrapped, for from three weeks to forty days in the bottom of the refrigerator. Air should be able to pass on all sides. Some mold may develop. As it does not penetrate the meat it can be burnt or cut off. However, meat which begins to smell, indicating intense bacterial activity, should be trimmed and cooked immediately. After aging, clean and bone the shell. In actuality, meat is much less perishable than imagined. Some meat for connoisseurs is aged as much as forty days above the surface of the water in a deep well. Some yachtsmen without refrigeration aboard keep cut steak above the bilge for three or four weeks with only delicious results.

The cuts from the hindquarters (sirloin, top sirloin, loin end, short loin, sirloin tip, top round, and bottom round) should be aged. The tenderloin need not be.

The cutting of the choicer portions of beef is almost the same in France and America, except that many of our sirloin steaks (wedge bone, pin bone, etc.) are not cut, nor is the porterhouse.

The fillet itself is cut into several smaller pieces, the chateaubriand (not chateaubriant) of 20 ounces, taken from the heart of the fillet, tournedos of two or three ounces taken from the tail, grenadins of five ounces cut in tear shapes and of three ounces trimmed round, and filet mignons which may be portions from the head of tenderloin which branches off into a piece resembling a whole, small fillet or from the fillet itself.

All meat is composed of muscle, connective tissue, and fat. The proportions of these tissues dictates the cooking process. Some connective tissue softens in moist cookery, while muscle hardens. In dry cooking, the connective tissue toughens, while the muscle tissue becomes more palatable. The external fat melts in both processes. However, its presence within the lean seems to result in thinner connective tissue and, therefore, more tender cooked meats.

It follows that cuts high in connective tissue and low in internal fat should be moist-cooked by slow processes, while cuts with high muscle content, high internal fat, and low connective tissue, can be cooked by fast dry cooking.

It will also be discovered that meats with a high fat content cook faster than those with a low fat content. In other words, Prime cooks faster than Choice, Choice faster than Good.

AMERICAN	FRENCH	ENGLISH
Round	Tendre de tranche Gîte à la noix Tranche gras	Round
Top round	Tendre de tranche intérieure	
Bottom round	Milieu du gîte	
Rump	Aiguillete Culotte Romsteak	English rump is part of round. American rump includes top of steak piece.
Loin (Strip)	Aloyau (Contrefilet)	Sirloin
Sirloin steak (delmonico, loin strip)	Contrefilet (faux filet)	
Ribs	Plat de Côtes couvert	Ribs
Chuck	Plat de Côtes découvert	Neck
Plate (includes English shoulder)	Poitrine	Part of shoulder, part of flank, part of brisket.
Brisket	Milieu de poitrine	Brisket
Shank	Gîte de devant	Shin
Bottom of Chuck	Macreuse Jumeaux	Bottom of neck

N.B. These equivalents are merely indications of cuts which are found in the same general anatomical areas. What is "trim" in one country often is an integral part of a cut in another. As well, butchering within countries differs considerably from one major city to another.

▼▲

XXV

Veal

While beef enjoys an almost universal popularity, veal's appeal is more limited. It figures prominently in countries where cattle do not produce first-quality beef. It is least attractive in countries where the emphasis is on red meat.

In my opinion veal, that is, young bovines up to the age of three months, should have smooth, velvety, grayish-pink lean meat, soft, pliable, white, abundant fat, and narrow, very red rib bones. Calves, young animals older than three months, but under a year, have darker lean meat, harder fat, wider and less red rib bones than veal. The best meat will come from unweaned calf of four to eight weeks, weighing less than one hundred pounds dressed.

This milk-fed veal will be very pale pink, sometimes even a little bluish, with a moderate amount of fat around the kidneys (but nowhere else). As the animal is fed solid food, the flesh is colored and becomes redder.

Most veal is marketed as choice in retail butcher shops. Rarely, does one find prime veal.

In any animal the fat over the kidney should be plentiful, white and relatively firm, the veins in the shoulder should be blue or bright red, no other color. The flesh should not be spotted or clammy to the touch. It should not be moist at all in the higher grades.

Veal and calf cuts approximate those of beef. They are, however, from a half to two-thirds smaller. The only substantial difference comes in the broader use of the forequarters which are tender in veal and tough in beef and in certain cuts taken from the hind legs. Naturally, the relatively small size of the carcass indicates some cuts. One can reasonably cook a saddle of veal, that is a double loin with fillets, while the equivalent cut, the baron of beef, is a spectacular.

The choicest pieces of veal resemble those of beef, the loin, the leg cuts, the rack, the fillet, and the sirloin. The shoulder which yields blade roasts, arm steak, and rolled shoulder roasts is desirable.

As far as the best cuts of veal are concerned, American, English, and French butchering is relatively close. The secondary cuts, however, differ considerably as retail butchers break up the original primal cuts into different retail cuts.

AMERICAN	FRENCH	ENGLISH
Leg	Jarret	
Round	Cuisseau	Knuckle
(includes part of	(includes noix, sous	
quasi)	noix and fricandeau	
	muscle cuts)	
Loin	Quasi	Fillet
Fillet	Longe	Loin
Rib		
Shoulder		
(includes Epaule and		
côtes découvertes)	Côtes découvertes	Middle Neck
	Epaule	Shoulder
	Collet	Scrag End
Breast	Poitrine	Breast

N.B. These equivalents are merely indication of cuts which are found in the same anatomical areas. What is trim in one country often is an integral part of a cut in another. As well, butchering within countries differs considerably from one major city to another.

A great deal of veal is cut into slices. In America, a cutlet to be called a cutlet must come from the hind section; similar pieces from the forequarter must be called steaks. The French equivalent cut is the escalope which is properly translated as collop, the word *cutlet* would seem to have more relation to *côtelette* (rib chop, or côte de veau).

Veal can be cooked in any fashion. As it is tender, one can interchange most of the cuts in a recipe. It lends itself to braising. In fact, braised veal dishes, the sautées escalopes taken from the rack, and the roasted loin represent the best veal preparations. Almost complete lack of intramuscular fat (marbling) precludes the dry cooking of most cuts. Roasts, other than the rack and the loin should be larded. Escalopes from other cuts should be mechanically tenderized with a mallet, a heavy cleaver, or a special tool.

The breast is usually cut with a pocket and stuffed with bread or sausage meat and roasted or braised. It is eaten with caper sauce, horse-radish, tomato sauce, or the thickened braising liquid.

The individual ribs are larded with anchovies, ham, bacon, mari-nated, fried, sautéed in butter and deglazed with white wine to which cream is added. They are stuffed by splitting them toward the bone, or the meat removed from the bone, chopped and reformed on it. They are cooked in casseroles, in paper, with a variety of garnitures.

Many cuts of veal are bargains in American butcher shops (especially the very cartilagenous portions), because most American customers generalize from their experience with beef and avoid these portions. A tough gristly cut in beef is often delicious, tender, and quite appealing in veal.

The saddle is often braised, with the meat carved and sandwiched around either a farce or thick sauce. The entire piece is then glazed with another sauce and served with the braising liquid made into a sauce. Orloff which is now in vogue, Metternich, Romanoff, Tosca, Versailles are all variations on this treatment. Unfortunately, many home cooks are not up to neatly carving and reforming the piece, to making three good sauces, to keeping the piece attractive and, finally, to serving the preparation. It really should not be generally attempted, because, even when done in a good restaurant, it sounds better than it eats.

The shoulder is mainly boned and rolled; the leg is braised or cut into cutlets or larded (at each major muscle) and roasted.

As most American butchers do not cut the leg into its component muscles, the home cook might do well to buy an entire small leg, butchering it by following the natural seams and freezing those portions which cannot be used immediately.

The high content of gelatin makes veal well suited to cold prepara-tions. A galantine of veal can be prepared from the boned breast or shoulder, beaten flat. Cover it with ham and a stuffing, place some garnish like truffles, hard-cooked egg yolks, tongue in the center, so that the garnish appears in the middle of the loaf when it is cut. Roll the galantine, wrap it in a towel, and tie it at both ends and several places in the middle. The galantine is cooked in simmering water or stock, cooked between boards, then unwrapped and decorated.

Water cookery of any veal results in a large quantity of scum, result-ing from an abundance of soluble proteins, which first rise and then

155

METHODS AND MANNERS OF COOKING

sink. When they do rise, they should be removed, otherwise the sauce made from the cooking liquid will be dull.

In some cooking, for example in stews and blanquettes, and fricassées, the veal can be preliminarily blanched, and that first water be discarded.

XXVI

Lamb and Mutton

Although many of the preparations of lamb and mutton are similar, and the characteristic taste, compared to beef, is the same, lamb is lamb and mutton is mutton. A sufficient distinction is seldom made. In America, almost no mutton is eaten because people consider it old and therefore inferior lamb.

Lamb is a white meat like veal, mutton is a red meat like beef, and they should be judged and treated accordingly. For example, lamb should be eaten fresh, mutton should be hung.

Lamb is at its best before weaning; mutton should be eaten in its fifth year, except for those varieties which are bred for mutton butchering and mature fully in two years. Between its infancy and fifth year the animal is not a gourmet meat. The yearling mutton which appears in some markets from July to October has neither the appeal of mutton nor the appeal of lamb. Unfortunately, it is the mutton most people know because five years of feeding makes first-class mutton an expensive proposition.

Lamb eaten in its second month, generally called *hothouse* or *genuine spring* lamb, is at its peak of delicacy. It does, however, preserve most of its qualities until the fifth month when it is sold as *spring lamb*. A very young lamb is distinguishable by the "break joint" of the foreleg. A lamb foreleg breaks into four well-defined smooth moist ridges which appear red with blood. As the animal matures the bones become hard and white and the breaks are jagged. In the mutton stage, the leg does not break at this joint. The pinker and softer the fat the younger the animal. Mutton fat is white and brittle. The exposed bones in the shoulder of a cut carcass are another indicator; they are smooth and round in a lamb and brittle and jagged in a mature mutton. The color varies with age; from light to dark pink in lamb; and from light red to medium red in a

157

yearling; and from light red to medium-dark red in a mutton. The grain is finest in milk-fed lamb and becomes coarser with age.

Sex is not usually a consideration in lamb, but it is in mutton. A fully developed ram would be too coarse and too woolly for most tastes. It is recognized by a bluish-red, spongy flesh and the massiveness of the carcass. Most mutton available is either ewe, which provides excellent meat, or wether (the equivalent of a beef steer), which is first-class mutton.

In general, the grading characteristics of beef apply (*see* Beef).

Lamb is in season all year round. However, because of religious associations the spring remains the best season. Mutton is also in season year round, but is least attractive in the fall when the woolly taste is most apparent.

Sheep butchering in Europe and America is quite similar. The carcass is divided into shoulder, rack, loin, and leg sections with the shank, breast, and flank as by-products.

From the shoulder, the equivalent of the chuck in beef, comes the square shoulder, the boned, rolled shoulder, the cushion shoulder, arm chops, shoulder chops, and boned "saratoga" chops (the name applies to any boned piece prepared for grilling).

The rib section, or the rack, yields the rib roast, which can be made into a "crown roast" by removing and discarding the back bone attaching it to at least one other rack, and leaving the rib chops intact. While these preparations are often thought attractive, the flavor of the meat is not improved by being cooked in this form, and a great deal of juice is lost when the crown roast is carved into chops.

The loin is boned and rolled, cut into loin chops, cut into double chops (two loin chops, called English chops), rolled around the kidney and cut.

Noisettes, the equivalent of the tournedos in beef, are also taken from the loin. Their butchering involves a great deal of waste and they are rarely used. They can be treated in the same manner as tournedos.

The hip section, the equivalent of the sirloin in beef, is either left on the leg, or roasted as a sirloin, boned, cut into double sirloin chops or "steaked out."

The leg appears with or without the sirloin, with or without the shank, or with the shank meat boned out and folded into the thigh. Sometimes lamb steaks are cut through the bone; sometimes two legs or two legs and a portion of loin are roasted together.

Mutton produces a fillet which is an excellent piece for steak. A good butcher will also bone the rack or the leg and tie them for roasting or steaks.

Cuts of Lamb and Mutton

AMERICAN	FRENCH	ENGLISH
Leg	Gigot	Leg
(with sirloin)	(without sirloin)	(with sirloin)
Loin	Selle	Loin
	(double loin)	(include first ribs)
Rib	Côtellettes	Best end of neck
Shoulder	Epaule	Middle of neck and
(includes chuck	(includes côtellettes	shoulder
section)	découverts)	
Neck	Collet	Scrag end of neck
Breast	Poitrine	Breast

N.B. These equivalents are merely indications of cuts which are found in the same general anatomical areas. What is "trim" in one country often is an integral part of a cut in another. As well, butchering within countries differs considerably from one major city to another.

In roasting lamb—whole racks, legs, rolled roasts—the skin, called the fell, should be left on to shorten the cooking time and conserve juices.

Mutton should be aged at least ten days in the average home refrigerator. As the woolly taste which many people dislike is strongest in the fat, it should be removed after aging. Marination in a game marinade; in oil and vinegar; lemon juice, thyme, and bay; in white wine with shallots, thyme, sweet basil, garlic, and allspice, will also moderate the flavor.

Even mild lamb will profit by some marination. Young lamb can be marinated to good effect in buttermilk.

Lamb and mutton can be cooked by any process: braising (all pieces), boiling (the leg of mutton), sautéing (escalopes of the fillet or the rack), grilling (chops, steaks), and roasting (leg, rack, rolled roasts, and loin). When cooked by dry heat the meat can be eaten rare. Nothing argues for the traditional method of cooking lamb and mutton well done, except tradition. Even so, it should not be overcooked; an internal thermometer should be used.

159

Many treatments tend toward sweet, pungent, and fruity sauces (like cranberry, mint, currant, chutney) because of the dryness of the meat when well done. A stock is seldom made, brown sauce or veal stock serving for braising and for moistening stews. Many Middle Eastern dishes, and those which have invaded French cuisine, combine lamb and mutton with tomato sauces.

Lamb and mutton also lend themselves to treatment as *civets,* and as *blanquettes*.

Lamb and mutton dishes must be served very hot or very cold, as the fat tastes furry and unpleasant in the middle temperatures. Hot it is liquid and cold it is brittle.

XXVII

▼▲▼▲▼▲▼▲▼▲▼▲▼▲▼▲▼▲▼▲▼▲▼▲▼▲▼▲▼▲▼▲▼▲▼▲▼▲

Pork

Pork presents the cook with some unique problems. Only recently has any conspicuous progress been made in breeding the pig to produce meat destined to be eaten fresh rather than as lard, cured, and as delicatessen products. The meat is still far from perfect; the present fattening procedures do not produce meat that "eats well" and is economical.

At the moment a sort of compromise is achieved by the packers' trimming a good deal of fat, but ultimately a lean pig that can be fattened for butchering will have to be developed.

Some improvement has been made and the recipes in older books might be reconsidered and roasting temperatures lowered for a greater yield and more tender meat.

Unfortunately, the grading system is not oriented to fresh meat; weight and utility as a cured product heavily influence the judging. As no grade identification appears on the animal, the home cook must defend himself by demanding certain characteristics. The lean should be very tight, the piece should not be at all flabby. It should be well muscled, a bright grayish pink; dark meat indicates age; too light meat, an undesirable flaccidity. The fat should be firm, dry, and white. Any squared cut should hold its edge. The bones should be soft and red. There should be no odor whatsoever. Cuts from smaller animals have less fat and waste than those from heavy pigs.

Fresh pork is highly perishable. It should be wiped with a cloth and stored (for a very short period) unwrapped or in very loose wrapping.

Pork is hard to freeze. The fat becomes rancid, and pork can be kept only a matter of weeks. Oddly, curing processes exaggerate this problem.

The danger of trichinosis from underdone pork limits its preparation. It should be cooked well done. The use of a meat thermometer is the

161

only effective way of determining this point (175°). Actually the trichinae are destroyed at a far lower temperature. We continue to cook pork this well done because of the effective publicity given this disease. Canned or precooked hams which require further cooking can be cooked at 145°.

The popular method of waiting for the meat to turn from pink to gray is ineffective as some pork will not turn gray. When the thermometer registers well done, it should be inserted several times in the cut to determine that this reading is the lowest temperature, then the meat should be removed. Overcooking only destroys the palatability. Nowadays, as pork is less fat and more tender, the effects of overcooking are especially noticeable.

Trichinosis is in actuality relatively rare and could be completely eliminated by either grain-feeding all hogs or cooking all feeds, and keeping the farms free of rodents. Should danger-free pork be available the possibilities of rare pork, which is red meat, will be interesting.

The French butchering of pork is quite similar to the American. The English presents some difference and a set of parallel terms for bacon.

AMERICAN	FRENCH	ENGLISH	BACON
Foot	Pied		
Shank half of ham	Jambonneau	Knuckle (includes foot)	Gammon
Ham	Jambon	Fillet includes sirloin section)	
Bacon and spareribs	Poitrine	Belly	Streaky
Picnic shoulder	Plat de Côtes	Hand	Hock
Loin	Filet	Hind Loin	Back and Long
Back	Carré	Fore Loin	
Shoulder Butt	Palette	Blade bones (and part of spareribs)	
Pork Hock	Echine (lower portion)	Spareribs	Collar

Only the ham and the loin have had any acceptance in fine cookery. Other cuts simply have too much fat intermingled with the lean. They don't cook well, they don't look good, they're expensive. Again, if the apparent progress in breeding continues, this problem will be substantially eliminated.

Some hams are dried-cured to be eaten raw: Westphalian, Braden-ham, Irish ham, Wiltshire, York, and Proscuitto. The scraps and ends are ideal for seasoning purposes.

In general, hams are poached until about three-quarters done before roasting or braising. One allows fifteen minutes a pound, and uses a thermometer in the final stage. High quality hams need not be poached. Smoked ham (and other smoked products) should be soaked at least eight hours and up to forty-eight depending on the age of the ham.

"Fully cooked" hams need not be soaked or poached and are baked to 130°. A ham that has been completely cooked in water for sandwiches should be cooled in the liquid and, ideally, cooled in the liquid in the refrigerator for minimum weight loss.

Virginia ham, which can be considered as among the world's best hams, requires somewhat special treatment. The cheesecloth or burlap covering is removed. The ham is scrubbed with lukewarm water and a stiff brush. The ham is then soaked from twelve to twenty-four hours depending on size. It is then slowly boiled for three hours, then cooled in the water. The fat is trimmed and the small lateral bone is cut out. The ham is then roasted for about six hours, while being basted with brown sugar and mustard mixed with beer, red wine, or cider. It may be eaten hot or cold, in thin slices.

The razorback hogs, which once ranged widely in the Ozarks and are now occasionally available locally, provide excellent ham, rivaling any European product.

Bacon which is taken from anywhere on the pig is widely used as a breakfast meat and as a flavoring element. For flavoring, the less expensive cuts of bacon (the term bacon refers to a processing procedure) can be used. Bacon square is the best for flavoring.

Only belly bacon is used for entrées. It should be well cured and smoked, about 50 percent lean, 50 percent fat. The fat should be white, very firm, and brittle.

Often bacon is purchased sliced, which not only limits its use for cooking purposes but increases the possibility of rancidity. Brand is extremely important in sliced bacon as the arrangement of slices in the package is often deceptive.

Canadian bacon, the eye of loin, is always extremely lean and generally used as breakfast meat.

Pork is very good braised. It is probably the best way of preparing it; the meat is tender and highly palatable. It can be done in white wine, port, burgundy, sherry, champagne, beer. It is served with sauerkraut, endives, spinach, noodles, chestnut purée, pea purée, mushrooms; with

Robert sauce, piquante sauce, madeira sauce, tomato sauce, and the English cold sauces.

While pork does not accept marination as well as other meats, cuts left for a few hours in a bath strongly perfumed with bay, sage, onions, thyme, juniper, and cloves are improved.

When roasting pork it should be cooked very slowly to render some of the fat from the meat. After cooking, as much fat as possible should be removed. The racks make excellent roasts; the fillets can be treated like veal escalopes.

Suckling pig, which is surely a gourmet meat, is a bit difficult for the home cook. Figuring a pound per person, one must have at least twenty guests, and an expert carver.

The animal should be obtained in the freshest possible condition. Freshly killed is ideal as the meat deteriorates hour by hour.

Assuming the animal has been properly cleaned, brush the skin thoroughly. Stuff the cavity with a veal forcemeat, a bread and sausage stuffing, rice and chestnuts, etc., and sew it closed. Truss the pig with the legs at the side. Roast in moderate oven for about two hours, basting with oil to crisp the skin. A meat thermometer inserted in the thick of the thigh will indicate the overall temperature. Remove from oven, let the meat set for a few minutes, and proceed to carve.

A great deal of pork (as well as the less desirable cuts of other meats) is made into sausage and meat products of infinite variety. While these cannot be considered as particularly valuable in formal cuisine, as a food they are generally excellent.

XXVIII

Fowl

Chicken is by far the most popular fowl. It is tenderest when young and most flavorful when old. A new-born chicken, although relished in some cultures, has a consistency that is repellent for most Occidentals. At seven weeks, the squab chicken (poussin) enters cuisine. Recently a particular breed of squab chicken—the rock Cornish—has been widely promoted and has introduced a great many people to these younger birds. The spring or broiler or fryer chicken (poulet de printemps, poulet noveau) of between two and three months is the youngest chicken widely used. The broiler industry now brings these birds into the market as early as nine weeks. The roaster (poulet de grain, poulet de reine, slightly older) of about six months and the capon (chapon), an unsexed male chicken of less then ten months, probably represent the best compromises of flavor, tenderness, and economy. Pullets (poulettes, a young spayed hen, and poularde, an older bird) are older female birds not generally used in America although they represent a considerable economy and have a finely developed flavor.

Few stewing fowl (poule) or roosters (coq) are available in retail markets as there is almost no demand for them, and an extremely limited production in an industry geared to broiler chickens.

A young chicken will have smooth fine-grained moist white skin (except in certain breeds with yellow skin) with a bluish tinge. The feet will be proportionately large but with short claws. The neck will be fleshy. The most certain indicators are the tip of the breast bone and the wing ends which are very pliable in young birds and rigid in older ones. For the most attractive presentation, the chicken should be blocky rather than long. Any bird should be plump with heavy thighs.

The breast bone should be unbroken. Some merchants will flatten the breast bone to give the breast undeserved fullness.

Chickens are graded by lot rather than individually so that in some legitimately grade A lots, there are some inferior examples. This is not particularly serious as a grade B chicken is generally only slightly less attractive, with a few minor defects, and cooks just as well.

If possible, poultry should be purchased at a market specializing in freshly killed birds (they may legally be up to three days old and be called fresh-killed) as cold storage and freezing conserves everything but the flavor.

When one has the opportunity to shop in a live poultry market, dry picking should be specified. Many gourmets prefer poultry that has been electrocuted (an increasingly common process) to poultry that has been killed by more traditional methods.

In any case, the home cook generally encounters poultry that is oven-ready, that is, it has been plucked, eviscerated, cleaned, and singed. What further processing the cook undertakes is largely a matter of personal preference. The bird should be inspected for pinfeathers and hairs and for bits of entrail. Some cooks soak the bird in salted water. While this may alter the flavor, it does have the effect of protecting the stock, sauce, or soup from becoming cloudy. Other individuals scrub the bird with warm water and baking soda, which eliminates the slight slickness often characteristic of chickens that have been scalded before picking. Others, myself among them, do not wash chickens, rather we wipe them thoroughly so they will brown well.

Salting, a common practice, may effect some absorption of body fluids, but this does not seem a very significant end.

When poultry is purchased frozen, it may be defrosted in the refrigerator over a period of time, or in cold or warm running water relatively quickly. Recent tests have demonstrated that there is no appreciable difference in either the taste or the loss during cooking among these methods. Defrosting at room temperature is risky as the bird may become contaminated.

Of the types of chicken available, squab chicken are least economical, as well as being the least flavorful. They are ridiculously expensive and have all the taste of a glass of water. The Cornish hens are not much better. For the most part they are both boned, stuffed, and cooked in a casserole. Spring chickens are used for broiling, frying, and sautéing—the short cooking processes. Older birds are generally roasted, braised, or poached. Chicken is never boiled because the proteins are too delicate for high temperatures. During protracted cooking, the breasts are covered with bacon and sometimes larded to moisten and protect them while the tougher dark meat sections are cooking. In roasting, if a

166

V-shaped rack is available the bird may be cooked breast down so that the breasts baste in the juices rendered from the heavier portions.

Only the breast sections of the chicken (the suprêmes) are widely explored in classical cooking. They are extremely tender and quick cooking—by any fast cooking process. A stuffing or garnish can be placed between the two sections of each breast.

Otherwise, the chicken can be sectioned in a variety of fashions and used in sautés and stews. The legs can be boned and denerved, stuffed, tied, and cooked by moist cookery processes.

The age and relative tenderness of duck is indicated, as it is in chicken, by the state of the cartilage, determined by feeling the beak, the feet, and the windpipe. Broiler ducks (or duckling) and roaster ducks are almost always very well cleaned and frozen. The finest breeds are the Nantais (French), Rouennais (French, a domestic mallard), the Long Island (American), Aylesbury (English). Only the Long Island type is widely available in this country. The teal ducks (sarcelles), the canvasback, the mallard, black scooter (macreuse) and shoveler (souchet) are among the most excellent wild birds. Wild duck should be hung about a week, like most game birds, if it has been cleanly killed.

Two things should be immediately said about duck: it need not be greasy and it need not be à l'orange. All visible fat should be cut from the bird when it has been defrosted, especially the fat on the inside of the thighs, and the lower portion of the breast. The duck, no matter how it is to be finished, may be steamed for fifteen minutes with a cup of sherry to further melt the fat. In braising, the fat is constantly skimmed off the top of the sauce. In roasting, the duck is cooked on a rack, started at a high heat, then slowly cooked to render the fat. It can ultimately be as dry as chicken.

Wild duck and duckling, especially of the more distinguished species, are acceptable somewhat fat for they are best eaten rare. Brown the duck on each side, just pass the breast under the broiler. The savor of its juices compensates for the fat. Wild duck should not be elaborately garnished: the duck is flavorful enough.

Ducks of the Rouen sort, which are smothered or electrocuted to conserve their juices, are also roasted rare.

While duck is excellent with fruit (oranges, figs, pineapples, cherries), it lends itself admirably to treatment with sauerkraut and bacon, turnips, braised cucumbers, chestnuts, olives. It can be either braised or roasted, with sauce made from the braising liquid or the deglazings of the pan cleared of grease and combined with some appropriate wine. It can also be treated as any game, as a salmis, a civet, en daube, etc.

167

The emphasis on roast turkey has left other treatments of this most valuable bird relatively unexplored. Young turkeys under sixteen weeks can be fried or broiled. Older birds (young hen or young tom) can be braised, poached, or steamed. Water-cooked, the shrinkage is 25 percent less than dry-cooked.

Much progress has been made in marketing large, broad-breasted turkeys with good flavor and texture. Tom birds of twenty pounds are certainly the best buy. Turkeys can be judged like chickens by the condition of the cartilage. There should be no pinfeathers, and skins should be white.

There are significant differences between brands of turkey, both in the flavor characteristics and the cooking qualities. The home cook might do well, if the bird shows inordinate shrinkage or dryness, to try another brand.

Turkey is also available boned and rolled, and in a preformed loaf. While some of these preparations are excellent (again a question of brands), they do not compare with well-roasted whole turkey. The better brands will have solid, juicy, well-flavored meat with a minimum of additives. Inferior brands break apart in cooking and are dry and unpalatable.

Goose and gosling (recognized by pliable feet) should be thoroughly cleared of fat like duck. They can then be treated like turkey, roasted, prepared en daube, poached in white wine and served with a velouté made from the poaching liquid, braised in white wine and finished with cream, braised and finished with sour cream.

Traditionally goose is reserved for less formal occasions, except for foie gras and smoked breast.

Both goose and turkey are improved by moderate aging. This, however, obliges the cook to pluck and clean the bird which is not particularly pleasant.

Guinea fowls are very much like pheasant (see Game), although the meat may be a little juicier. They are treated with any pheasant garniture. Beyond broiler age they are rather tough.

The flavor of pigeon deteriorates rapidly after killing. A frozen pigeon is really quite worthless. As there is very little meat on the wings, and the legs are short and tough, the breast is the only portion that deserves attention. Because of this, young birds, squabs, that have not toughened their breast muscles by considerable flying, are favored over older birds, which can only be used for pies. Pigeon is treated like chicken.

Rabbits are customarily considered with fowl, as the flavor of a domestic rabbit is not far removed from that of chicken. As well, rabbits are often available in stores that sell fowl. Fryers of three to four pounds, roasters of five to six pounds, and stewing rabbits of six to ten pounds are available. The best are short, thick, full-fleshed with broad back and hips. Plentiful interior fat is another good sign. For sautéing, the rabbit is cut into sixteen or eighteen pieces; three leg cuts, two foreleg cuts, two neck and six pieces across the saddle.

The home cook should really purchase rabbits live and undertake the butchering himself as the blood is an important element in the confection of rabbit dishes. It is stabilized with a few drops of vinegar and then used as a thickening agent (*see* Thickening).

Rabbits are often treated like chicken, especially in sautés. They also lend themselves to treatment as game, with a sweet or a sweet and sour marinade. The fillets, cut from the loin, can be skinned and fast sautéed, or flattened and treated like red meat escalopes.

XXIX

▼▲

Variety Meats

The variety meats—the internal organs and the extremities—do not figure largely in formal cookery. With the exception of cock's kidneys and combs, veal sweetbreads, chicken livers, veal brains and kidneys (more or less in that order), this large category of meats is employed only in bourgeois cookery and regional cuisines.

This, of course, in no way reflects on their usefulness to the home cook. For family meals, the variety meats are nourishing, inexpensive, and in many instances extremely tasty.

Part of the problem for the home cook has been proper cleaning. In general, outer membranes, hair, trailing appendages, external vessels, fat, and the white portions of red meats, and the red portions of white meats should be removed.

Almost any neighborhood butcher will clean variety meats. He may charge a few pennies more (well worth it), but will clean them if asked. Tripe and feet are generally sold cleaned and sometimes partially cooked. Otherwise, these particular tidbits would not be worth the effort.

The liver and giblets of foul are the choicest morsels in this category. After any green parts have been removed, they should be cooked fast and rare in hot fat, then immersed in a sauce to prevent blackening and the bitter taste that comes with it.

They are eaten with red wine sauces, with fine herbs, with tomato sauce, in rice pilaf, with madeira sauce, with mushrooms, with bacon. A little lemon juice in any of these preparations improves them immensely. Often the livers are used in pâtés and terrines.

The hearts, gizzards, necks, or wings may be cooked in a white stock strongly seasoned with herbs and then browned in butter or oil and served with cream sauce, with onions, with garlic, with tomato sauce, with "spring" vegetables, or with stewed fruits.

The white variety meats from beef, veal, lamb, pork are often allowed to soak in cold running water to remove the blood and then blanched to firm the outer layers, or cooked in a "blanc" to prevent blackening (*see* Vegetables).

Calf's head is boned, soaked, scalded, rubbed with lemon juice, and finally cooked in blanc (a quart of water mixed with half a cup of vinegar and a teaspoon of salt). It is then cut in squares and served with highly seasoned sauces: Robert, Piquante, Gribiche, and Ravigote. The heads can be boned and made into pies or galantines. They can be sautéed and prepared with tomato sauce, with cream sauce, au gratin, sautéed with olives, with madeira sauce, with curry sauce, with brown sauce, with "turtle herbs," in a stew with ham, bacon, and anchovies. It can be made into a fine salad with potatoes, beets, carrots, and mayonnaise mixed with vinegar.

The brains and the spinal marrows (amourettes), which have the same properties, are blanched in a quart of water mixed with half a cup of vinegar and a teaspoon of salt. This blanc is also used for vegetables which darken in air. They are cooled and kept in water for future preparations. They may be served with Béarnaise sauce, with brown butter, with red wine sauces, with sauce Allemande. They can be sliced, dipped in a batter and deep fried, or prepared in a matelote (*see* Stews). They can be made into salad or into croquettes.

The ears, because of their cartilaginous character, are either cooked very crisp to emphasize it, or cooked very slowly to minimize it. First they are singed to remove all hair, then scraped, then blanched, after which they are scrubbed with a rough cloth to remove the skin. At this point they can be stuffed, baked, poached, grilled, dipped in egg and bread crumbs and deep fried. When stuffed, they are either cooked until the stuffing is done and then crisped under the broiler, or cooked by some moist method (braising, poaching) until the cartilage is reduced to jelly. In the latter case it is wise to wrap the ears in a cloth to retain the stuffing. Sometimes ears, especially pig's ears, are available cooked.

The palate (generally of beef) is soaked, scalded, skinned and cooked in a blanc until very well done and white throughout. It can then be cut in squares, floured and fried in oil, simmered in medeira sauce, in light béchamel, in red wine sauces. It can be cooled and coated with sauce Villeroy as can any white variety meat and then rolled in bread crumbs and deep-fried. (Sauce Villeroy is a very thick Allemande sauce, highly seasoned.) Or it can be prepared like tripe.

Beef snouts have only one current use. After being blanched, scraped and skinned, the muzzle is slowly simmered for about eight hours to

171

develop the gelatin and then chilled between plates with some pressure from a weight. Cold, it is sliced and served as an hors d'oeuvre.

Tongues are among the more choice meats. Fresh, they should be allowed to soak for several hours either in running water, or soaked in salted water overnight and the skins removed. They may be blanched to facilitate this. They can be braised or poached in a well-seasoned stock. Tongues are generally served with piquante sauce, tomato sauce, port wine or madeira sauce; with fruits (stewed apricots, raisins, dried figs); with chestnuts; with morels (morilles); with green peas; with pepper sauce; with mustard sauce.

Sweetbreads of beef, lamb, and veal are trimmed, tubes and gristles cut off, then soaked until they are white. They are then blanched, the skins, nerves, and small blood vessels removed, and the sweetbreads pressed between two plates. They are braised white; sliced, fried in butter; partially cooked in salted water; breaded and fried; braised *en cocotte;* larded and braised; with Suprême sauce, with Madeira sauce, Diane sauce, Chivry sauce, Colbert sauce. They can be scooped out and stuffed; cut in two and sandwiched around a stuffing or a slice of ham; breaded and fried. They can be poached and used cold in aspic.

The lungs (generally of veal) are beaten flat to expel any air they contain. Then they are blanched in a white stock until cooked. At this point they may be cut into convenient pieces and sautéed, deep-fried or stewed and garnished with any preparation used for any other variety meat. A frequent treatment is stewing in white stock with capers, lemon peel, parsley, anchovies, and rosemary.

The liver is by far the most well-known variety meat. The outer skin is stripped off and the white portions and tubes removed. It can be sliced, grilled, or fried, garnished with bacon and fried tomatoes; with fried bananas; with any mushrooms; with herbs; with grapes and raisins; with tomato sauce; with Béarnaise sauce; with a deglaçage with vinegar; with chasseur sauce; madeira sauce; or white wine and cream.

The whole skinned liver may be larded and braised in white wine with shallots and demiglace; with light beer and root vegetables; with sour cream; with any braising treatment of red meats.

It can be marinated, cooked in a pig's caul by stewing. Liver can be chopped and used as a stuffing for vegetables and pastry dishes, re-formed as croquettes or made into soufflés.

The livers of lamb and veal lend themselves to quick cooking, while mutton and beef are best cooked by the long-cooking processes. Milk-fed veal liver, which is very mild and almost creamy, is not as popular as the older calf's liver which has more character. Lamb livers are milder than pork or beef. Pork is probably the best liver for braising.

The kidneys of veal and lamb are generally cooked underdone after the skin and the gristle have been removed. They can be sliced and sautéed, with Bercy sauce; with cream and white wine; with Bordelaise sauce; with a deglaçage of champagne; with curry sauce; with tomato sauce.

When the whole kidney can be used, the skin and some fat is left on. Whole kidneys are cooked in casserole with veal gravy, and any of the standard garnitures.

Mutton, pig, and beef kidney should be cut and soaked for two or three hours in cold running water. They can be cooked like liver or like other kidneys, but stewing in thin slices in a wine sauce is best.

Heart, which is oily and hard, is too coarse for most tastes. Split open, cleaned of blood, soaked for six hours in cold running water, and stuffed with a highly seasoned preparation, it is satisfactory when braised or roasted. The real heart lovers like it sliced and fried like liver, or grilled. It can be broiled and simmered in wine sauce, or cooled and treated à la Villeroy.

The tripe or the edible portions of the several stomachs of ruminants is bought partially cooked, or at least cleaned. It is then boiled, broiled, or stewed and served with some highly seasoned sauce. The name *gras-double* is properly applied to the first stomach but is currently in modern French cookbooks for all tripes.

It can be fried; simmered in tomato sauce; in sauce Hongroise; in demiglace with allspice and vinegar; with cream sauce; and with any of the brown sauces.

Calf's udder is soaked in water, blanched, and then skinned. It can be beaten flat and used in wrapping the stuffing in a cromesquis, or in place of pig's caul. Or it can be cut in squares and used like beef palate.

Feet are marketed cleaned. Pig's feet are best boiled in a white stock with onions, parsley, bay, thyme, rosemary, and sage, then cooled between plates.

At this point they can be boned, or partially boned and stuffed. They can be cut in pieces and treated à la Villeroy. They can be dipped in mustard, rolled in bread crumbs and grilled; or chopped and re-formed with any sauce.

Sheeps' trotters are steeped in cold water, blanched, and cooked in a blanc, after which they are generally boned. They can be simmered in tomato sauce; in poulette sauce; grilled or treated like pig's feet.

173

The tails are stewed (large end) and used in soups. They can be braised in wine with brown stocks; boiled with root vegetables and served with cream sauce; stewed in light beer; boiled and simmered in brown stock with ham; deep fried; boiled and served with vinaigrette sauce.

The gonads of the male sheep, after being skinned, may be poached, grilled, or fried, with tomato sauce, with brown sauces, with any treatment used for sweetbreads. Euphemistically, these are called Rocky Mountain oysters or fries in English; ris, properly the word for sweetbreads, is used on some French menus.

The mesentery of veal or lamb can be used effectively as a hot entrée. After being scrupulously cleaned and scraped, they may be boiled, then breaded and deep-fried; chopped and seasoned as croquettes; poached and served cold with vinaigrette.

Mesentery is not often available, as most of the internal organs which are not particularly distinguished, although sold in European butcher shops, are used in making meat products and sausages here.

The one exception is chitterlings—the small intestine of swine—which are widely sold, cleaned and ready for frying or deep-frying.

XXX

▼▲

Game

Although several species of game that were gourmets' meat in past centuries must be absent from our tables, having opposed the juggernaut of industrialization with their frail bodies and lost, game itself is increasingly available in the major markets of Europe and America. Game farming, freezing, easier commerce, better transportation, and a measure of conservation-oriented hunting result in more game, a longer season, and a greater variety of game each year.

Unfortunately, intensive marketing has also established the mediocre as a standard. We compromise considerably. A frozen quail from Virginia, or a quail raised in a cage, while not worth a prime wild quail, is far more satisfactory than those poor skinny birds full of shot that were also part of any downed covey. We accept that game, which feeds tranquilly on wild herbs, is rarely available because we are glad not to encounter those injudicious animals who ate all sorts of trash and had to be buried for a day to eliminate the rankness.

Game birds can be bought dressed, trussed, and literally oven-ready, or they can be bought "freshly killed" leaving the cleaning and the aging to the cook.

Aging is really a matter of personal taste. In the case of pheasant, woodcock, and snipe, moderate aging of a week or so radically changes the flavor and texture for the better.

The bird, cleanly killed, is hung upside down until a slight decomposition results, indicated by a change in the color of the belly and a slight odor. If the bird is at all messy, that is, if the flesh has been considerably damaged by the shot, it should be cooked immediately as aging will encourage the wrong type of bacterial action.

Woodcock, snipe, thrush, lark, and reedbird, which do not have a gall

175

bladder, are not cleaned, except for the gizzard, before cooking by roasting. Rather, the plucked birds are cooked, then emptied, and the innards are made into a stuffing with spices, mushrooms, and truffles, or puréed and spread on a canapé served with the bird. Or they may be pounded in a mortar, passed through a sieve and added to the sauce as a liaison.

The use of the entrails for a liaison distinguishes many preparations of game birds. The bird is roasted, there is a deglazing (*see* Frying), and the deglazed material is moistened and a sauce developed which is thickened in this manner.

Game which has a strong character is generally lightly garnished. When roasted, it is cooked underdone. Game can also be poached, braised, grilled, sautéed, or fried.

Except for the red partridge, which is thought to be superior when mature, game birds are best young. Older birds are braised, made into galantines, terrines, or salmis (*see* Stews).

Pheasant (Faisan)

Young birds are identified by gray legs and a soft breastbone. Pheasant should be larded before being roasted. It can be stuffed, roasted, and deglazed with various liquids, such as cognac, madeira, pineapple juice, white wine, champagne, port, or cream. It can be eaten cold with any cold game sauce (*see* Sauces); prepared in a cold mousse; in a galantine; or browned and braised, like a white meat. Pheasant breast is also sautéed white or browned in butter and used with suprême sauce, sauce périgourdine, and with various sauces developed with a deglazing liquid. Roasted rare, it can be cut in pieces and treated with duxelles (*see* Forcemeats), rolled in eggs and bread crumbs, and deep-fried.

Woodcock (Becasse)

Woodcock can be prepared like pheasant, but is as well excellent à la bourguignonne; cut in pieces, sautéed rare, deglazed with brandy, and seasoned with lemon juice and mustard; deglazed variously with champagne, cognac, applejack, and a sauce, which is thickened with the entrails, developed. Woodcock can be split lengthwise, sautéed blood rare and finished as a sauté (*see* Stews); boned, filled with goose-liver forcemeat, wrapped in a cloth and poached.

Snipe (Bécassine)

Prepared in the same manner as woodcock.

Figpecker (Becfigue) and Reedbird (Ortolan)

Small birds weighing less than two ounces are an extremely delicate and delicious food. They are boned, stuffed, and poached; wrapped in a cloth, fried, and finished in a puff paste shell; roasted (for a matter of minutes) and served in a baked potato or a pastry case with a variety of sauces and garnishes—pitted cherries, grapes, mushrooms, truffles, crayfish, oysters. They are preferred simply roasted.

Bustard (Outarde)

Bustard are prepared like wild duck (*see* Fowl).

Partridge (Perdreau)

After one year, the partridge is known as the *perdrix* and is more suited to moist cooking processes than dry. It can be prepared in salmis; roasted and deglazed in various fashions: with sour cream, demiglace; red wine; suprême sauce; chasseur sauce; with game stock and with sherry. It can be treated à la provençale, split at the back, skewered, and grilled; deep-fried like chicken; cooked in a casserole (the sides of the casserole can be rubbed with garlic).

Hazel Hen (Gelinotte des Bois), Grouse, Prairie Chicken, and the French grouse types (Lagopèdes, Tourterelles, Tétras)

Prepared like partridge.

Plover (Pluvier) and Lapwing or Green Plover (Vanneau)

Prepared like pheasant or quail.

Quail (Cailles)

Quail are smaller in Europe than in America. They are wrapped in a vine leaf (or leaves) and bacon, roasted, deglazed with cognac; boned, stuffed with a goose-liver forcemeat, poached, and served with sauce Allemande; split, dipped in butter and chopped truffles, wrapped in a pig's caul and grilled; roasted and served with a sauce in a pastry shell; marinated in brandy with quince peels, cooked in butter with the brandy (but not the peels), and served with sauce made from the brandy, with quince jelly on the side; marinated in scotch whiskey, roasted, and deglazed with the marinade.

Thrush (Grive) and Blackbird (Merle)

These are prepared like any other small bird, but are excellent as well baked in the proverbial pie or flambéed with gin which contains the juniper on which they ideally feed.

Teal Duck (Sarcelle)

Cooked like duck (*see* Fowl).

Lark (Alouette, but called mauviette in France in the season when it is hunted.)

The lark is protected in America and almost never seen on tables here. In France, these tiny birds (about an ounce) are highly appreciated. They are baked in pies; browned in butter and served in baked potatoes; cooked in a cocotte; added to rice and made into a pilaf which is then molded and served.

Venison (Venaison)

Three types of deer generally encountered: the roe deer (chevreuil), the fallow deer (daim), and the red deer (cerf). Chevreuil is most appreciated in France, daim in England.

178

Specifics of Preparation

Only the chops, the saddle, and the hind legs are considered first quality meats. The neck meat should be ground, mixed with pork, and cooked as a meatloaf. The front legs can be boned, rolled, and braised. The spareribs can be barbecued, and the flanks cut up for modest stews.

Venison must come from a young animal, the younger the better. After three years, no deer is edible even with intensive marination. While daim and cerf are almost always marinated, chevreuil need not be. A few days' aging (all deer should be aged if cleanly killed) and the chops, fillets, rump steaks of chevreuil can be grilled and eaten rare.

A marinade is a mixture of carrots, onions, celery, shallots, garlic, parsley, thyme, bay, peppercorns, cloves, with one part vinegar, two parts wine, and one part oil. It is either cooked by browning the vegetables in the oil, or it is used raw. A marinade tenderizes the meat and accentuates the particular game flavor. Meat should stay in a marinade between twenty-four and forty-eight hours, depending on the cut and the age of the meat.

After marination the deer is roasted, grilled, or braised. Tender cuts can be sautéed. Most often, it is served with sauce Poivrade, made by browning parsley stems, bay, thyme, carrots, onion, and celery in oil, adding one part of marinade, two parts wine, reducing the mixture to almost dry, then adding one and one half parts of demiglace.

Venison can also be served with pitted sour cherries added to the pepper sauce, with Diane sauce, with chestnut purée, with applesauce, cranberry sauce, Cumberland sauce, with deglazing liquid (chevreuil) and game stock; with thickened reduced orange juice; with a hot compote of pears marinated in brandy with allspice and cinnamon; with compound meat butters; with a gravy made from the roasting juices.

Roasted and braised pieces accept all the standard beef garnitures and are seasoned highly.

The tenderloin of the roe deer is among the most choice pieces in cookery. Two or three make a portion, and they are generally served sautéed on a canapé spread with foie gras.

Other animals can be prepared like deer. For example, antelope, moose, caribou, elk, are occasionally available. Reindeer can also be prepared like deer, but it is often seen roasted or braised with a sour cream sauce and some kind of cucumber garnish. Buffalo can be marinated and treated similarly, but is also well suited to treatment with madeira sauce and garnishing with goose liver and truffles.

179

Bear (Ours)

Bear is available in most specialty markets. The choicest parts are the ham, which is braised after being marinated or cut into "steaks" through the round. It is well suited to sour cream sauce, and is excellent smoked, after which it is soaked, baked in a crust, like ham, and served with unsweetened whipped cream mixed with horseradish (like roast beef). The paws are treated with cooked marinade for two days, then parboiled in the marinade and additional wine after which they can be grilled with the garnishes for pig's feet. The saddle is marinated and braised.

Wild Pig (Marcassin)

The wild pig is represented by its young, the marcassin, more often than by the mature animal, the sanglier. The saddle, the legs, and the tender portions are prepared like venison. The rack, the equivalent of pork chops, may be sautéed with game garnish or with ham garnish, while the ham can be treated like a pork ham after marination (*see* Pork).

Hare (Lièvre)

Hare lends itself to soufflés, molds, and aspics. It can be roasted after being larded and served with the gravy. The meat can be ground either raw or cooked and made into patties or forcemeats. Older hares are treated this way, and then fried or deep-fried like croquettes, with any game garnish.

The fillets can be removed from the sides of the hare, skinned and larded with bacon—the large Canadian hares are excellent prepared in this fashion. They can be pan-fried; sautéed, and deglazed with cream, or game stock; roasted with game garnishes; or stewed.

The whole saddle can be roasted. If the flanks are left long, the saddle (râble) can be stuffed with the liver, heart, and lungs of the hare, chicken livers, etc., tied, and roasted or braised.

Small Furry Game

Rabbit is treated like chicken (*see* Fowl) or prepared like hare.

Opossum, commonly called possum, is almost always roasted. It should be bought alive, if possible, fattened on persimmons, and killed by slitting its throat. It should then be skinned and carefully gutted. Before roasting, the possum is stuffed with peeled, seeded persimmons, peeled, cooked sweet potatoes, and a bread crumb mixture moistened with beef stock, and well seasoned with herbs. It should be started in a hot oven with constant liquid basting for a half hour, then the oven reduced to 300° and the possum cooked for two hours.

Squirrels may be treated like rabbit, or cleaned, disjointed, and cooked like a small game bird.

▀▚▀

XXXI

Vegetables

In menu planning, especially for family meals, the vegetables should be varied. There are about sixty different vegetables currently being used in restaurants; the home cook should enlarge his usually meager repertoire to thirty or forty. He can also experiment with the more exotic vegetables occasionally found in the markets and small foreign specialty stores: Chinese cabbage (Pe-Tsai), Chinese artichoke (Crosne du Japon), Purslane (pourpier), nettles (orties), chayote and helianthus (hélianthe).

He might well buy those vegetables, which have several varieties like peas and asparagus, by type and season. The local greengrocer will know what is going to be available and its season at least a week before the vegetable appears. Through him the home cook can be in on the first endive and learn to discriminate between kinds of asparagus.

Another good source of information are the radio stations which broadcast between five and six in the morning. They are obliged to devote time to agricultural subjects and announce those crops which have arrived in the wholesale markets, their quality, and their price.

Vegetables should be carefully prepared in an effort to conserve and accentuate their color and flavor. It is really not worth the effort to present soggy green beans, smelly cabbage, blackened mushrooms, tipless asparagus, woody turnips, as no one will eat them.

Green vegetables tend to change to olive black-green in the presence of acid. For this reason, professional chefs add baking soda, an alkali, to the water both to neutralize the water and to compensate for the vegetable acid that becomes dissolved in the water during cooking. Baking soda (sodium bicarbonate) will also accelerate the cooking process, soften some of the vegetable fiber—sometimes to an undesirable degree —and destroy some of the vitamins. It can be used and should be used moderately except in cooking for the ill or for children. An eighth of a teaspoon per quart of water is a fairly satisfactory compromise.

Green vegetables are cooked uncovered so that the volatile vegetable acids can escape and the temperature of the water remains moderate (*see* Water Cooking). These vegetables should be cooked crisp in most cases, that is, until they are just tender. There is some argument for cooking very young green vegetables with a cover to accelerate their cooking, compensating for the increased presence of acid by a reduced cooking time.

Green vegetables that are excessively grassy can be cooked with a peeled potato, which will soak up some of the vegetable acids released.

Green vegetables that are naturally bitter, like chicory and turnip greens, should be blanched (briefly immersed in boiling salted water) before being finished by some other cooking process. Blanching in the case of a vegetable to be braised is really partial cooking.

The vegetable to be braised—for example, artichokes or celery—is blanched, cooled, placed in a casserole lined with bacon strips, onions, carrots, and "sweated" to force some of its liquid into the braising. Then it is moistened with a stock and slowly cooked.

When blanching is the entire cooking process, as in the case of peas and Brussels sprouts, the vegetables are not cooled but are immediately finished with butter, cream, or whatever, and used. Cooling under cold water causes a considerable loss of flavor and keeping them warm causes a loss of vitamins, color, and character.

The dried vegetables, like beans, split peas, chick peas, lentils, can be cooked without soaking if the cook has the time and the patience to add water as it is absorbed. This is the best approach for dried vegetables of the season just passed.

The practice of soaking dried vegetables overnight is unsatisfactory. Sometimes there is a partial germination which reduces the starch content and gives a bitter flavor to the preparation; other times there is a degree of fermentation. Two or three hours' soaking is the longest recommended. The process can be reduced to less than an hour by bringing the vegetables to a boil and allowing them to soak up the hot water, or by adding baking soda to the water (there will be, however, a degree of softening), or both.

Vegetables like salsify, which blacken in contact with the air, are cooked in an acidulated solution of flour in water (blanc pour légumes) in an effort to conserve their whiteness. Combine two tablespoons of flour with four tablespoons of water and three tablespoons of vinegar or the juice of one lemon, and dilute with four cups of water. A few parsley stems, half an onion stuck with cloves, a pinch of thyme, a bay leaf, improve the flavor of the blanc.

The cabbage family (cabbage, cauliflower, broccoli, kale, Brussels sprouts) are cooked quickly and in an open pot to minimize the characteristic odor. Overcooking must be rigorously avoided; it does not soften the woody portions and only succeeds in reducing the delicate parts to mush.

Cauliflower is improved by the addition of a small quantity of lemon juice, or by being cooked in half milk and half water.

The stronger cabbages might well be cooked with raisins or walnuts, which will eliminate much of the odor.

The tubers and the roots (beets, carrots, Jerusalem artichokes, parsnips) are best cooked unpeeled and then peeled after cooking.

The red vegetables, with the exception of red cabbage, should be cooked in a covered pot.

The cucumbers, the squashes, and the vegetable marrows are split and liberally sprinkled with salt. Then they are allowed to throw off their water for an hour. It may be that this makes them more digestible. It certainly intensifies the flavor. After an hour they can be lightly squeezed between plates. Eggplants, which are traditionally treated in this way, need not be as the procedure is not very effective in their case.

Most of the flavor of these vegetables is just below the skin: peeling should be avoided.

In preparing any vegetable, it should be thoroughly washed but soaked only in cases where the dirt cannot be readily removed; for example, cauliflower, spinach, and greens.

Consideration in cooking should also be given to eye appeal. Vegetables should be either used whole, turned in imitation of their form when whole (carrots, turnips), or cut in some simple geometric shape. Uniform pieces are most attractive and cook at the same rate.

The most common manner of finishing vegetables is au beurre. The vegetables are drained, salted and peppered. To achieve a buttered look, the butter is added away from the fire and the vegetables tossed in it.

Vegetables are treated à la crème by draining them and adding partially reduced cream and seasoning, then further reducing the cream. As the vegetables cook in the cream, they should be quite firm at the beginning of cooking.

Mornay, hollandaise-based sauces, tomato sauces, demiglace, Bordelaise sauce, go well with vegetable preparations.

184

To these sauces one can add anise seed, marjoram, oregano, saffron, sage, tarragon, cumin seed, dill, fennel, basil, and coriander.

In addition to braised, sautéed, boiled, steamed, and fried vegetables, purées of vegetables (any vegetable can be puréed but the more watery ones should be mixed with a third quantity of mashed potato for body), and vegetable soufflés provide menu variations.

Artichoke, Globe (Artichaut)*   Italian—long-head
December–February   French—round

> *Buy:* The best artichokes are bright green, stubby, short stemmed, symmetrical, with close-fitting leaves and a heavy feel. The leaves should be uniform and free from brown spots.
>
> *Treatment:* Trim the points with a scissor. Rub bottom with lemon juice, tie with string. Remove the choke (hairy cup found at the center of the flower) after blanching. Steam: braise, serve with braising liquid; stuff, with tomato sauce. The leaves can also be fully trimmed to the "bottom" and the choke removed. The bottom is then cooked in a blanc and can be used as a base, as a vegetable, as a garnish, or as an hors d'oeuvre. Young artichokes can be used whole; blanched, sautéed, etc. They must be very young.

Artichoke, Jerusalem (Topinambour)

> *Buy:* This is a tuber and unlike the globe artichoke. The best are unblemished, resembling a knotty potato.
>
> *Treatment:* Treated like a sweet potato; baked; boiled and mashed; blanched and fried; puréed.

Asparagus (Asperge)   All green, green with white
April–June   butts, and all white.

> *Buy:* Asparagus with deep purple tips, as close to picking as possible as sugar is reduced and toughening begins early. Best are straight, firm, with closed buds, little white butt. Fifteen to the pound is the best buy.
>
> *Treatment:* The stems should be peeled and trimmed regularly. Cook in a high pot so that the tender tips are steamed while the stalks are boiled. The stalk ends can be split to facilitate this. Tips are creamed; with butter; with hollandaise sauce; with butter and chopped egg; in omelettes; deep-fried; in soufflés. Whole asparagus can also be cooked in a special asparagus poacher. Generally, whole asparagus is served in a special holder or napkin.

* Common name appears at the left, French name is in parentheses, months refer to best season, varieties appear at right.

Banana (Banane)
May–December
  Buy: Unblemished, plump yellow bananas with green tips for cooking.
  Treatment: Banana sections can be dipped in a batter and deep-fried, or the whole banana can be baked.
Bean, Broad (Fève de marais)
June–September
  Treatment: Remove skin after blanching. With bacon, and sautéed onions; with cream; simmered in oil with onions and diced tomatoes.
Beans, Dry (Haricots Secs)   Blackeye (cowpeas), dark red kidney, small white, marrow, yellow-eye, pea (navy), pink-white kidney, pinto, chickpeas.
  Buy: U.S. Choice Handpicked
  Treatment: Water-cooked, then baked; stewed; sautéed; cold as hors d'oeuvre.
Bean, (Flageolet)
  Buy: Flageolet are only available in cans here.
  Treatment: (*See* Beans, White)
Beans, Green (Haricots verts)
June–September
  Buy: Snappy, grass-green, firm, unblemished, thick, heavy for size, with small seeds.
  Treatment: Blanched. With diced bacon and chopped onions; with almonds; with mushrooms; au beurre; with carrots; with cream sauce; with diced ham; with shredded sorrel.
Beans, Lima, fresh (Haricots de Lima)   Fordhook Baby Fava
June–September
  Buy: Beans should be well-defined in pods. Pods should be well-filled, bright fresh green. Shelled beans should be plump, whitish-green.
Beans, Wax (No French equivalent)
  (*See* Beans, Green. Color should be bright yellow.)
Beans, White (Haricots blancs)
  Buy: Plump, full well dried, mature U.S. #1.
  Treatment: Blanched, stewed in butter; with bacon; baked, with onions; boiled; as an hors d'oeuvre.
Beansprouts
  Treatment: These are purchased canned. They should be drained and washed. Then they can be creamed; sautéed; used in oriental dishes; made into croquettes.

186

Beets (Betterave)
July–October
> *Buy:* Clean, deep red, small. With tops if the tops are to be used as salad or vegetable. Without tops if the tops are to be discarded.
> *Treatment:* Boiled or roasted in oven. Peeled. Eaten in slices with chopped onions; with sugar, vinegar and cloves; in croquettes; creamed; with a sauce of thickened orange juice. Baby beets are especially excellent.

Broccoli (Brocoli)
December–March
> *Buy:* Tender, compact, closed, stubby, deep green-purple stalks, about six inches long.
> *Treatment:* Steamed; with brown butter; with tomato sauce; with hollandaise sauce; with browned bread crumbs and melted butter.

Brussels Sprouts (Chou de Bruxelles)
October–January
> *Buy:* Tight budded, firm, unblemished, hard to the touch, moist end cuts, medium or small, cabbage green.
> *Treatment:* Trim outer leaves and hard stem. With butter; with chopped fried onions; with Mornay sauces; with grated parmesan; tomatoes; puréed, with chestnuts.

Cabbage, Chinese, Michikli
> *Buy:* Long, tight, crisp leaved heavy heads.
> *Treatment:* A long tapered loose leaf cabbage with a mild flavor. Generally blanched, and sautéed.

Cabbage, Red (Chou-range)
All year
> *Buy:* Hard, bright red, smooth pointed heads of ten ounces.
> *Treatment:* Shredded raw and cooked with apple and vinegar to prevent discoloration. Braised; with caraway seeds; with onions.

Cabbage, Savoy (Chou-vert)
October–December
> *Buy:* Light green leaves, crisp, loose head, flat profile, crinkly.
> *Treatment:* Same as white below.

Cabbage, White (Chou-blanc)
December–May

Danish, applied to storage cabbages. Domestic, not as compact as Danish, either flat or round while Danish has a profile in between. Domestic is more tender.

Buy: Unblemished heads, heavy for size, hard.

Treatment: Blanched and braised; with apples; with chestnuts; with cream; with diced ham; with tomato sauce.

Cardoon (Cardon)

Buy: Medium sized, well-shaped, without excessive hard stems or wilt.

Treatment: Stalks or ribs of inner leaves are cleaned, cooked in a blanc. Fried in batter; simmered in butter; with red wine sauces; with meat juices; with marrow. Main root can be boiled and sliced, often used in salads; creamed; fried; au gratin; with gravy; with marrow.

Carrot (Carotte)

All year

Buy: Firm, clean, light orange color, smooth, blunt, full straight, fresh tops, one inch diameter at base with a crisp snap. Baby carrots are an interesting variation but not good for general use.

Treatment: Baby carrots can be blanched. Others are peeled, turned or sliced, braised; creamed; with madeira sauce; cream sauce; with marrow; with chopped shallots and diced tomatoes. The woody core should be removed from old carrots.

Cauliflower (Choux-fleur)

September–November

Buy: Tight, hard compact, very white, heavy heads surrounded by crisp green leaves. About two and half pounds.

Treatment: Boiled, with fresh butter; creamed; mashed, au gratin; in soufflé; milanaise; fried.

Celery (Céleri en branches)   Golden (Blanched)

All year   Pascal

Buy: Regular stalks, good green (Pascal) solid, compact, no spread with good bright leaves. Golden is more tender.

Treatment: Stripped of strings, blanched, braised; creamed; with madeira sauce; cream sauce; with marrow; with chopped shallots and diced tomatoes.

Celery Knob—Celeriac (Céleri-rave)

All year

Buy: Medium-sized, clean creamy brown knobs without soft spots.

Treatment: Cooked in water, then peeled. Braised; with hollandaise; fried; with tomato sauce; creamed, deep-fried.

Chard (Poirée à carde)

October–November

Buy: Avoid tough and pithy stems.

Treatment: Ribs are peeled, cooked in blanc, finished like cabbage.

Chayote (Chaiote)
All year, where available
> *Buy:* Generally imported from South America. Standards as for squash.
> *Treatment:* Like cucumber or eggplant.

Chestnut (Marron)
November
> *Buy:* Plump, dark, glossy, heavy kernels.
> *Treatment:* Skin pierced, immersed in deep fat, outer skin removed. Blanched, inner skin removed. Braised; puréed; stewed in white stock.

Chicory (Chicorée)
November–December
> *Buy:* Bright, clean crisp tender stalks (determined by twisting a leaf).
> *Treatment:* Like spinach. Blanched; in cream; boiled and rubbed through a sieve; simmered in butter with onions and fennel.

Chinese Artichoke (Crosne du Japon)
September–December
> *Buy:* Smaller firm roots, without soft spots and with regular conformation.
> *Treatment:* Thoroughly cleaned, boiled, blanched and braised, creamed; croquettes; au gratin; tomato sauce; puréed. This must be highly seasoned.

Corn (Maïs)
May–October

Field—early maturing, may be tender but never really sweet
Sweet—a smaller darker-leaved corn; used for corn on cob, etc.

> *Buy:* Well-filled, green ears, brown tasseled, plump kernels. Milk should burst from kernel under pressure. Most important to be fresh picked.
> *Treatment:* On the cob. Husks removed, silk stripped. Cook covered in water or milk and water about seven minutes. Do not add salt, rather sugar. Kernels are creamed; sautéed; au gratin; with lima beans as succotash; in fritters; in pancakes.

Cucumber (Concombre)
All year
> *Buy:* Hard, dark-green, well-formed, slim cucumbers, without soft spots or excessive bulges.
> *Treatment:* After treatment with salt, trimmed, seeds removed.

189

Blanched, sautéed; braised, stewed; with cream; with sour cream; fried in butter; stuffed; with hollandaise.

Eggplant (Aubergine)
All year
Buy: Heavy for size, dark purple, no soft spots, glossy, smooth, regular eggplants of between one and two pounds.
Treatment: Baked, peeled. Peeled, fried, sautéed; with cream sauce; with tomato sauce; marinated in brandy and white wine; fried, with various stuffings.

Endive (Endive)
July–November
Buy: Absolutely pure white, crisp, regular tender leaves without spots, marks or blemishes.
Treatment: Simmered in butter with lemon juice. Braised; with hollandaise, Mornay; brown sauces.

Fennel (Pied de fenouil)
Buy: Small, well-formed bulbs with crisp, bright green leaves.
Treatment: Blanched; fried in batter; with tomato sauce; braised; au gratin; with sauce Mousseline.

Greens (Herbes Potagères)   Beet tops, mustard greens, collard, dandelion, turnip tops, kale, borecole, broccoli greens
June–July
Buy: Fresh, tender greens with crisp stalks, definite "snap" when broken.
Treatment: Blanched, stewed; sautéed; chopped; in general, like spinach.

Helianthus (Helianthe)
October–December when available
Buy: Heavy regular, medium sized.
Treatment: Scrape, cook in a blanc, treat like oyster plant or potato. Fry; cream; sauce Allemande; sauté in butter; purée. Season highly. Do not cook too soft.

Hop Shoots (Jets de houblon)
Buy: Not available except home grown.
Treatment: Like young asparagus.

Kale (Chou vert non pommé)
January–April
Buy: Crisp, compact with dark green curling leaves.
Treatment: Strip leaves from stems, wash, cook like spinach. Steamed; braised; sautéed; creamed; au beurre.

190

Kohlrabi (Choux-raves)
June–November
>   *Buy:* Pale-green, small, young tubers.
>   *Treatment:* Wash, trim off red end, and vinelike stems. Water-cook, then peel and trim. Use like broccoli; cream sauce; au gratin; sauté in butter. Leaves are cooked like spinach.

Leeks (Poireau)
September–November
>   *Buy:* Leeks with fresh blue-green tips and medium-sized necks and dry tassle bottoms. Crisp tender, white within two inches of root.
>   *Treatment:* Washed, blanched, with butter; simmered in stock fat with raisins; fried in oil; cold as hors d'oeuvre.

Lentils (Lentilles)   French—yellow green to dark brown
                                        Egyptian—reddish
>   *Buy:* Hand-picked with minimum of dirt.
>   *Treatment:* Preliminary soaking, water-cooking. Cook in stock; garnish with fried sausage; with marrow, simmered in red wine and bacon.

Lettuce (Laitue)
May–September
>   *Buy:* Solid, crisp green heads.
>   *Treatment:* Braised. With marrow; with brown butter; stuffed, water-cooked.

Mushrooms (Champignons)
November–May
>   *Buy:* Firm, moist, closed buttons, medium-sized, pink juicy gills, unblemished.
>   *Treatment:* Creamed; au gratin; sautéed; pickled; broiled. Should be treated with lemon juice before processing to conserve color. (Sautéed in lemon juice and butter for example.) Need not be peeled except when very old.

Nettles (Orties)
>   *Buy:* Gathered in spring.
>   *Treatment:* Picked young, blanched like spinach.

Oca (Oxalis)
>   *Buy:* Tubers at least two months after harvest.
>   *Treatment:* Scrape, cook in blanc; creamed; sautéed in slices; cooked in stock.

Okra (*Gumbo*) (Cornes Grecques)   Long pod green, dwarf green, long white pod
July–November

Buy: Young, two-to-four-inch pods, rich green, crisp, regular.

Treatment: Blanched; drained; sautéed; Parmesan cheese; breaded and fried.

Onions (Oignons)
All year

Buy: Button or pearl onions.

Treatment: Small onions are skinned, boiled; with cream sauces; glazed; rings fried in batter; sweated, with pork fat, puréed; in tarts.

Parsnips (Panais)
October–April

Buy: Unblemished, well-washed, small parsnips, firm.

Treatment: Like knob celery; tender shoots can be peeled and prepared like carrots; boiled; with cream; fried; puréed.

Peas (Pois)
July–August

Buy: Bright green, heavy, regular, well-rounded pods with a definite snap. Very fresh.

Treatment: Generally quick-blanched or cooked in very little water. Simmered in butter; with chopped onions; with shredded lettuce; with chopped ham; with bread crumbs fried in butter; with mint; with cream.

Pea Pods (Mange-tout)
July–August

Buy: Same standards for fresh pea pods.

Treatment: Trim ends, cut into two or three pieces, cook like regular peas.

Peppers (green) (poivron doux)   Long, short, bell, bullnose
July–October

Buy: Well-shaped, green, red, or red and green, firm, full plump, heavy for size.

Treatment: Peeled, by blanching or passing through hot oil. Seeded, filaments removed. Simmered in tomato sauce; fried; fried in butter; used as vegetable case.

Plaintain
All year

Treatment: Similar to banana but better for cooking purposes.

Pumpkin (Potiron)
October

Buy: Regular, rounded, hard, thin-shelled pumpkins of a bright yellow-orange color without soft spots. Four pounds is the best vegetable size.

Treatment: Blanched, braised; in purée; with tomato sauce; simmered in butter with chopped onions.

Purslane—Pigweed (Pourpier)

Buy: Gathered in spring and summer.

Treatment: Blanched; creamed; like spinach or greens. Stalks can be dipped in batter and deep-fried or creamed.

Radish (Radis)

June–July

Buy: Tiny round olive-shaped, with hard feel and a symmetrical appearance.

Treatment: Can be sliced and sautéed; peeled and braised; deep-fried; creamed.

Rhubarb (Rhubarbe)

June

Buy: Firm, unblemished, crisp, unwilted green leaves.

Treatment: Only the stems are used, the leaves are injurious. Stems are strung, sectioned, and blanched; stewed in butter; sometimes with fruits or berries.

Rutabaga

January–April

Buy: Light-yellow, hard, smooth, middle-sized.

Treatment: As in any treatment of turnip. Used, mashed, at Christmas.

Salsify—Oyster Plant (Salsifi)

October–December

Buy: Smooth, firm, well-shaped roots, small or medium-sized, with a regular conformation and the color of parsnips.

Treatment: Cooked in a blanc after being scraped. Croquettes; deep-fried; au gratin.

Sea Kale (Chou-marin)

September–October

Buy: Crisp, dark green stalks of medium size, or the very light forced. Blanched sea kale is much tenderer.

Treatment: Stalks are treated like asparagus.

Sorrel (Oseille)

September–October

Buy: Regular, dark green, relatively clean; unyellowed.

Treatment: Blanched, shredded, smothered in butter; omelette filling.

Spinach (Épinard) Flat, Curly
April–June
  Buy: Clean (minimum of sand and dirt), full-leaved, bright green crisp spinach.
  Treatment: Scrupulously washed, blanched, stewed in own juice; puréed, with cream sauces; simmered in butter; with fennel seed; with anchovy fillets; fried with garlic.
Spinach, New Zealand (Tétragone)
  Buy: Long, thick, whitish green leaves, crisp, clean.
  Treatment: Like ordinary spinach.
Squash (Pâtisson, Courge à la Moelle) Summer: Scallop, Vegetable Marrow, Straight-neck, Early Yellow, Zucchini Crookneck
  Winter: Hubbard, Acorn, Butternut
  Buy: Heavy for size, unblemished, soft for most summer, hard for most winter.
  Treatment: Most winter squash are boiled, or baked, summer squash treated like cucumbers. Fried; breaded, diced, fried with bacon; deep-fried in a batter; mashed; baked with sugar.
Tomato (Tomate)
All year
  Buy: Red, but not soft, well-rounded, smooth, firm.
  Treatment: Blanched, skinned, seeded; fried in batter; creamed; au gratin; sautéed in butter; stuffed; mixed with other vegetables.
Turnips (Navets) Green, purple or white crowns
September–April Round root or long root
  Round root tastier
  Buy: Turnips of about two inches in diameter, with smooth skins, regular shape.
  Treatment: Boiled, mashed; with cream sauce; with butter; simmered in gravy; fried like French fried potatoes; braised; glazed.
Watercress (Cresson) Broadleaf
All year Narrowleaf
  Buy: Bright green, well-leaved, fresh cress.
  Treatment: Trimmed of stems, blanched. Puréed; creamed; sautéed.

XXXII

▼▲

Starches

French-fried, baked, boiled, and mashed potatoes are overworked. Many cooks have ignored the other preparations of potatoes and have restricted the other starch foods overly to specific roles: rice with curries, noodles with goulash, sweet potatoes with turkey, when, in fact, their use is much more considerable. Few cooks have explored the possibilities of gnocchi, spätzle, polenta, buckwheat groats, hominy, barley, or couscous.

The home cook should have at least fifty different starch preparations in his repertoire. Bland starch dishes can be used to complement any meat; they will accept almost any sauce. Absolutely nothing argues for continuing traditional combinations. The text is not arranged alphabetically, but according to use.

Potatoes (White) (Pommes de terre)

Potatoes with a waxy, hard, yellowish inside are best for frying, and those with white soft insides are good for baking and boiling. The moisture and starch content of potatoes will determine their suitability for different purposes. Those potatoes with high specific gravity will be less moist and better for baking or mashing. Potatoes of low specific gravity are for frying. White Rose and Russet Burbank (generally known as Idaho potatoes), for example, and Maine Katahdin are dry, while mature Triumph and Irish Cobbler are moist. There will also be a difference within a kind of potato. The home cook might do well to test a potato for use prior to cooking, by mixing two ounces of salt in a pint of water: potatoes of baking quality will sink.

New potatoes of any type and potatoes just out of storage will have an

195

undesirably high degree of sugar. It is the sugar that causes dark potatoes. New potatoes should be reserved for specific uses, steaming for example, while storage potatoes (which also develop a bitter substance) should be seasoned in a warm dark place for two weeks (or just until the buds form on the surface) before being used. The best possible potatoes are the just harvested, *mature* potatoes, which have a very low percentage of sugar.

To give variety to fried potatoes, other cuts than standard "French" might be considered. Stores that deal in imported kitchen equipment stock a device called a "mandoline" designed for cutting potatoes into matchsticks, chips, waffles, and slices for soufflé potatoes.

Raw potatoes cut in slices or in a small dice can be cooked in butter with chopped onions, with sour cream, with bacon, with ham, with mushrooms, with tomatoes and garlic. Slices can be baked in a casserole with cream; parmesan cheese; artichoke bottoms; bits of ham; etc.

Plain boiled potatoes can be cut into slices and browned in butter; chopped and browned in bacon and formed into an "omelette," mixed with bread crumbs; with cream; with cream and browned; tomato sauces; capers and brown butter.

Often boiled potatoes are sieved, mixed with egg yolks and a little butter, floured and fried as croquettes or pancakes, or, forced through a pastry tube and deep-fried or baked in the oven.

Genuine baked potatoes are improved by greasing the skins with butter, starting them at 500° for 15 minutes and then lowering heat to 400° to finish their cooking. There is more edible potato with a more appetizing skin by this method than by cooking them with any other. Potatoes cooked in foil must be considered dry-steamed (*see* Water Cookery).

Potatoes (Sweet) (Patate)

Yams and sweet potatoes are treated similarly in cookery. The only difference worth noting is that yams have a tendency to break up and will not maintain their form when removed from the skin and cooked.

Sweet potatoes are of two types: the moist (yellow to salmon-colored skin) and dry (darker yellow). Moist, which are low in starch, are the more popular. Like white potatoes, they must be mature and seasoned before use, and the moisture content must be considered.

Sweet potatoes can be boiled, peeled and mashed; mixed with egg yolks and formed into croquettes; baked; boiled and fried; French fried; candied; made au gratin; grilled after being parboiled.

Rice (Riz)

While rice is widely used, few cooks observe that there are different qualities by the different results they get. Few recipes specify a type or brand.

Just harvested, rice is brown. After minimal processing, some of it is sold as brown rice which contains most of the nutrients and fats of the original grain. The bulk of the crop is hulled and polished leaving the familiar white kernel. This whiteness is emphasized by a coating of glucose and talc, which washes off in cold water.

Converted rice is white rice that has been steamed, forcing some of the nutrient into the kernel while others have been added. It is then redried. The most popular brand of rice is a converted rice.

Instant rice is cooked rice which has been dehydrated and is simply reconstituted with the boiling water.

Rice is classified as long grain or head rice, medium, and short grain. Long grain rices give the best appearing rice: firm, clean with separate grains. Most long grain rices are marked long grain, but *brands* should not be mixed even if marked long grain, because the cooking time varies by as much as 50 percent.

Rice (polished or brown) is cooked by one of three methods. After being washed in cold water, it can be added to two and one half times its volume of boiling water; it can be steamed in a closed pot over moderate heat or in a double boiler, adding it to one and three quarter times its volume in boiling water; or it can be started in hot fat with one and one half times its volume in cold water added after the grains have become translucent, brought to a boil and finished in a closed pot in a moderate oven. This last method (called the pilaf method) is the most attractive; the grains are separate, smaller; the flavor is more developed by the initial cooking. The actual cooking time will depend on the brand (actually on the variety of rice, but rice is not sold by varietal name). Read the package.

The addition of a modest quantity of lemon juice tends to make the rice white.

Rice may be mixed with fragments of meat, pork sausage, green peas, artichoke bottoms, marrow, tomatoes, asparagus tips, parmesan cheese, salt pork, onions, fried ham, green peppers, etc. It can also be bound

197

with egg yolks and parmesan cheese, after cooking, shaped into croquettes and fried.

Brown rice has a pleasing nutlike taste because of the hull and is an
interesting dish with game.

Wild Rice (Riz Sauvage)

Wild rice, a type of grain which grows wild in three areas (St.
Lawrence, Minnesota and Southern Canada, and Louisiana) is cooked
like white rice but takes almost three times as long to cook. It can also
be puffed in deep fat for one minute at 375°. Most people, rather than
experiment with cooking it by absorption like white rice, prefer to cook
it in an abundance of boiling water until done, and then drain it.

Macaronis (Pâtes Alimentaires)

Macaroni products are shaped and dried doughs to which flavoring,
coloring, eggs, and seasonings may be added. Quality is determined by
color and brittleness; the best macaronis are semitranslucent and break
cleanly like a glass rod. They are made from semolina (refers to part of
the wheat kernel) and from hard durum flours, and have a typical
yellow color. The combination of high-grade farina with semolina will
tend to make the macaroni whiter without materially affecting its
quality. Poor farina will give the macaroni a gray color, and these
products should be avoided as they become mushy in cooking.

Macaroni comes in a variety of forms:

Solid Round Rods	Vermicelli (smallest)
	Spaghettini (double the size)
	Spaghetti (triple the size)
Plain Hollow Tubes	Foratini, Maccaroncelli, Forati,
	Percatelli, Mezzarrelli Mezzani,
	Macaroni, Mezzani, Zitoni
Ridged Hollow Tubes	Mezzani regati, Zitoni rigati
Noodles	Broad, Medium and Fine ribbons
Sheets	Lasagne, Reginette, Margherite
Elbows	Tuchetti (small), Ditali lisci (large)
	Rigatoni (corrugated), Bonballati
	(hexagonal)

In addition there are many small shapes, and fancy cuts—shells, horns,
crowns, etc.

198

Macaronis, whatever their forms, are cooked in a large quantity of boiling lightly salted water (1 part macaroni to 5 parts water) until they are almost done, then allowed to finish cooking in hot water without heat. Good quality products will retain their shape even when over-cooked; however, good macaroni is just tender and cooked through. Some professionals add a few tablespoons of oil to the water to coat the strands as they are removed. In any case, when finished, the macaroni is drained, washed in cold water to stop the cooking process before the cook begins to garnish it: with tomato sauce; brown sauces; butter; goose liver; fried ham; and a multitude of vegetable garnishings.

Noodles are treated similarly. Fresh noodles, which are now widely available, only require a few moments of cooking.

Chestnuts (Marrons)

Chestnuts are excellent meat accompaniments. To remove the shells, split the shells and either roast them in the oven, or put them in the deep fryer until the shells are easily removed. Then the underskin can be removed by blanching. They are then simmered in stock for twenty minutes. At this point, they are braised; fried in butter; made into a purée with cream or brown sauce; or, stewed in stock with seasoning. The commercial preparation of chestnut purée and chestnut flour (imported from France) are excellent.

Polenta (Polenta)

Polenta is prepared by cooking corn meal (one pound to about eight cups of water: the exact proportions depend on the grind) until it is thoroughly cooked. Then it can be drained in a cheesecloth and eaten with butter, sauces, or combined with cheese or even baked in a loaf. Cornmeal can also be made into corn bread, cooked with milk to form a mush, or cooked and formed into cakes to fry.

Cornmeal is available as either white or yellow meal.

Hominy

Hominy is in the inner part of the corn kernel. It is prepared by soaking corn in lye to remove the outer layer and then it is dried. Once it is dried, it is ready for use. Pearled hominy or samp, a dry meal like cornmeal, is cooked in milk or water similarly to cornmeal.

Grits are finer than samp and widely available in several grinds. The hominy is cooked by a wet cookery process and then often re-fried with pork and seasonings.

Buckwheat Groats (Gruau)

Kasha (buckwheat groats), or, for that matter, any kind of groats (oats for instance), are mixed with butter, moistened with hot water or stock, seasoned, and cooked in a slow oven in a covered vessel. They are eaten with sour cream or melted butter. Kasha can also be mixed with raw egg, buttered, moistened with hot milk and cooked.

Bulgur

Bulgur is cooked much like rice pilaf with butter. The bulgur, a coarse, crushed, roasted wheat, is sautéed; then twice its quantity in stock or water is added. The mixture is then brought to a boil and covered and slowly cooked. It can be served like wild rice, which it vaguely resembles.

Barley (Orge)

Several types of barley are available: Pearl barley is the grain cleaned of its outer layers; Scotch barley is coarsely ground grains; and Pot barley is much like brown rice. Any form can be cooked in twice its volume of liquid by the pilaf method and used as a starch vegetable.

Couscous

Couscous is a fine-grained paste, not unlike pearl tapioca, made in North Africa from millet flour. It is bought packaged and ready to be cooked. Wash the couscous in a sieve under running water, then drain and allow to stand for five minutes. Wash again under running water and fluff the grains with a fork.

For every cup of couscous, bring two cups of liquid to a boil, add two tablespoons of peanut oil and one half a teaspoon of salt. Slowly pour the couscous into the water and continue to boil, stirring occasionally, until the water is almost absorbed. Remove from the heat, cover tightly and let stand for fifteen minutes. Fluff with a fork, and then garnish with sauces, with almonds, meats, spicy vegetables, gravies, etc.

Fried Cakes, Croquettes, Plain Dumplings

A host of small preparations are used as the starch element in a meal. Johnnycakes are made by mixing white cornmeal, boiling water, and eggs into a batter and frying them on a griddle; the various vegetable fritters and croquettes and timbales, small soufflés, fried cakes, popovers, might also be considered.

XXXIII

▼▲

Dumplings, Croquettes, and Pancakes

In almost every national cuisine there is some preparation of dough, often with meat or vegetables enclosed, that serves as a garnish or as a light main course: Nocken, Piroguis, Varenkis, Won Ton, Ravioli. They fall into three broad categories: the dumplings, croquettes, and the pancakes.

For the home cook these dishes are valuable as hors d'ouevre, late suppers, cocktail tidbits, and buffet chafing dishes.

Dumplings include nocken or noques, plain dumplings, ravioli, and international ravioli types.

Although there are many ways to make nocken (some of which can be eaten as a sweet) good main-course nocken is prepared by forming small balls of chou paste which are poached for about ten minutes in broth. Variations include using a potato chou paste mixture, or an Austrian variant which is formed in finger-size rolls. Gnocchi and spätzle may also be included in this type.

Plain dumplings are essentially an elaboration of nocken. However, some leavening, either due to chemical leavening agents or to the leavening of egg yolks, is often implied. When they are cooked, a glass cover or pot comes in handy as they can be observed without disturbing the cooking.

Dumplings can also be made of already cooked doughs. Bread crumbs can be soaked in boiled milk, mixed with butter and eggs, formed and poached. Knedlich (matzo balls) are of this type, made of matzo meal and chicken fat.

Filled dumplings are usually made of noodle dough, prepared by combining flour, egg yolks, salt, and water.

For ravioli, the dough is rolled out and trimmed square, then divided into two equal parts. The filling (vegetable purées, or meat preparations) is placed at intervals on one part in portions of about a half teaspoon. Then the other half is put over it, and pressed around each bit of filling. The ravioli are cut from the sheet with a special crimping device or a sharp knife. Without the ravioli cutter, the edges should be pinched to insure their closing. The same dough can be cut into squares, the filling put into the center and the sides drawn up like a purse. Moistening the edges will facilitate closing them.

Some forms of piroguis (others require pastry doughs) are made like ravioli. Sometimes from noodle dough but more generally from chou paste. The individual pieces are then breaded and deep-fried. Polish pelmeny are closer to ravioli, but they are smaller and the filling is coarser. Won Ton are less rich than ravioli, and may have some rice flour mixed with the wheat, otherwise they are quite the same.

Fillings are entirely a matter of personal taste: chopped beef, ham, chicken, creamed spinach, braised beef, oysters, etc.

The only imperatives are that the filling be thick enough to handle and highly seasoned.

Croquettes and fritters are both deep-fried. They differ in that the croquette is homogeneous, made of chopped, ground, or puréed base mixed with Allemande sauce (or béchamel sauce and egg yolks) and formed, while a fritter is made of base dipped in a batter.

The typical croquette is compounded of chicken, livers, lobsters, mushrooms, diced oysters, sweetbreads, ham, tongue, hard-cooked eggs, shrimp, mixed with a thick sauce, cooled, formed into cork shapes, balls, pears, rolled in egg yolks and bread crumbs and then fried.

Subrics are a form of croquette that is not breaded and is fried in clarified butter instead of deep fat.

Fondants are croquettes made of hash or purée of ingredients and are breaded.

The basic fritter batter is made with four cups of flour, half a teaspoon of salt, two tablespoons of melted butter and enough water to make a paste. Just before being used the whites of two eggs, beaten to a froth, are mixed in. Batter left to rest for a few hours adheres better. Any of the mixtures used for croquettes can be enclosed in a batter and fried as fritters. Also, firm fruits or vegetables, like eggplant, celery, apples, pears, can be treated as a fritter (*see* Breading).

203

There are many recipes for pancakes to enclose a meat or vegetable preparation. They almost all include flour, milk, eggs and salt, the proportions varying almost as a matter of whim.

Roti, an Indian pancake which contains no eggs or milk, is a notable exception. Tortillas, used for tacos or enchiladas, which contain corn-meal, water, and fat, are another.

Pancakes which include a leavening agent are more common in America than abroad. Their use is almost entirely restricted to breakfast or snacks, although, conceivably, they could be used enclosing a filling.

Blinis, small yeast-leavened buckwheat pancakes of Russian origin, are in fact used to envelop caviar.

Most pancake envelopes resemble French crêpes.

A completely satisfactory formula, which has the virtue of being easy to remember, is one pound flour, one dozen eggs, one quart of milk and one stick of butter (four ounces). Because of the high proportion of butter, this crêpe is easy to work with, no other fat is needed in the pan. Mix the eggs and milk, add the flour, whip the butter in. Let the mixture rest and adjust the consistency, by adding water, so that it will pour like heavy cream. Heat the pan, fry one crêpe to cure it. After discarding this crêpe, continue. This quantity of batter will make 120 pancakes or standard crêpes; a professional using six pans at once will go through the batter in twenty minutes.

Crêpes made with these proportions can be stacked, separated by two squares of wax paper, and frozen. A few seconds in a slow oven will loosen the top pancakes without disturbing the rest.

They can be filled with any croquette mixture, any salpicon like sweetbreads and asparagus tips, truffles and goose liver, chicken hash, diced shrimps and oysters, macaroni and tongue, flaked fish and mushrooms, livers in madeira sauce.

One can also take the crêpe, fill it with a croquette mixture, fold it into a pouch and prepare it for deep-frying in a batter. This dish resembles the cromequis which are really prepared with pig's caul or calf's udder in place of the crêpe.

One can also fill the crêpe with a soufflé mixture and puff it in the oven, or spread purée between pancakes and roll them.

With the same crêpe made with oil instead of butter, one can make Chinese spring rolls by mentally imposing a square on the circular crêpe and folding the right and left wings over the filling, then rolling the crêpe from the top down and securing the top flap with egg white. The spring roll is then fried in deep fat. The substitution of a little cornstarch for some of the flour makes a stronger wrapper. In addition to the traditional filling of shrimp, pork, bean sprouts, garlic, and Chinese cabbage stewed in a little sherry, spring rolls of any salpicon, or any stewed fruit, can be prepared.

▼▼▼▼▼▼▼▼▪▪▪▪▪▪▼▼▼▼▼▼▼▼▪▪▪▪▪▪▼▼▼▼▼▼▼▼▪▪▪▪▪▪▼▼▼▼▼▼▼▼▪▪▪▪▪▪▼▼▼▼▼▼▼▼▪

XXXIV

Salads

In a meal the salad sometimes serves as the hors d'oeuvre, sometimes as the main course, sometimes as the garnish for the main course, sometimes as the dessert. There are different salads and different types of salad for each of these roles, but the basic elements of salads are almost always prepared in the same way.

More indications of the proper preparation of salad elements are found in the chapters treating vegetables, fruits, meat seasonings, etc.

Apples: Wash, core, remove spots and bruises. Cut into rings and then dice. Leave in lemon juice to prevent discoloration until time to use. Can also be marinated in white wine.

Apricots: Blanch to remove skins, separate halves and remove seeds.

Artichokes: Use either canned hearts or bottoms. Wash. The hearts are used split or whole, the bottoms in julienne or dice.

Asparagus: Cook in salt water. Cut into sections, discarding the bottom third.

Avocados: Ripen at room temperature. Peel, cut into halves, remove seed. Slice, dice, or cut into balls with melon baller. Leave in lemon juice to prevent discoloration.

Bananas: Remove skins and unattractive portions. Cut into strips, slices, or wedges. Leave in lemon juice.

Beans, navy: Soak, cook thoroughly, cool.

Beans, green: Trim ends, split or cut into lozenges. Cool. Marinate in oil and vinegar.

Beets, roots: Wash, cook, peel, and cut in dice, slices, or julienne.

Beets, leaves: Trim like spinach.

Cabbage: Remove the outer leaves. Wash, cut in eighths, remove center core, shred the remaining portion. Allow to crisp in ice water for one hour before use.

Carrots: Peel, shred, cut in rounds or strips, or cook and cut into dice.

Capers: Use in sauces, whole and crushed, and whole over salads as a garnish.

Cauliflower: Remove all green parts and blemishes. Separate into small sections. Cook in salt water with an ounce of vinegar per quart. Trim stems. Or, separate into small sections and marinate overnight in oil and vinegar dressing.

Caviar: Use as a garnish.

Celery: Remove outer stalks. Peel inner stalks and cut into small rounds, or in julienne.

Celery Knob: Peel and cut in fine julienne.

Cherries: Wash, split, remove seeds.

Cheese: Grate for parmesan; cut in julienne or force through food mill for gruyère; cut in cubes, julienne, or balls for port salut and the like; crush for the blues.

Chicken: Cook by boiling, skin, remove bones and gristle. Cut into cubes or julienne.

Croûtons: Cut white bread in dice of about a quarter of an inch (day-old bread cuts better, as does cold bread) and fry these croûtons or prepare them in a moderate oven. Other croûtons of a larger size are useful in introducing garlic into the salad. Rub it on the croûton, mix the salad with the croûton, then withdraw it.

Eggs: Hard cook, chop, shred, or cut into pieces, force through strainer, or mash. Generally the egg whites and yolks are prepared separately.

Endive: Remove outer leaves and blanch remaining vegetable. Separate leaves and cut into julienne.

Fish: Lobster, crayfish are cooked by boiling, shelled, and then cut into slices or dice. Fish like salmon is flaked after the bones and skin have been removed. Herring is cut into strips, bits, or tiny squares. Anchovies are used whole, crushed, or chopped. Shrimp are treated as crayfish and lobster or used whole.

Flower: The petals of chrysanthemum, carnation, rose, nasturtium (the pickled seeds can also be used) make effective decorative elements and surprisingly add to the flavor.

Grapes: Split, peel, and remove seeds.

Grapefruit: Peel by cutting off both blunt ends. Place one end against the cutting board and cut down sufficiently deep into the flesh to remove the white with the skin. Then section by inserting knife between meat and membranes.

207

Green Peppers: Split, remove tops and seeds. Cut into strips, dice, or chop.

Herbs: Herbs for salads—basil, burnet, chervil, fennel, marjoram, mint, parsley, rosemary, tarragon, thyme (basilic, pimprenelle, cerfeuil, fenouil, marjolaine, menthe, persil, rosmarin, estragon, thym)—chopped, washed, with undesirable parts removed, are used in the salad or in the dressing.

Meats: Cooked ham, cold cuts, boiled beef, tongue, fowl, cooked game are all trimmed of fat and gristle and cut in julienne.

Mussels: Poached, removed from shell and marinated in white wine.

Mushrooms: Can be used raw marinated in oil and vinegar.

Mustard Greens: Prepared like spinach, should be blanched if bitterness is not pleasing.

Nuts: Removed from shells, chopped, slivered, or crushed.

Onions: Peel, cut into rounds, pieces, or chop. Wash pieces in cold running water to prevent discoloration.

Oranges: Peel, cut into rounds or sections.

Oysters: Poach, remove from shell.

Peas: Shell, cook.

Peaches: Blanch to remove skins. Cut into halves or sections, put in lemon juice to prevent discoloration.

Pears: Pare, cut in half, remove seeds and cut into wedges or slices.

Pimentos: Remove from can, wash, chop, dice, or cut into julienne.

Pineapple: Cut off top, pare down, and remove all eyes. Cut into sections and remove center core. Cut into pieces. Sprinkle with sugar and kirsch and let marinate overnight.

Potatoes: Peel, square off or round with knife and cut into rounds, squares, cubes, or dice and cook; or, cook in skins. Then remove skins and cut into rounds. Or, marinate rounds raw in oil and vinegar.

Radish: Red radish can be cut in slices or chopped. White radish is treated in the same manner. Horseradish is grated and marinated in vinegar.

Salad Greens: Cabbage, chicory, corn salad (mâche), dandelion (pissenlit), lettuce, greens (mustard, kale, turnip, collard, watercress, raw spinach) are washed, trimmed, and crisped in ice water for one hour. Should the bitterness of some be objectionable, they can be blanched.

Chicory (Endive): A broad-leafed green with upright, spreading growth and long round-ended leaves. When it is forced and blanched, it is called (properly) French or Belgian chicory, but more often described as French or Belgian endive or Witloof chicory. It is a tight, compact, elongated bud, very white and appears on the market in the winter.

Endive (Chicoree): True endive, a spreading green with a white or white yellow heart and a multitude of curly leaves, is found on the market all year except in the summer. It is properly called curly-leaf endive, but is often described as curly chicory.

Escarole (Scarole): Escarole resembles true curly-leaf endive; however, the leaves are broader, darker, and less curly. It, too, spreads.

Lettuce, Bibb (Laitue gotte, nearest equivalent): Cup-shaped head of compact pale green leaves. A soft, delicate lettuce.

Lettuce, Boston (Reine de Mai, nearest equivalent): A loose head of large crisp leaves, generally very well leafed. Also called white Boston lettuce. Big Boston, which is called Butterhead, is less solid than Iceberg with silky soft leaves that are not as crisp as Boston.

Lettuce, Butterhead: (*See* Boston)

Lettuce, Cos: (*See* Romaine)

Lettuce, Iceberg: Solid, heavy head of lettuce with white butt, light green outer leaves, round or pointed head. Interior generally very white.

Lettuce, Leaf: Also called garden lettuce, generally comes loose leaved.

Lettuce, Limestone: (*See* Bibb)

Lettuce, Romaine (Laitue Romaine): Also called Cos. An elongated lettuce, generally trimmed before marketing to five or six overlapping leaves. Strong flavored. Should be very crisp.

Shallots: Cut into fine dice, wash in cold water.

Spinach: Blanch, remove coarse stems, and use as salad greens.

Tomatoes: Blanch to remove skins, split in two halves horizontally and squeeze to remove seeds. Cut as desired in rounds, or chop.

Turnips: Remove tops, peel. Shred or cut into strips. Or, peel, cook, and dice.

Hors d'oeuvre Salads:

Hors d'oeuvre salads tend to spicy combinations of vegetables, seafood, and, in the Anglo-Saxon countries, fruits (the fruit cocktail).

—Artichoke hearts marinated in oil and vinegar with fennel, coriander, pepper, thyme, and bay.

—Celery knob with remoulade sauce.

—Crêpes marinated in vinegar, oil with garlic, thyme, bay, and then cooked for ten minutes in boiling water, then served in the marinade.

—Cucumbers in sour cream with vinegar, salt and pepper.

—Eggplant, fried, diced with tomatoes, oil, vinegar, and saffron.

—Beets diced in oil, vinegar, and chopped onions.

—Navy beans with chopped tomatoes and onions.

—Cole slaw (sliced cabbage, shredded carrots, chopped green pepper, seasoned with sugar, vinegar, mayonnaise, and white pepper) with anchovies.

—Cabbage stuffed with rice; blanched cabbage leaves cut in rectangles, filled with cooked rice, chopped onion, salt, pepper and garlic, rolled on themselves and dressed with oil and vinegar.

—Macedoine: Blanched tiny onions, pieces of cauliflower, green beans, pickles, pimentos, macerated in vinegar, then served with oil and vinegar.

—Antipasto: Sardines, tuna, pickles, capers, olives, artichokes, mushrooms, generously splashed with oil seasoned with oregano and garlic. Elements are not mixed but served separately on the plate.

—Shrimp cocktail: Large pink shrimp, cooked in a court bouillon or in beer, peeled, deveined, served with a sauce composed of horseradish, chili sauce, and lemon juice.

—Endive, first braised, then marinated in oil with lemon juice, crushed garlic, fennel, saffron, salt, pepper, and tomatoes.

—Fennel knobs, prepared like endives above.

—Oranges, tomatoes, and green peppers with oil and vinegar.

—Raw mushrooms, red pepper, and artichoke bottoms with a mustard mayonnaise.

—Sauerkraut, apples and boiled potatoes with oil, vinegar, chopped hard-cooked eggs, chopped pickles, tarragon, etc.

—Potatoes, celery knob, olives, shrimp, ham, garlic sausage in vinegar and oil with sherry wine.

—Mussels and potatoes marinated in chablis and dressed with oil and vinegar.

—String beans in mustard mayonnaise.

—Diced carrots, turnips, pickles, mushrooms, potatoes, with bits of chopped herring in oil and vinegar.

Main Course Salads

Main course salads are good summer meals, luncheons, late snacks, and a casual way of turning a cocktail party into an informal dinner.

Some listed here exist in classic cuisine. Others are merely attractive combinations.

Alexander: Shredded ham, sliced cooked mushrooms, celery knob,

210

beets, apples, and endives marinated in vinegar, served with mayonnaise.

Bagraton: Strips of chicken, celery, artichoke bottoms, with tongue, truffles, and hard-cooked eggs, dressed with mayonnaise.

Beef: Strips of beef, potatoes, pickles, tomatoes, and hard-cooked eggs with mustard diluted with vinegar and cream.

Chef's Salad: Assortment of cold cuts in julienne with watercress, cabbage, lettuce, Swiss cheese and truffles.

Café Anglais: Morels, truffles, and shrimps in mayonnaise.

Dame Charmante: Half a melon scooped out, the flesh diced and mixed with diced chicken breast, rice, tomatoes, and orange and replaced in the melon with mayonnaise sauce and a julienne of red pimento on top.

Dumas: Mussels, truffles, potatoes, oil and vinegar.

Egyptienne: Cold cooked rice mixed with diced chives, diced ham, artichoke bottoms, mustard, green peas, and red peppers, with oil and vinegar dressing.

Françillon: Sliced potatoes marinated in white wine, sliced truffles, and mussels in oil and vinegar.

Grande Duchesse: Assorted cooked vegetables, strips of fillet of sole, anchovies, shrimp, and pickles, with oil and vinegar.

Imperiale: Shredded chicken, asparagus tips, green beans, arranged on lettuce, with oil and vinegar.

Italienne: Carrots, turnips, potatoes, tomatoes, green peas, anchovies, salami, capers, with mayonnaise and herbs.

Jamaique: Finely diced bananas, oranges, grapes, stoned cherries, and chopped nuts with mayonnaise filled in the banana skin.

Monegasque: Round potatoes sliced, whitefish, and artichoke bottoms, with diced tomatoes, black olives, oil, vinegar, mustard, and anchovy purée.

Mayonnaise: A salad of elements like lobster, chicken, shrimp, bound with mayonnaise sauce is called a mayonnaise. It can be garnished with any garnishing elements.

Nantese: Shrimp, smoked salmon strips, and asparagus tips, with hard-cooked egg, oil and vinegar dressing.

Niçoise: Mixture of tuna fish, red tomatoes, pimento, black olives, red peppers, green peppers, chopped onion, capers, pickles and anchovies, seasoned with a mixture of mustard, mayonnaise, oil and vinegar, with fine herbs, and garnished with egg slices.

Norvégienne: Strips of beef, celery, sliced onions, beets, apples, tomatoes, pitted olives, in a mustard mayonnaise.

Olivier: Diced potatoes, cucumbers, shredded lettuce, with mayonnaise, garnished with hard-cooked eggs, crayfish, or shrimp.

Paillard: Flaked poached sturgeon (any white fish will serve), pickled cucumbers, hard-cooked eggs, shredded lettuce.

Princesse: Shredded broiled veal kidney, asparagus, celery, red peppers, and cucumbers.

Reine Isabelle: Sliced lobster, shrimp, cooked salmon, chopped anchovies, julienne of pimento, oil and vinegar.

Reine Margot: Large halves of tomatoes stuffed with shrimps, chopped radishes, and watercress.

Russe: Diced ham, tongue, sausage, pickles, cucumber, green beans, peas, anchovies, red peppers, capers, oil and vinegar.

Suédoise: Sliced beef, potatoes, red beets, apples, seasoned with oil, vinegar, mustard powder, pepper, salt, and garnished with raw oysters and hard-cooked eggs.

Salads as Garnishes

Salads sometimes accompany the roast and are sometimes served as a separate course after the main course. While this is largely a matter of individual preference, the practice now is to serve the salad after the entrée in Europe and with the entrée in America.

Plain salads can well be served with the entrée and certainly composed salads can be served with cold joints, but the practice of serving a composed salad with a hot entrée tends to confuse the dinner with too many flavors at once.

The plain or simple salads are made of greens, singly or in combinations: watercress, escarole, lettuce, mâche, dandelion, pourpier, romaine, spinach greens, turnip greens, salsify sprouts, etc.

The composed salads are made of various vegetables, greens, and fruit elements. As these salads are sometimes the fourth or fifth course, it is imperative that they be appetizing and not filling.

The considerable use of fruit—bananas, oranges, grapefruit, apples, nuts, grapes, etc.—is relatively common in America but has not found a wide acceptance in Europe. On the other hand, the very traditional (in French cuisine) practice of making salads in gelatin, which has passed from vogue in Europe, is, in a somewhat different presentation, popular in America.

Composed Salads

(*Without Fruit*):

—Cooked salsify, sliced tomatoes, and cucumbers.

—Green peppers, endives, and artichoke bottoms.
—Tomatoes, green peppers, boiled rice, chopped onions, parsley, garlic.
—Cucumber, red pepper, mâche, watercress, sour cream dressing.
—Carrots, mushrooms, asparagus tips.
—Boiled potatoes, celery, red beets, mustard.
—Turnips, carrots, celery knob, scallions.
—Artichoke bottoms, celery, truffles, green asparagus tips.
—Celery knob, apples, mushrooms, and cucumbers.
—Red pepper, raw mushrooms, artichoke hearts.
—Celery, red pepper, tomatoes.
—Red peppers, celery, shredded spinach, watercress.
—Tomatoes, cucumbers, lettuce, radish.
—Cooked diced root vegetables, peas, green beans, cauliflower, watercress.
—Red peppers, tomatoes, boiled rice, chopped onions.
—Cooked vegetables, anchovies, olives, and capers.
—Chrysanthemum, mâche, and watercress.
—Beets, olives, potatoes, cooked asparagus tips.
—Diced tomatoes, endives, sliced cooked mushrooms, potatoes marinated in white wine.
—Artichokes, tomatoes, pumpkin blossoms, black olives, garlic.
—Green beans, asparagus tips, cucumber, with tarragon mayonnaise.
—Lettuce, watercress, cucumber, beets and radish.
—Lima beans, julienne of cooked potatoes, green beans.

(*With Fruit*):
—White grapes, grapefruit, apples, oranges.
—Romaine with grapefruit and pears, chopped pimento, hard-cooked egg.
—Celery in julienne, apples, Brazil nuts, and guava jelly diluted with vinegar.
—Celery, apples, pineapple, romaine with mint.
—Monk's beard, avocado, mushrooms, red peppers, white grapes, and green beans.
—Pineapples, apples, grapes, tangerines, with crushed olives.
—Tomatoes, bananas, blood oranges, with cream dressing.
—Pimento, chopped hard-cooked eggs, chicory, watercress, apricots, with oil, vinegar, and saffron.
—Romaine, pineapples, apples in julienne, oranges, black grapes, and melon balls.

—Tangerines, celery knob, apples, strawberries, lettuce, pineapple.

—Celery, apples, bananas, walnuts.

—Grapefruit, pears, julienne green or red peppers.

—Bananas marinated in oil and vinegar with chervil.

—Tomatoes and pineapples with sour cream and lemon juice.

—Melon balls, rice, cream with ginger.

—Orange pieces, diced pineapple, cream with lemon juice.

—Pears, apples, grapefruit, bananas, oranges, cherries.

—Lettuce, mâche, beets, pears, hard-cooked egg, oil and vinegar with mustard.

—Diced cooked cèpes, pears, and cucumber.

—Shredded carrots with pineapple.

—Lettuce, mangoes, rice, pimento, mayonnaise with ginger and chutney.

—Romaine, hearts of palm, oranges, mayonnaise with zest of orange.

—Lettuce, oranges, apples, grapefruit, with mayonnaise tinted with pomegranate juice.

Salads in Gelatin

A preparation of salad in gelatin is either molded in a special mold or made in a pan two inches deep, then cut from the pan attractively.

In general, about one envelope of pure gelatin (one tablespoon, one-fourth ounce, four sheets of sheet gelatin) to a pint of liquid to about the same volume of salad material are the proper portions. One package (3 ounces) of prepared gelatin requires the same liquid. This depends, however, on the brand of gelatin. Salads which incorporate pineapple or papaya will not gel properly if these fruits are used raw because an active enzyme affects the gelatin's proteins.

The gelatin is dissolved in half of the liquid, brought to a boil. The remaining liquid is then added cold. The mixture is cooled and the salad mixture either mixed in or placed in the mold. The gelatin may be partially gelled to facilitate the even distribution of the salad material.

Port, sherry, cognac, fruit juices, consommé can be substituted for part of the liquid.

Flavored gelatin can be used, and unflavored gelatin can be flavored with two tablespoons of vinegar or lemon juice and one teaspoon of salt per quart.

214

Fruit Salads

Fruit salads are basically a macedoine of fruits macerated in various liqueurs, cognac, port, sherry, served with a cream dressing. Other elements which can be added are ice cream, fresh cheese, crystallized flowers, rice, purées of various fruits (bananas, raspberries), nuts like hazel, pistachio, Brazil; vanilla syrup, various strained jellies, prunes, raisins, preserved fruits, and candied ginger.

Dressings

Salad dressings are based in mayonnaise, oil and vinegar, cream (heavy or sour), plus seasoning and garnishing elements.

Mayonnaise dressings are of two types: those made with an already prepared mayonnaise and those made of a mayonnaise mounted in the salad bowl with either a base of raw eggs or hard-cooked egg yolks.

Mayonnaise sauces built in the salad bowl with raw egg are made in exactly the same manner as regular mayonnaise (which see). For an egg yolk of average size never attempt to incorporate more than three quarters of a cup of oil.

Mayonnaise made with hard-cooked egg yolks or a mixture of raw eggs recall the old recipes for sauce tartare and sauce gribiche. Naturally the egg yolks when hard-cooked do not absorb as much oil—(it is no longer an emulsion itself)—an additional quantity of oil—one-third more—is very satisfactory.

Roquefort: Mayonnaise with Roquefort cheese, cayenne, and cream or milk to desired consistency.

Escoffier: Commercial bottled Escoffier sauce or any steak sauce, mayonnaise diluted with water, chili sauce, lemon juice, cayenne, and chopped chives.

Cheese: Grated Parmesan cheese mixed with paprika, mayonnaise, and celery seed.

Chatelaine: Mayonnaise beaten with an equal quantity of whipped cream (for fruit salads).

Thousand Island: Minced onions, chopped pimentos, chili sauce, chopped hard-cooked eggs, pickles, cayenne, and mayonnaise.

Tarragon: One part mayonnaise, one part whipped cream garnished with tarragon and diluted with tarragon vinegar.

Russian: One part chili sauce, four parts mayonnaise, garnished with Worcestershire sauce, lemon juice, onion juice (pass an onion through the meat grinder).

Fruit Salad: Mayonnaise with red currant jelly and lemon juice.

Catalane: Mash two hard-cooked egg yolks in the salad bowl. Mount this base with oil as for a mayonnaise, then add chopped pimento, chopped garlic, chives, and the chopped white of eggs.

Tarragon-Red Wine: Hard-cooked eggs sieved, raw egg yolks. Mount with oil and add vinegar, mustard, red wine, and chopped tarragon.

Deauville: Raw egg yolks, one teaspoon of honey for every yolk, mounted like mayonnaise in salad bowl with wine vinegar, garlic, and mustard.

Albignac: Tomato paste and egg yolks, salt and paprika mounted with oil, seasoned with tarragon vinegar, and finished with chives.

Chiffonade: Mayonnaise plus chopped hard-cooked eggs and beets. Mayonnaise can be mixed with almost any vegetable purée, herbs, and aromatic seeds.

French Dressing—
Oil and Vinegar Dressing (à l'huile)

French dressing or oil and vinegar dressing is the simple combination of one part vinegar to three or four parts oil, seasoned with salt and pepper. A little water aids mixings. Mustard is almost always added in making the "house dressing" of French restaurants.

Oil and vinegar dressings can be made from any oil and any vinegar, however, olive oil and wine vinegar are the most satisfactory combination. Some gastronomes prefer oil derived from nuts or poppy seeds; others enjoy the tasteless oil of peanuts. In a preparation where a sour-sweet taste is wanted, cider vinegar is satisfactory, but it must be recalled that it is less acid than wine vinegar. The use of other oils (soybean, cottonseed) or other vinegars (beer, marc, distilled) is not advised for salad purposes.

A number of seasonings can be added to the basic French dressing: fennel, parsley, chives, chervil, capers, burnet, crushed anchovies, lemon juice, chili powder, chopped hard-cooked eggs, shallots, sour cream, sweet cream, orange juice, Roquefort cheese, celery, cheese, saffron, and curry powder.

Cream dressings for fruits are made from sweet cream with the addition of cinnamon, ginger, cloves, allspice, mint, peppermint.

Sour cream dressings:

Mustard: Sour cream with mustard and lemon juice.

Roquefort: Roquefort cheese, sour cream, lemon juice, and cayenne. Buttermilk can be added.

Anchovy: Anchovy paste mixed with sour cream, sieved hard-cooked eggs, mustard, and paprika.

Fruit Salad: Sour cream and red currant jelly.

Bacon Dressings

Some dressings can be made with hot bacon drippings. The bacon is heated, then the hot fat is poured over the greens, usually dandelion or chicory. Then the salad is seasoned with vinegar and treated as a salad with an oil and vinegar dressing.

▼▲▼

XXXV

Fruits

Although fruits are figuring more and more as appetizers, soups, salads, and garnishes for meat and sauce (see those chapters), their traditional use as a dessert course remains their most frequent employment.

Fruit are of six major types which more or less dictate their uses. The pome, the apple and the pear for example; the drupe fruits, like the cherry, the peach, and the plum; the berries like the currant and the blueberry; the citrus fruit, for example the grapefruit and the orange; the melons and the nuts. Some fruit, like the pineapple, the banana, and the strawberry as well as some of the more exotic types are not as easily classifiable.

The large fruits (apples, pears, peaches, etc.) are almost always preliminarily prepared by passing them quickly through boiling water, and then transferring them to ice to remove the skins, then poaching them. The poaching liquid is traditionally made by adding two cups of sugar (vanillaed or not) to two cups of water, stirring the sugar until it dissolves, boiling the mixture five minutes, simmering it twenty minutes. The syrup can be made in modest quantities and stored. These large poached fruits can be used with ice cream or sherbet, with fruit purées, with pudding, sweet fillings, and rice pudding. They can be sliced, flamed, combined with sweet sauces or liqueurs. They can be eaten simply with whipped or heavy cream.

It should be remembered, in cooking fruits in a sweet syrup, that the amount of sugar in the syrup will affect the condition of the fruit after cooking. No exact prescription can be made because the sugar content of the individual fruits also enter into the problem, but a very sweet syrup will leave the fruits reasonably whole, while a weak syrup will draw sugar from the fruit and leave it shriveled and formless in syrup flavored by the juices and sugars extracted from the fruit. Either effect is desirable depending on the use to which the fruit is being put.

A similar comment can be made about soaking or macerating fruits in liqueurs. High alcohol-low sugar spirits will draw sugar and flavor from the fruit. Sweet liqueurs will not have the same effect. In preparing fruit and liqueur combinations, a careful hand and a judicious use of extra sugar might be suggested if the fruit flavor is to remain.

Also, fruit of these sizes can be rolled in marzipan crumbs (after being poached) and deep-fried; stewed quickly for a filling for tarts, pies, flans. They can as well be baked; stewed into compotes; made into butters; macerated with seasoned liqueurs and made into sauce.

The drupes may, of course, be treated like apples and pears, but they also lend themselves as well to fritters, jams, tarts, and cakes. Cherries are almost completely poached, stoned, bound with some liqueur, jelly, or sauce.

Currants and gooseberries are best employed as sauces, flavoring agents, purées, in such foods as meringues, creams, tartlets, jellies, fresh heavy cream and sweet whipped cream.

Blackberries, raspberries, and the like, in addition to the constant possibilities for fruit (pies and tarts) are often eaten fresh with sweetened cream, or used as a garnish or filling for other fruit preparations, as purée for flavoring sauces, sherbets, cakes, and ice cream preparations.

The citrus fruits which do not take particularly well to cooking are protected by a leathery skin which is unpleasant in all but the smallest quantities, and contains a quantity of white membrane which is bitter. The fruit, then, is generally sectioned before being used. Sometimes, however, the entire fruit is hollowed and the skin used as a container for fruit preparations.

Citrus fruit sections can be caramelized in boiling honey (which is then solidified by immersion in ice water); made into soufflés, ices, cakes, etc.

A very pleasant variation often used in preparation of citrus fruits that is equally applicable to other fruits, is a chocolate fondue. The chocolate is melted in a chafing dish double boiler and the fruit, impaled on long forks, is dipped in it.

Melons are almost exclusively eaten raw.

Nuts can be used roasted, as garnishes; candied, and combined with syrups for sauces; puréed and used as lining in pastry; made into puddings; added to soufflés, breads, cakes, and pastry fillings.

Apple (Pomme)*
September–December
>*Buy:* Mature apples with good variety color characteristic, firm but not hard flesh, rich fruity apple aroma. For use as raw fruit, choose crisp, juicy, moderate low-acid apples high in sweetness. For baking, soft, moist, tough-skin varieties. For cooking, high acidity. For pies and applesauce, Baldwin, Jonathan, Grimes Golden, McIntosh. For baking, unripe Rome Beauty or ripe Gravenstein.
>*Treatment:* Baked; peeled, cored, poached; filled; pies.

Apricots (Abricots)
June–July
>*Buy:* Plump, firm, golden, medium-size. Tree-ripened best quality.
>*Treatment:* Raw; stewed; syrups; puréed as sauce; macerated, poached in liqueur; baked; peeled, wrapped in puffpaste, baked.

Avocado (Avocat)   Fuerte—green and pear shaped
October–December   Lula—heavier, flecked with tiny yellow dots
>*Buy:* Heavy avocado for the size, with the least bit of yield to finger pressure. Avocado ripened at room temperature.
>*Treatment:* While the avocado is properly a fruit, its more extensive use is as a vegetable or salad element. It can be treated as a dessert: peeled, cut in half, remove seed. Fill with jellies; ice cream; berry purées; rice pudding. Macerate in sugar and brandy. Cook in a ginger-flavored syrup.

Banana (Banane)
>*Treatment:* Custard; baked; puréed; fruit cups; fritters. While the skin cannot be eaten, it is useful as a vessel for banana or fruit preparations. For example, a banana soufflé mixture can be baked in the skin.

Berries
June–August
>*Buy:* Uniform-colored berries of bright color for type, whole, well-fleshed, firm, clean, in clean boxes.
>*Treatment:* Raw with sugar and cream; stewed; baked; sauces; puréed; pies; tarts; turnovers.

* The common names appear at the left, the French names appear in parentheses, varieties are given at the right and the months refer to the best season.

Cherries (Cerises)   Sweet
June–August   Pie
  Buy: Sweet varieties for eating, with stems, bright clean appearance, plump, uniform. Sour varieties for cooking, tart, dark red.
  Treatment: Stoned; poached in red wine; tarts; puddings; poached in kirsch.

Cranberries (Airelles)   Small dark
October–December   Large bright
  Buy: Small, plump, dark berries, with bounce, high shine, hard feel.
  Treatment: Although cranberries are generally cooked and used as a garnish for meats, they make a good pie filling or pudding when cooked.

Dates (Dattes)   Fard: Dark, hard
                                        Persian: Light brown, large, soft
                                        Hallowi: Gold brown
                                        Khadrawi: Brown, dark, soft
  Buy: Waxy, golden, plump smooth dates.
  Treatment: Although excellent fresh they are generally marketed dry, and should be stored at about 60° at low humidity. They can be made into cakes; boiled in sugar syrup and pitted; stuffed with chopped nuts; with vanilla cream. Puréed, they also make an excellent pastry filling.

Figs (Figues)   Light green (Calmyrna)
June–September   Yellow (Kadota)
                                        Purple (Misson)
  Buy: Firm, sweet-smelling fig without blemishes and good characteristic color. Peel for raw service, generally lighter varieties are better for cooking.
  Treatment: With cream; macerated in liqueurs; poached in white wine, lemon juice; poached in port.

Granadilla
  Passion fruit, which is available as a juice in cans.
  Treatment: Can be used as the liquid in a pudding preparation or for making ices.

Grapes (Raisins)   American-Slip Skin
August–December   European
  Buy: Compact bunches, high variety color, sweet, tight bunches, brown cluster stems, full, brown seeds.
  Treatment: Raw; jams; fruit mixtures; meat garnishes.

Mangoes (Mangue)
November–January

Buy: Solid mangoes of red, green, yellow without brown spots, allow to ripen at room temperature. Half pound mangoes are the most useful size.

Treatment: Generally eaten raw, like a melon. When green made into preserves.

Medlar

Treatment: A small fruit which is eaten raw when very ripe. It has a pleasant guava-like taste and is suitable for jams, jellies, preserves.

Melons (Melons)   Muskmelons, Cantaloupes, Watermelon, Cranshaw, Casaba, Santa Claus, Honey Ball, Honey Dew, Persian

Buy: Vine-ripened melons (melons do not ripen well after picking), firm melons with a heavy aroma, full color for variety, and soft blossom end.

Treatment: Eaten in slices, balls, chunks. Used as a vessel for fruit, entrée (chicken in sauce), dessert preparations. Peeled; filled with vanilla cream; wrapped in puffpaste, baked.

Nectarines

July–August

Buy: Plump, firm, creamy with red tinge.

Treatment: A smooth peach which may be either cling or freestone. Treated like a peach.

Nuts (Noix)   Almonds (Amandes)
September–December   Filberts (Noisettes)
Peanuts (Cahuètes)
Walnuts (Noix)

Buy: Current crop, clean, dry, uniform in size and color, free of loose pieces, chaff, and dirt, with intact shells.

Treatment: Before use, some nuts must be shelled and blanched to remove skins. However, pecans, hickory nuts, butternuts, walnuts skins are acceptable. Almonds are blanched by simmering for three minutes and then slipping the skins. Brazil nuts and filberts should be bought blanched. Nuts are used as a decoration; with meats; in fillings; in cakes; and as a garnishing element for vegetables, salads, hors d'oeuvres.

Oranges (Oranges)   Sweet (Juice)
December–August   Mandarin (Tangerines)
Seville (Sour)

Buy: California for dessert purposes, Florida for juice. Well-colored, no green, firm, round, smooth, unblemished, no cracks.

Treatment: Peeled, sectioned, removed from membrane; with liqueurs, flambé. Peeled, sectioned; stewed; preserved; soufflés; mousses, custards, etc. Used as a vessel for fruit preparation, ices, soufflé mixtures.

Papayas (Papayes)

Buy: Spherical, thin-skinned, orange papaya without excessive spotting. Fruit should be just ripe and firm.

Treatment: Puréed and sieved, for custards, sauces, syrups. Treated like a melon.

Peaches (Pêches)   Freestone
June–September   Cling

Buy: Firm, regular peaches with a large area of red blush, plump.

Treatment: Blanch, poach. Slices or halves with cream; with liqueurs; with wines. Flambé. Pies; tarts; ice cream; baked in puffpaste; filled with creams, sweet rice mixtures. Puréed.

Pears (Poires)   Bartlett, Howell, Bosc, Comice,
August–October   Anjou, Kieffer

Buy: Mature pears, but not necessarily tree ripened. Soft at base, good yellow color for kind, bright, clean, without scars or indications of mishandling.

Treatment: Blanched, poached: in port, in white wine, in vanilla syrup. With ice creams; with chocolate sauce; with fruit preparations; berry purées; tarts. Macerated, dipped in butter and deep-fried.

Persimmon (Kaki)   Oriental (black spot)
October–February   California (seedless)

Buy: Slightly soft, plump, completely red-orange, medium-sized persimmons with a good gloss and a slightly wrinkled, thin skin. Oriental are best.

Treatment: Raw; puréed; soufflé; vessel for fruit or ice cream preparations.

Pineapple (Ananas)
All year

Buy: Must be bought ripe, orange-yellow, copper, fragrant, skin with fully developed squares. Leaves should be easy to remove, bottom dry. Fruit should feel heavy for size.

Treatment: Peeled, poached in slices; baked with meringues; glazed; soaked in liqueurs. Puréed: sauces, syrups, ice cream preparations. As a vessel for ices, soufflé mixtures.

Plums (Prunes)   Purple: Italian, Damson
July–September   Red: Climax, Hungarian
                                              Yellow: Kelsey, Green Gage

Buy: Plump, firm, full-colored from top, soft ends, unbruised, lustrous.
Treatment: Peeled, stoned, poached in vanilla syrup; used in tarts; pies; cakes; with jelly.

Pomegranate (Grenade)
November
Buy: Bright red with good gloss and no brown spots, regular. No soft spots.
Treatment: Syrup used for flavoring and coloring. Fruit cups.

Quince (Coïng)
September–November
Treatment: Baked like apples. Used in jams, jellies; stewed in compotes.

Strawberries (Fraises)
June–July
Buy: Fully red, firm, dry, bright, clean berries, of a regular shape with attractive hulls on.
Treatment: Hulled. Tarts; pies; ice cream preparations; syrup; poached in wine; macerated in liqueurs; in meringues; puréed.

XXXVI

▀▀

Puddings

The accepted meanings of the word *pudding* include an incredible variety of preparations ranging from mousse-like puddings, through custards to dumpling-like puddings.

Some classification is possible. Among the major types are the cream pots and cup custards; the jellies; the Bavarian creams; the farinaceous puddings of semolina, rice, and baked products; soufflé puddings, and the English boiled and steamed puddings.

Custards are very simply made but they do involve egg yolks, which if overcooked will curdle and if abused will become tough. When a delicate custard is wanted, like cream pots, one egg or one egg yolk to each cup of liquid is all that is necessary for minimum thickening, but a custard this light will not unmold. Generally about twice this quantity of eggs is used. China or ovenware glass cups are well suited to custard preparations (and other puddings) as the smooth surface allows the pudding to be easily removed. Most custard should be baked at 350° in a three-inch pan two-thirds filled with water. Take care not to overcook custards.

The word *blanc mange*, like *pudding*, has no really specific referent. Commonly it refers to an almond milk preparation, made by pounding sweet almonds, and a few bitter ones with a little orange water. Then gelatin and milk are added and the mixture set to cool. The basic mixture can be blended with chocolate, jams, liqueurs.

Plain gelatin desserts are extremely popular in America and available in a number of brands, as are preparations which are close to Bavarian creams. Homemade gelatin is a possibility but the cost would be prohibitive. Commercial plain gelatin does merit consideration, as gelatin desserts contain sugar (which is cheaper than gelatin) and flavorings which are often poor. It is far better to prepare gelatin desserts with plain gelatin and good flavoring. Use only enough gelatin to set the mold; too much is ruinous.

Metal molds and vessels are better for gelatin desserts as the heat is lost more quickly and the dessert has a sharper outline.

Mixing only half of the gelatin with hot water and stirring in the rest cold speeds the gelling process. Fruits can be positioned in the gelatin by first gelling part, then adding the fruit and covering it with the remaining gelatin.

Any gelatin dessert is easily removed from the mold by a quick dip in very hot water.

Bavarian creams bridge the custards and blanc manges, containing both gelatin and egg yolks.

The farinaceous puddings are of two types, those resembling bread puddings, made from bread or cake, and those resembling rice puddings, made from rice, semolina, tapioca, or even arrowroot.

The most common variety of bread pudding consists of small slices of bread spread with butter, placed in a greased pie dish, garnished with raisins, currants and candied fruits. Then the dish is filled with a custard mixture and baked.

Another approach, less attractive, involves soaking the bread in milk or wine, seasoning it, sieving it, and then combining the mixture with egg yolks and sugar and finally, with egg whites like a soufflé. It can, in fact, be made in soufflé proportions using the bread paste instead of the usual roux milk base.

Cabinet pudding and other charlottes are made in a mold like a bread pudding; often the mold has a special name which it lends to the pudding, but the basic preparation remains the same. The mold is lined with a cake, garnished with candied fruits, filled with custard, sometimes in layers, and poached.

Rice, semolina, and tapioca puddings are prepared in the same manner. The bases are boiled in milk until soft, sweetened and flavored to taste, bound with egg yolks, finished with egg whites like a soufflé, poured into a mold, and poached.

Soufflé pudding hardly differs from soufflés themselves (see Eggs).

Steaming or boiling characterizes the English puddings, although close to the same mixture could be baked for similar results. Cumberland pudding is as good an example as any. Peel, cored and chopped apples are added to chopped beef suet. How fine the suet is chopped will affect the consistency of the pudding. If the fat is rubbed with flour after being chopped (this is rather difficult with suet, but quite easy with butter) the pudding will be substantially richer. The apples and suet are mixed with flour, seasoned with nutmeg and salt, and moistened with eggs. Then the mixture is put in a buttered pudding basin (any kind of moldlike receptacle with cover, or tie a floured and buttered cloth over it so that the cloth forms a pouch with a tied end). The whole contraption is boiled for two hours. The mold must be at least two-thirds covered, and the water kept boiling constantly and slowly. As it evaporates more boiling water is added. Plum pudding, a similar preparation, made with raisins, currants, citron, orange peel, mace, molasses, brandy, combined with flour and bread crumbs into a homogeneous mass, filled into a mold, covered, and steamed-boiled three or four hours. It is cooked and left to develop for two days and then boiled another couple of hours.

Rennet pudding is a rather interesting type of pudding which has not been well-explored because of its identification with invalid feeding. Although it is easily digestible, it is also quite good and can be well-flavored. The rennet necessary to produce junket curd can be purchased in supermarkets under brand names, or in many drugstores.

XXXVII

▚▚

Frozen Desserts

Extremely efficient modern freezers and freezer units in refrigerators allows the home cook to make a great many frozen preparations that once required a special ice cream freezer: ice cream, coupes, bombes, ices, mousses, parfaits, and sorbets.

Ice cream, store bought or homemade, is of three major types. French ice cream is rich in egg yolks, regular American ice cream has less eggs and generally has some sort of binder, Philadelphia style ice cream is a mixture of cream, or cream and milk, and generally does not contain eggs; it is the least rich.

Commercial ice cream will vary from 8 percent butterfat to 18 percent. Most good ice cream is about 14 percent butterfat. Low-fat ice cream is somewhat richer than milk ice but not as rich as ice cream. Frozen pudding is richer than low-fat ice cream but not as rich as regular ice cream. Usually nuts and fruit are added to frozen pudding.

The air incorporated in the mixing is also an important consideration. A gallon (a unit of volume) may weigh as much as seven pounds or eight pounds and as little as four. In comparing prices, compare weights.

While homemade ice cream may be as rich as the home cook desires, a number of factors affect the final product. If the base elements for ice cream, or for that matter any dessert, were simply frozen outright, the dessert would be a solid block impossible to eat until it melted.

The freezing procedure and the addition of other ingredients to the base elements prevent the solid block from forming by keeping the liquid in tiny droplets, separated from each other, so that when they freeze, the crystals formed are small and the mixture semisolid.

The basic liquid of ice cream is milk and cream. The liquid portion gives body to the mixture, while the solid material (protein) suspended in the liquid keeps the crystals of ice cream small. The butterfat gives smoothness and texture. A great deal of cream gives a particular, not unpleasant, clinging texture. A very high butterfat content in the cream will insure small crystals. Cream should be partially whipped before being added to the mixture as the air incorporated gives a smooth, less icy ice cream.

Condensed milk, being very finely homogenized, makes excellent ice cream.

Plain milk when it is used should be scalded.

Egg yolk acts as a thickening and emulsifying ingredient, adding considerable velvetiness to the texture.

When eggs are used, some hot milk or cream is slowly poured over the yolks beaten with sugar, then the entire mixture slowly heated in the top of a double boiler to form a light custard, which is flavored. When cold, it is combined with other ingredients.

Sugar is a sweetener and prevents large crystals from forming. Excessive sugar will delay freezing and may in fact prevent it. One volume of sugar to four of liquid is a good ratio.

Corn syrup can also be used as part of the sweetening with good results.

A gelatin stabilizer is often added to ice creams that are low in egg yolks to insure good binding. It is dissolved in a little water prior to being added to the mixture.

Solids, fruits, nuts, candies should be added when the freezing process is well along to insure that the fruit is well distributed and to prevent the fruit from delaying the freezing process.

When fruit purées are added to an ice cream mix, the purée should be added very cold to the mix (rather than the other way around), as there is always the risk that a curd will form because of the acid in the fruit.

Although hand freezers and freezers run by electricity are available and excellent, the refrigerator will produce good quality ice cream with a texture only slightly different from the freezer product.

Generally there is a booklet with a refrigerator that will explain how to adjust the freezer compartment to its lowest setting.

If the freezer compartment can be partially emptied, a stainless steel bowl may be used which will facilitate the several whippings (to break up the large crystals) necessary during the freezing process. Otherwise, chilled ice cube trays may be filled with a cold ice cream mixture and the whipping done in a separate prechilled bowl.

Ice cream is commercially made in over two hundred flavors and there is no reason why the home cook should be more limited in combining liqueurs, fruits, nuts, extracts, perfumes, and the like.

A number of formal ice cream desserts called *coupes,* are garnished quite like sundaes, do exist and are whimsically named. These coupes can be used as fancifully as desired.

The following table might provide some ideas for the coupes of homemade ice cream or commercial ice cream. Combine any ice cream with any garnish and any sauce.

Coupes

ICE CREAM	GARNISH	SAUCE OR SECONDARY GARNISH
Strawberry	fruit macédoine	kirsch
Pineapple	pineapple	crushed macaroons
Vanilla	strawberry	strawberries
Asparagus	raspberries	whipped cream
Lemon	orange section	marmalade
Peach	blueberries	apricot sauce
Raspberry	mincemeat	crystallized violets
Chocolate	glacéed	chocolate cream
Hazelnut	puddings	applesauce
Banana	glazed chestnuts	mint sauce
Coffee	glacéed apricots	
Cherry	fruitcake	raspberry purée
Tea	cherries	chocolate chips
Orange	diced pears	curaçao
Red Currant	sliced pears	Benedictine
Tangerine	seeded currants	spun sugar
Almond	seeded pomegranate	grilled chopped almonds
Carrot	peanut brittle	port
Pistachio	marzipan	cocoa, caramel, English cream

Some confusion surrounds the use of the words *parfait* and *bombe.* Many authors feel that these are simply elaborated ice cream dishes: that a parfait is in reality a coupe and a bombe is a molded ice cream preparation.

Properly, bombe and parfait are made of the same mixture, called a bombe mixture in classic cuisine. This is a rather expensive, impractical preparation consisting of thirty or thirty-two egg yolks whipped in a double boiler with a quart of twenty-eight-degree syrup until firm, then cooled and whipped over ice. After flavoring it is lightened with stiffly whipped cream. For the parfait it is poured in glasses and chilled. Parfaits are always of a single flavor. For a bombe the mixture is used as the filling for a bombe mold.

The inside of the mold, which is generally elaborate in design, is lined with ice cream or ice, then the filling spooned inside, the mold covered and the whole mass frozen. Currently bombes are being prepared with one variety of ice cream on the outside and another variety on the inside.

The mold need not be a proper bombe mold; a pastry mold or pudding mold would serve, if covered with a piece of waxed paper.

To unmold the mixture, pass through cold water quickly.

The syrup (sugar water mixture) used for bombe mixture and for sherbet and ices is best measured on a saccarometer, or glucometer, or Baumé thermometer or hydrometer to determine the density of sugar in the water. Although these devices are inexpensive, they are not widely used. Most cooks rely on a candy thermometer that measures the temperature of the mixture or on identifying the stage (pearl, ball, gloss) the sugar is at as it becomes more dense.

As these methods will not work below twenty-five degrees of density, they are quite inefficient in making frozen desserts although adequate for candy. Of the professional instruments, the hydrometer is excellent and inexpensive and is the most readily available.

Simple water ices, for example, are easily made by combining fruit purées with thirty-two-degree syrup (in other words, syrup which is at the small pearl stage) until the mixture measures eighteen or twenty degrees on the device. Then freeze the mixture in the refrigerator like ice cream, whipping several times. The problems of fruits which are more acid or sweeter than others is completely solved by this method when it cannot be by any other.

A frappé is a water ice mixture that has been frozen to a slush.

Sorbets are very light water ices made with sweet wine or champagne and occasionally with fruit juices flavored with liqueurs. Light cold syrup, twenty-two degrees (in other words, the syrup had not reached gloss), is mixed with juice or wine until it is about fifteen degrees. Then this mixture is frozen to a slush and a quarter volume of Italian meringue or stiff whipped cream is added with a liqueur as flavoring.

231

Granites are simply sorbets without Italian meringue or whipped cream added. They are not stirred during freezing.

Spooms are sorbets which have more sugar (twenty degrees) and are half Italian meringue.

Sorbets and granites were once served as entremets, that is, between meat courses to settle the stomach. Nowadays they are simply dessert or part of dessert.

Sorbet might well be translated *sherbet* in English but the preparation we call sherbet is much closer to a lightly bound milk ice than to the proper sorbet. Usually the commercial sherbet contains milk, fruit juice, and some gelatin or other stabilizers.

XXXVIII

▀▄▀▄▀▄▀▄▀▄▀▄▀▄▀▄▀▄ ▀▄▀▄▀▄▀▄▀▄▀▄ ▀▄▀▄▀▄▀▄▀▄▀▄▀▄▀▄▀▄▀▄▀▄▀▄

Pastry

The basic pastries used for hundreds of dishes, both desserts and main courses, are made from flour and fat and a very small quantity of liquid.

The manipulation of these ingredients determines the quality of the pastry whether it is simple piecrust or a complicated puff pastry.

Plain piecrust dough is extremely useful for main dishes as well as fruit desserts. The basic crust is made with sugar for dessert and without sugar for covering meat pies or pâtés.

Piecrust should be flaky, which in effect means that the gluten present in the flour (*see* Baking) must not be allowed to develop. To this end, manipulation is reduced, a minimum of liquid is used, and the entire mixture is kept cold.

The fat is cut into the flour with a pastry cutter or two knives until the particles of mixture are pea sized. Fingers may be used if the home cook is quick enough to keep from heating and melting the fat.

A small quantity of ice water is sprinkled over the surface of the mixture to dampen the top slightly, then this dampened flour is moved aside and another layer moistened and so on until the entire mixture is dampened and can be formed into a ball.

The dough must be kept cold. It should be prepared in a cool place, on a cool pastry board (ideally of cold-keeping marble) and, if necessary, refrigerated periodically.

In very hot weather, a hot water pastry can be made (often with baking powder). Boiling water is combined with the shortening to make a soft, semisolid mixture which is beaten creamy, then the flour (and the baking powder when called for) is added to the fat mixture and mixed enough to combine the ingredients. It might be wise to chill the entire dough quickly before using.

No pastry dough should be overmixed as this will definitely give tough, solid piecrust. If overmixing does occur, the dough should be used for the bottom of fruit pies because it will withstand moisture better than flaky crust.

After mixing, the dough is gathered and either stored (it will last three or four days in the refrigerator) or formed into roughly the shape desired and rolled with a covered rolling pin. Take care that large quantities of the flour that covers the board (which should be of the same type as the dough flour) is not rolled into the dough.

Small shells can be made by placing the dough inside an ungreased mold of the desired size, taking care to avoid air between the dough and the mold. When the dough has been fitted, trim the overhang and crimp or flute it. Prick the shell to prevent steam from developing under it.

At this point another similar mold may be placed inside, or even more effectively, a piece of aluminum foil can be cut to size, placed on top of the dough and filled with lentils and the shell baked.

When baking two-crust pies, it is necessary to close the pie firmly by moistening the bottom shell and pressing the top to it before the edges are trimmed. When a great deal of activity is anticipated inside the pie during baking, it is wise to make a flour-water paste and use it as a sealer around the edge. After baking, the flour paste can be removed.

The pie should also be vented, either by pricking it liberally in some attractive design, or making a chimney for the middle out of rolled parchment paper or a hollow tube of macaroni.

To prevent the bottom crust from becoming too soggy—it will become soggy no matter what is done—it may be sprinkled with crumbs or a little flour, or brushed with egg white.

Puff paste, or half puff paste, has a great many uses in French cuisine but it is often abused, as a vogue for food in a crust continues and everything conceivable ends up in a pastry shell or *en croute*.

Puff paste might be restricted to its legitimate dessert uses, to dishes that absolutely require a vessel, and to preparations that are made demonstrably more attractive (visually) by being enclosed in pastry.

Puff pastry is not difficult to make but it is useless to pretend that it does not require some attention and some practice.

Puff pastry, like plain pastry, is made from chilled butter and an equal quantity of flour combined quickly to prevent the development of gluten.

Knead the butter under cold running water to wash away some of the milk solids and some of the water it contains. If the water is left in the butter, it will toughen the pastry. Make sure it is well chilled before proceeding.

Sift the flour and any seasoning required and then dampen it with ice water. The dampening is best accomplished by sifting the flour into a mound and making a well in the center which is filled with a small quantity of ice water. Push the flour and the water together.

Just form a small ball of the dough and set it aside for about a half hour in the refrigerator.

Form the dough into a rough square and roll it to a thin square about a quarter-inch thick. As this dough will be folded, it is necessary to keep the edges and corners regular.

Place the chilled lump of butter in the middle of the bottom of the square and fold the top over it, pressing the sides and corners firmly.

The butter should be about as plastic as the dough so that they blend easily. If a very large quantity is being made, some of the flour may be reserved and kneaded with the butter to insure better mixing of the butter with the dough.

Roll this new rectangle out again to a square a quarter inch thick.

Fold the bottom third of the square onto the second third, then fold them both onto the top third and firmly pinch the edges.

As the dough is now beginning to warm, it is necessary to chill it (covered to prevent the surface drying) for twenty-five minutes.

After chilling, remove the folded dough from the refrigerator and roll it out again, rolling first along the length.

Repeat this process for as many turns as are required in the recipe. Take care not to break the dough or allow the butter to come through as it is the air entrapped between the layers of fat covering the dough that will puff the pastry.

Puff paste is generally baked in a hot oven. The presence of some steam in the oven (produced by brushing the puff paste with water) aids it to rise. If puff paste begins to color highly, it is shielded with oiled parchment paper.

While puff paste dough keeps well in the refrigerator, puff paste products do not.

Puff paste shells are made by cutting out rings of rolled puff paste, stacking them and describing a circle with a sharp knife in the upper layer. This small circle becomes the "cap."

When puff pastry is used as a crust, the ingredients within must be precooked, unless they can be cooked in the time it takes the puff pastry to bake. The most considerable indictment of articles *en croute* is that they often must be cooked, and then reheated as the puff pastry bakes. A filet of boeuf is not at its best reroasted.

The scraps of puff paste, from cutting various shapes, are rerolled into half puff paste, which does not puff quite as well. It is used for decoration and for garnishing soups.

The various strips, braids, butterflies, and squares of puff paste used as desserts are all made similarly. The puff paste is cut into the required shape, placed on a cookie sheet slightly moistened with cold water, and the whole pan chilled for thirty minutes, after which it is baked.

XXXIX

▗▄

Cakes

Only three kinds of cake figure importantly in cooking: the butter cakes, the spongecakes, and the angel food cakes. Although plain cakes, made with a small proportion of rubbed or melted fat, and chiffon cake, made with oil and chemical leavening, represent distinct types, examples are limited.

Butter cakes, made with butter or hydrogenated shortenings, represent a large class of cakes which includes one-egg cakes, butter cakes made with whole egg, egg yolks or egg whites, of varying richness and "quick" butter cakes, cupcakes, and many cookies.

They are distinguished by being made on an emulsion (like an emulsion sauce) that depends on the particulation of the fat globules. This particulation is accomplished by creaming and beating, which also serves to incorporate air into the mixture. The fine, smooth, velvety texture of the best butter cakes is directly determined by the attention paid to creaming and beating.

The three different methods normally used in butter-cake making—the muffin method, the cake mixer method, and the standard butter cake method—differ in results because of the different degrees of creaming.

Although most recipes emphasize continuous creaming, that is, complete beating after every step, this does not seem to be necessary if the total creaming is sufficient. Shortening that has not been adequately creamed can be compensated for by additional creaming after the egg yolks have been added.

While the proportions in these various baked goods varies considerably and the addition of incidental ingredients may alter the preparation, they all have much in common.

The initial step in making a butter cake by the standard method is sifting and measuring the flour. This need not be done more than once, as the notion that sifting incorporates air (after the first time) into the flour does not seem to be valid. The flour is then sifted with the leavening agent and seasonings called for in the recipe.

In the second step the shortening is creamed. It is important that the shortening be of a consistency to combine easily with the other ingredients. The closer the consistency of the creamed shortening to that of the other ingredients, the better and easier the emulsion.

Hard shortening or butter should be softened. In hot weather, where there is risk of the butter or shortening oiling, it should be chilled in the refrigerator after each of the preliminary steps (until the dry ingredients are added). It is also useful to add the eggs cold in hot weather.

After the shortening is creamed, the sugar is added and the mixture beaten well. At this point it is important to incorporate air into the mixture. It is not important whether the creaming is done thoroughly at this point or in the next step.

After the sugar has been added and the mixture preliminarily beaten, the egg yolks (or whole eggs) are added one by one and the whole mixture beaten until it is very light and fluffy. This is the last real opportunity to incorporate leavening air into the mixture and the final texture of the cake will be determined by the character of this mixture.

In the case of whole eggs, if the eggs are separated and the whites and yolks added separately, there will be some difference in the cake.

When the mixture is fluffy the flavoring is added to the entire mixture. It is wise to add the flavoring at this point rather than earlier because the beating in the preliminary steps tends to cause some of the flavor to be lost.

The dry ingredients are added alternately with the liquids.

Add small quantities of liquid. Never add more than a sixth of what is called for in the recipe as there is the danger that the liquid will cause the emulsion to break. Add a quantity of the flour and stir carefully only until the flour is dampened, then beat vigorously for a few moments. Vigorous beating after each portion of the flour should take about five seconds; the initial stirring another five.

At this point it is important to work quickly, as the leavening is beginning to act in the moist mixture.

After the flour and liquid have been added (as called for in the recipe), the entire mixture is beaten for a period of time, which should also be specified in the recipe, to allow the baking powder to begin to work. The final beating time will depend on the type of baking powder used; if the author has not specified a type, consult the can. (*See* Incidental Ingredients.)

Stirring, Folding, and Beating

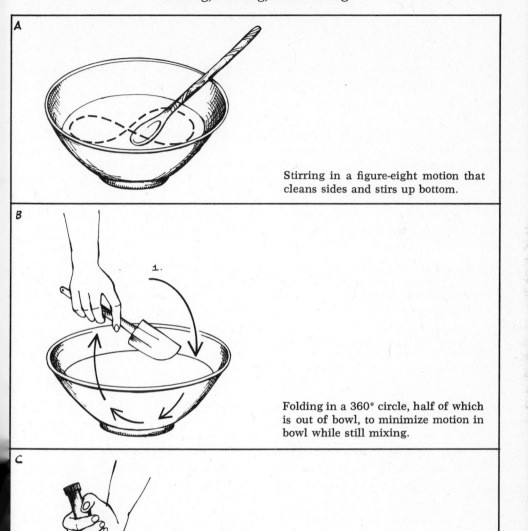

A

Stirring in a figure-eight motion that cleans sides and stirs up bottom.

B

1.

Folding in a 360° circle, half of which is out of bowl, to minimize motion in bowl while still mixing.

C

Beating with a wire whisk, using to-and-fro wrist motion.

The final step is combining the stiff egg whites, which act as further leavening (*see* Eggs), to the cake. They should be folded into the batter rapidly until they are dispersed.

At this point, take care not to stir the batter, as any further beating will tend to make it lose volume. It may be baked immediately or left for a short time with equal results.

Pour the batter into greased baking pans and bake according to the recipe.

The muffin method produces a good light cake with considerably less beating and creaming. However, it will lack the moist, smooth, velvety texture. The flour is sifted and measured. Combine the flour with the baking powder, salt, and sugar, and sift the mixture. Beat the egg until foamy. Measure the milk and combine it with the egg. Melt the fat (it is necessary to use liquid shortening or melt the fat) and add it to the egg-milk mixture. Combine the fat, egg, and milk mixture with the dry ingredients and stir until the dry ingredients are moistened and the batter relatively smooth. Some small lumps are acceptable. Add the egg whites (if the recipe calls for them) last, folding them in.

The cake mixer method for butter cake is also acceptable but the cake does not equal the standard butter cake.

The shortening, sugar, egg yolks, and flavoring are combined in the mixing bowl. The ingredients are creamed at the lowest speed. Then the sifted dry ingredients and liquid are alternately added.

After the mixing has been completed the egg whites are folded in and the cake poured into greased pans and baked.

Most cakes are best baked in a pan with ungreased sides but with a greased bottom or oiled paper on the bottom. Temperatures and times will depend on the recipe but these cakes should not be overbaked.

Unlike the butter cakes which contain chemical leavening, sponge-cakes and angel food cakes rely on the air which has been incorporated into the egg whites for leavening.

Nor do these cakes, when they are made traditionally, contain shortening except that contributed by the emulsifying action of the egg yolks in spongecake.

It is important, then, to combine the egg thoroughly with the other ingredients, and it is important that in combining them that air is not lost from the beaten whites.

Folding serves the same function in these cakes that creaming did in butter cakes. However, the processes are quite different. The object of folding is to combine the ingredients in the gentlest possible manner, by gently cutting down through the ingredients being mixed with the whip or rubber spatula and then cutting up the other side of the bowl. The folding tool describes a 360° circle, part of which is in the bowl.

For spongecake, sift and measure the flour, then sift with whatever seasonings are called for in the ingredients. Beat the egg yolks (or whole eggs) thoroughly, as this will aid their shortening property. Slowly add the sugar and liquid flavoring to the eggs. At this point the mixture should be stiff enough to peak. Add whatever liquid is called for. (If the liquid is boiling water, add a small quantity at a time and beat thoroughly after each addition, then let the mixture cook.) Add the flour mixture gradually, a sixth at a time, folding but not beating excessively. Add the beaten egg whites by folding, until they are dispersed. Bake in an ungreased pan.

Angel food cake differs most obviously from spongecake in that it has no yolks and the ingredients are folded into the white.

The sifted flour and half the sugar are sifted together as this mixture is more easily folded into the whipped whites. Salt and cream of tartar (both for enforcing the eggs and keeping the cake white) are sprinkled over the surface of the eggs and the whites beaten until soft peaks are formed (see Eggs). The sugar is folded into the whites a little at a time and then the sugar-flour mixture. The flavoring is added last and the folding continues for a minute or two.

After baking in an unoiled tube pan, the cake is inverted immediately on a rack, so that there is an air space between the bottom and the table.

XL

╼╾╼╾╼╾╼╾╼╾╼╾╼╾╼╾╼╾╼╾╼╾╼╾╼╾╼╾╼╾╼

Kitchen Equipment

The present emphasis by homemakers on electric equipment is unfortunate. Most of these machines do not do the job as well as the old-fashioned utensils they replace. They only do it more quickly.

A blender, for example, will make a mayonnaise in seconds; however, the egg yolks are so brutalized that they lose some of their taste. In blending meats and vegetables there is a substantial reduction of flavor in many instances because of the exposure of the flavor elements to enzymes from which they were naturally isolated.

Hamburger run through a meat grinder has no texture; while, when chopped by hand with a knife, enough of the fiber remains to give it character.

The speed of an electric mixer reduces the opportunity to incorporate air into a dough, preventing some of the chemical processes which, to be effective, depend on air. A juicer not only juices, it pulverizes the pulp and the membranes of the fruit. It even extracts some of the oil from the skin, giving machine-produced fruit juice an unnatural consistency and a bitter taste.

The newest toy, the electric knife, does not cut as cleanly as a carving knife and the cut meat is less appetizing.

Instead of buying any of this hardware, I would purchase solid tools and solid pots and pans of the traditional sort. Although somewhat more expensive than rinky-dink equipment, they give much better service and should last forty years.

Basting Brush
Bowls: of stainless steel, glass or earthenware (which usually has a
  ridged outer surface by which they can be held). A set is useful.
Broth Skimmer

243

Bulb Baster

Cake Cooking Rack

Cheesecloth: for straining stocks and emulsion sauces.

Cleaver

Colander: for straining pasta and vegetables.

Corkscrew

Cutting Board: an almost essential purchase is a cutting board in beechwood at least two inches thick. Cutting against the board is quicker, less dangerous, and better for the knives.

Deep-fat Fryer: either an electric device or a standard black pan and basket. It must be equipped with a thermometer. Several basket sizes should also be purchased. (*See* Frying.)

Double Boiler: in glass for puddings, chou paste, etc.

Flour Sifters: with coarse and fine wires, sturdy construction and securely fastened handles.

Forks: very few home cooks have an adequate fork. Perhaps two are necessary. A long-handled fork with firm, sharp tines and a well-secured handle for pulling fowl out of the stock pot, testing potatoes, pushing pans around the oven, and a short-handled two-pronged fork for turning meats and frying items. The fork should be stout enough to hook it through one of the handles of a full roasting pan without bending.

Funnel: several funnels in assorted sizes and diameter, one with calibrations, one in metal.

Graters: with drilled holes.

Gratin Dishes

Kitchen Shears: a large set for poultry and a smaller set for crayfish and lobster.

Kitchen Twine: for trussing, for tying vegetables, etc.

Knives: The best possible knife will be hand-forged with the blade running back through the handle. It should be high carbon or vanadium (noncorrosive) steel. Stainless steel does not keep an edge as well as nonstainless and should be reserved for cutting foods like lemons which would attack other metals. Knives that are forged or hammered from a solid piece of metal are much better than those cut from a sheet of steel. They have a better cutting edge because forging develops a finer grain in the steel. A hand-forged knife "sounds" with a high clean note when struck.

A knife should have spring and balance. The blade should be tapered from handle to point. When the blade is bent, the third next to the

The "French" Knife and Its Use

A

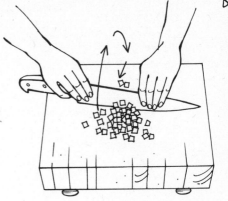

D

High quality "french" knife, hand-forged, full tang, well secured handle.

B

Chopping with knife, both hands gripping the knife out of way of blade; knife blade used to push food together and maximize effort.

C

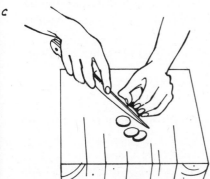

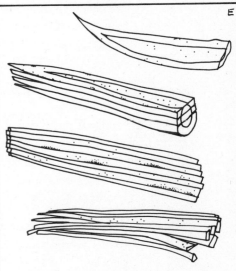

E

Slicing vegetables correctly, knife on board, fingers on left hand gripping the food, but out of way of knife, which is not raised above second knuckle.

Cutting a carrot-shaped vegetable preliminary to dicing.

F

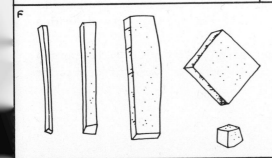

From left to right, vegetable cut in allumette, julienne, Brunoise, Losange, and dice.

handle should remain rigid while the two-thirds closer to the point are flexible enough to form a slight curve.

Good knives are recognized by the manner in which the blade is fastened to the handle. In a cheap knife the shank of the blade, called the tang, is narrowed to a point and pushed into a handle, where it is secured by a nail. The better knife has full tang and is secured by three large rivets.

While plastic handles are strong, they shatter and wood is therefore preferable.

I personally prefer German carving knives and French triangular vegetable knives (called *French* knives in America, and couteaux de cuisine in France). The French knife comes in a number of sizes. One should purchase the largest size that fits the hand easily, as the weight of the knife facilitates the work and the width protects the fingers.

The French knife is used effectively by placing the end on a board and rocking the knife with a sawing motion while at the same time advancing the blade with the other hand. In other words the knife remains in the same place and the food moves through the blade. The French knife is used for chopping by placing the end on the board under one hand and pivoting the knife through a half circle while chopping up and down.

A carving knife should be flexible with a definite spring to it. There are two basic types: the round-ended knife used for meat and the pointed knife useful for fowl. A good all-purpose bet is a medium-sized meat carver. A long flexible blade, tapered slightly at the point, will give the thinnest slices of cold meats and fish.

One should also have a heavy French knife for splitting lobster, beating veal cutlets, cutting through the bones in a rack of lamb or a loin of pork, and a utility knife of medium size with a straight or curved cutting edge for trimming meat, cleaning fish, and the like.

Paring knives should have a short blade to give leverage without undue strain on the finger muscles. They are available with a sharp, a spear, or a clipped point. Which you choose is a matter of personal taste.

A boning knife and a stout knife with a serrated blade for frozen foods, a clam knife, oyster knife, and a cleaver are useful tools; most other professional knives, especially some of the more exotic butcher knives, are almost worthless in the home kitchen.

Ladles

Larding Needles: in assorted sizes. The Germans have come out with a larding needle with an alligator clip end which facilitates larding enormously.

Mandoline: A French cutting device for potatoes and vegetables.

Measuring Cups: of aluminum with a large handle welded to the cup.

Measuring Spoons: It is important to check these against a standard cup as they vary.

Meat Saw

Molds: Baba, Charlotte, Dariole, tube mold, decorative molds and terrines, pudding molds.

Mortar and Pestle

Oilstone: for sharpening knives of high quality and all hollow-ground blades.

Parchment Paper: for lining pans, for paper cookery.

Pastry Bags: with a variety of tips.

Pastry Blender: either a several-bladed knife designed for this purpose or a small mill manufactured for pastry.

Pastry Board: in marble, plastic, or wood.

Pastry Cutter: fancy cutter that can be used for toast, for canapés, or cookies.

Pastry Wheel

Pepper Mill

Pots and Pans: Pots and pans are the most important pieces of kitchen equipment. Often they will mean the difference between satisfactory results and burned or scorched food. There are pots and pans of aluminum, enamelware, glass, stainless steel, and iron on the market. Some case can be made for each of these materials. Actually, the home cook should avoid buying a "set" of any one material and try to pick the material best suited to each cooking procedure. The kitchen does not look as sharp but the cooking is better.

Aluminum with a fraction of magnesium is suited to large pots that will be used in water cooking. It is light enough not to make heavy pots overly burdensome, and relatively stain resistant. A stock pot should have a spigot. It should be heavy gauge in any case; thin aluminum is to be avoided. Generally, aluminum utensils are finished with a highly polished exterior, a "Sunray" interior, and a satin bottom to help absorb heat. Dull bottoms on any pot are slightly better conductors than shiny bottoms. Some cast aluminum pieces are generally heavy with enamel coated exteriors and a "Sunray" finished interior. Cast aluminum makes excellent omelette pans. (*See* Eggs.)

Black iron is very good for quick sautéing, although thin sheet

248

metal has a tendency to warp. Pans that will be used for deglaçage should be heavy enough to make a sauce without scorching.

A new iron utensil should be washed and rubbed with cooking oil. It is then placed in a warm oven several hours to season. After seasoning it should not be scrubbed; in fact, even washing should be minimal. It must be reseasoned if scoured. (*See* "curing omelette pans" in Eggs.) Enamelware and glass are well suited to white sauces and egg preparations (including boiling eggs) which will react with metals. Hollandaise should be kept in these materials.

Stainless steel with copper bottoms or tin-lined copper pots (the tinning must be renewed periodically) are ideal for sauce cooking. The combination of stainless steel with another material is necessary for heat conduction. The second metal may be applied to the outside (two-ply) or sandwiched between layers of stainless steel (three-ply) which maximizes the advantages of all the metals: aluminum or copper for conduction and stainless steel for cleanliness and durability.

In general, plated utensils which appear to be bargains are unsatisfactory for long-term use. It is important to make sure that the metals are bonded together in an indivisible metal sandwich.

Earthenware and enamel-lined iron are excellent ovenware for long cooking times. Their virtues are considerable for long braisings, *daubes*, and other slow-cooking dishes.

As a rule, lightweight materials that heat quickly are for short-time use. Heavier materials that heat slowly are for long processes.

Almost every cooking utensil is being made with a nonstick finish. While advantages of nonstick surfaces are obvious—they clean quickly and easily—the material to which they are applied must be considered. A thin pan is still a thin pan. I personally feel that their use is rather limited. Fragile baked goods and food with a great deal of sugar must be greased. Good cooks don't burn pans; at the temperatures at which foods burn the coating is nearing the threshold of decomposition.

A pressure cooker has very few advantages in serious cooking over the old-fashioned waterless cooker which also doubles as a steamer. Meats lose their juices, vegetables are overcooked (few pressure cookers have a good pressure gauge or for that matter any pressure gauge). Oatmeal, for which it seems ideal, gums up the works nicely. In any case, a pressure cooker should have a tight fitting gasket, preferably one of synthetic rubber (fats react with pure rubber), a good safety valve, an accurate pressure gauge, and solid seamless construction. All pans should have seamless sides and flat bottoms. Pots should have rolled edges pressed to the sides to form a flat-bevel with no crevices to accumulate dirt. Covers should be tight fitting with a similar finish. Spouts should be shaped to direct liquid toward the center of the pouring stream. Handles should be heat resistant and joined to the pot with a clean joint to keep dirt from accumulating. If the handle is wood, a metal shank must connect it to the pot to eliminate its catching fire over the flame.

Glassware, earthenware, and ironware with detachable handles must have a completely reliable lock between the handle and the pot; otherwise disasters are inevitable.

Roasting and Baking Utensils: The best roasting pan has a smooth dark surface with a relatively large bottom area and a rack. Round corners which do not collect dirt are preferable to square. Several sizes should be purchased roughly paralleling anticipated cooking needs.

In cake and muffin pans, the material plays a dramatic role. Accepting tin as a standard, baking times must be shortened for enamelware; lengthened for aluminum; further lengthened if the aluminum is bright and new; shortened for glass. The shape is important. Sharp corners tend to cause a cake to brown more at the corner than in the middle. Shallow pans give a more coarse grain than a deep pan.

To insure even results, cookies and small pastry are best baked on a sheet rather than in a pan. (The side of the pan baffles the heat.) Again some consideration must be given to material. Pastry will burn on tinned steel when it would be perfect on aluminum or sheet iron. As most cookbooks do not indicate what material the author used—sometimes it can be divined from the list of recommended equipment—the home cook should try one or two pastries before committing the entire batch.

Baking dishes present some of the same problems. Heat-resistant glass is probably the best material, as it is nonabsorbent and free from tiny cracks and flaws. Because of its transparency and relatively low cooking rate, it is also the most controllable material for small preparations that will be served in the cooking vessel.

While a great assortment of baking pans in different formats are available, not all of them see enough use to justify their acquisition. One jelly roll pan (11 × 16), one tube pan (9″), one flan ring, one spring form pan (9″), one set of tartlet tins, two square pans (9″), one muffin tin, one flutted (10″) ring mold, a shallow pan (9 × 12), two pie pans, two cookie sheets, one loaf pan should be sufficient.

Rolling Pin: a French rolling pin without handles, or a rolling pin with handles and a cover.

Rubber Spatula: of synthetic rubber molded in one piece. A two piece spatula usually comes apart.

Salad Basket: either the traditional wire mesh basket, or one of the newer devices which work on centrifugal force and whirl the salad dry.

Scales: a standard scale calibrated in ounces from one ounce to twenty pounds.

Skewers: disposable bamboo skewers or ringed metal skewers.

Slotted Metal Spoon

Spatula: a flexible-blade spatula of stainless steel riveted to sturdy handles is used for turning foods, for aiding in omelette making, for folding egg whites into mixtures.

Spoons: While mixing spoons are made of everything from aluminum to graniteware, the wooden spoon remains the most useful. Aluminum spoons are brittle, iron spoons rust, all metal spoons scratch pots. A wooden spoon will not scratch the pots, react with the sauce, or become too hot to hold. They are inexpensive enough to throw away when they warp.

Strainers and Sieves: Three strainers are necessary to cookery: A very fine strainer for sauces and stocks, called a Swiss Bouillon strainer, fine enough to double as a flour sifter. A china cap, a conical strainer punctured by relatively large holes, which is used for straining semisolids. Those made of tin with thin and sharp drilled holes (rather than punched) are best. A regular all-purpose round strainer with a moderately fine wire screen fastened to a solid metal edge around the bowl is also necessary.

Tenderizing Hammer: with four sides for cubing, flattening, and tenderizing.

Thermometer: Candy, broiler, oven, deep fryer, floating.

Timer

Tongs

Vegetable Brush

Vegetable Peeler

Vegetable Scoops: several fancy scoops for turning and shaping vegetables.

Whips and Beaters: The whip is the traditional alternative to the mixer or rotary beater. There are essentially two kinds of whips: the sauce whip and the egg-white (ballon) whip. The sauce whip has fewer wires and is stiffer than the egg whip. The finer the wire, the more air

251

will be incorporated. Both are necessary. Specific whips for egg yolks, creams, and purées are handy, but can be dispensed with. The wire should be fastened smoothly and securely to make cleaning easier.

Wheel or rotary beaters should have sharp cutting edges and a turn ratio of at least five to one. The handle should be long enough to eliminate danger of contact with the fingers. Gears should mesh smoothly and the blades should permit the material at the bottom of the bowl to be mixed. There is also a horizontal rotary beater which mixes as effectively but does not "lift."

Wooden Bowl and Chopper: for nuts and the like.

Zester: for removing the zest of citrus fruits without excessive white.

PART

4

Appendices

▀▄

Incidental Ingredients

Small details are important in cooking. The incidental ingredients used in cooking—olives, spirits, capers, butter, vinegar—should be of the highest quality obtainable, otherwise the entire dish, regardless of the cost or quality of the other ingredients, is substantially cheapened.

Cooking with inexpensive cuts of meat and first-class incidental ingredients is far more sensible than economizing on the brandy and splurging on the filet. The difference in cost between quality of incidental ingredients is never more than a few pennies a dish.

Baking Powder

Most recipes which call for baking powder never specify brand or type. This is unfortunate as the amount of available carbon dioxide (the leavening force) will vary from 12 to 20 percent. In addition, the tartrate baking powders are quick acting and require a quick oven, as do the phosphate baking powders, while the double action acts slowly and requires a slow oven. It is necessary to buy a fresh can of a good brand and read the label and integrate its instruction with those of the recipe. Only small quantities should be purchased as the powder deteriorates rather rapidly.

Baking Soda

Sodium bicarbonate is used as a leavening agent (it produces carbon dioxide in the presence of an acid—$\frac{1}{2}$ teaspoon plus $\frac{1}{8}$ teaspoon cream of tarter = 1 teaspoon tartrate baking powder) and as a color stabilizer in the cooking of green vegetables.

Bouillon Cubes

Beef extract and bouillon cubes (one cube = 1 teaspoon of extract) are rather dangerous to use as they always bear a strong characteristic taste. At best they can be used in modest quantities as an "enricher."

Butter (Beurre)

In Europe, several different types of butter are available. While these same types are made here, only salted "sour cream" butter is widely available. Other types are sweet cream butter, which is creamy and bland, and unsalted, and unsalted sour cream butter (which is generally called sweet but is not necessarily made from sweet cream). The best butter is graded AA (93 score) and has a good flavor, body, color, and package. "Sweet" butter, in which defects acquired after grading are easily discerned, is the best for cooking. Summer butter is said to be better flavored than the butter produced from the cream of cows fed on silage.

Capers (Câpres)

Tiny buds of a bush sold either pickled or salt dried. A premium is put on the smaller sizes. Used with fish, salads, sauces of white meats. Bargain capers are generally nasturtium seed buds.

Chocolate (Chocolat)

For cooking purposes, plain chocolate without additional ingredients like spices, vanilla, milk fat, is best. As the additional ingredients are generally less costly than chocolate, this pure chocolate will be more expensive but the flavor is more intense and dependable.

Cheese (Fromage)

Three types of cheese are widely used in cookery: cottage, Parmesan, and Gruyère.

Unripened cottage cheese or some form of it is used as a filling for pasta, in blinis, and cheesecake.

Parmesan, properly called Parmigiano Reggiano, is the prototype for all the grating cheese on the market. The genuine, imported Parmigiano Reggiano remains the best cheese for cooking purposes.

Gruyère, from Switzerland, and imported Swiss cheese (properly called Emmental), which is similar, remain, despite the competition of a host of imitators, the best cooking cheese for omelettes, sauces, seasoning, and garnishing.

Cornstarch (Fécule de Maïs)

Cornstarch is the most widely used simple starch for thickening, while very useful there are other valuable liaisons (*see* Thickening). Waxy maize starches, which are now available and resemble cornstarches, are used for preparations which will be frozen, as they maintain their character better. They are also about 50 percent more effective than cornstarch.

Any of these products should be pure, without lumps.

Condiments (Condiments)

Bottled sauces, like catsup, A-I, Escoffier Sauce, chili sauce, Worcestershire sauce, have nothing near the versatility claimed by their manufacturers. In sauces (sauce piquante, some cold sauces, some mayonnaise sauces) where a sweet and spicy element is acceptable, they are quite useful, as is a good brand of chutney.

Pepper sauces, either the kind which contains the whole pod (in vinegar which serves as a carrier) or an extract of red peppers, are useful, as they are easier to use than cayenne for seasoning.

Soy sauce, especially the imported genuine Japanese sauces, are valuable condiments and can be used anywhere Worcestershire can.

Cream (Crème)

Cream is available with a butterfat content of from 18 to 50 percent, ranging from light to heavy. Cream to be used in a recipe taken from the French, which calls for double cream (crème fraîche), must have a butterfat content of at least 30 percent. Heavy cream which, in most cases, has at least 30 percent, is the lightest cream to be used. It is far better to inquire of the Board of Health in any area for the local standards than to guess the butterfat. This cream may be slightly acidulated to resemble French cream by the addition of lactic-acid-producing bacteria. This can be done by adding buttermilk (one tablespoon to one cup), heating the mixture slightly, and letting it work at room temperature for about ten hours or until it thickens, or by purchasing lactic acid starter from one of the companies listed under "Rennet" in the yellow pages, and following the directions. The lactic acid starter method is cheaper in the long run (in the absence of a passion for buttermilk) and much more controllable.

In whipping cream, 30 percent butterfat is sufficient. An excess will shorten the time but does not increase the whip capabilities. The cream should be cold, as should the room, the bowl, and the whip. Neither sugar nor acid aids whipping.

Fats and Oils (Graisses et Huiles)
(*See* Frying and Baking chapters)

An oil is liquid at room temperature while a fat is solid; their uses are in part determined by this difference. Oils are useful for salads because they pour at room temperature, and fats are preferred for baking because they do not.

Fats for baking must cream well, have sufficient plasticity and shortening power. This eliminates most of the hard fats and the very soft fats, leaving lard and the especially created hydrogenated fats.

Other fats are used for frying, for which they must have a high stability, a limited amount of free fatty acids, which largely eliminates animal fats. The smoking point must be high enough for use at frying temperature.

Oils are used for frying, for general cooking purposes, for salads and rarely for baking. The preferred oil for frying has traditionally been peanut oil. Corn oil is, as well, quite satisfactory. Cottonseed and soybean contribute off flavors to fried foods. Olive oil can be used for general cooking purposes and is the preferred salad oil. The best is cold pressed French olive oil; Italian olive oil from Lucca runs a close second. Unfortunately, the name Lucca is not strictly controlled. The term "virgin," while identifying the finest oil from the first pressing of sound ripe olives, may also refer to the first pressing of overripe and inferior olives. Taste is the final criterion. Good olive oil is free from strong odors and flavors.

Lard

Lard is made by rendering the leaf and backfat of hogs over low heat. This fat, well prepared and free from all impurities and admixtures, is excellent for pies, biscuits, yeast breads, cookies, doughnuts, and for browning of stews and roasts. The smoking point of lard ranges from 350° to 375°F.

Beef Fat

Beef fat, sometimes called beef suet, may be rendered in a similar way to lard.

Chicken Fat

Chicken fat is used in a similar way to goose fat. It is also good in making roux for chicken velouté.

Goose Fat

Goose fat plays an important part in the preparation of preserved potted foie gras. It is also excellent for the preparation of sauerkraut and green cabbage.

Margarine

Margarine is the chief fat other than butter used for cooking and as a spread. It is made from vegetable or animal fats, other than butterfat. In processing margarine, it is churned with pasteurized milk, which causes it to take up milk solids and to acquire butter flavor. Margarine is not counseled for serious cooking.

Shortening Compounds

Shortening compounds are usually made by combining a hard fat with a soft fat or oil to give the desired body to the final product. Shortening compounds are produced from all-vegetable fats or from all-animal fats or from a combination of the two. Compounds are also pure white, bland in flavor, odorless, and of good keeping quality.

Almond Oil

A nut oil, used exclusively in confectionary.

Beechnut Oil

An excellent table oil with a nutty flavor. As fine and subtle as the best olive oil.

Coconut Oil

The oil is a fat at room temperature. It is odorless, tasteless, and very digestible in the form it reaches us. Less refined products have a good, nutty taste.

Corn Oil

Corn oil is light, digestible. Modern processing reduces an otherwise pronounced flavor.

Cornel Berry Oil (Huile de Cornouiller)

An oil used in northern Italy, pressed from the seeds of the cornel berry. Used for cooking purposes.

Cotton Oil

A pale yellow, odorless oil, often used to adulterate more expensive oils. Limited gourmet use.

Peanut Oil

Peanut oil or ground nut oil is tasteless and is often made odorless. It is used where a light oil is wanted.

Poppyseed Oil

Extracted from seeds of the poppy, used as a table oil.

Sesame Oil

Sesame oil has a strong distinguished odor, like the sesame seed from which it is pressed. It is only used in salads, hors d'oeuvres, and baked goods.

Walnut Oil

A strong-tasting oil quite pleasant on bitter salad greens.

Flour (*see* Baking)

All-purpose flour: a mixture of hard and soft wheats with some gluten. Used for all baked goods.

Soft Flour: Low-gluten, high-starch for cakes and pastries.

Hard Flour: High in gluten for breads.

Whole Wheat Flour: Fine, whole grain flour.

Graham Flour: Coarse, whole grain flour.

Self-Rising Flour: Soft flour with leavening agents.

Patent Flour: A super-refined flour, better for baking because of a reduced ash and fat content.

Gluten Flour: A high-gluten flour.

While most baking is done with wheat flour (rye bread is made from rye and wheat in combination), other flours are available: buckwheat, corn, lentil, oatmeal, potato, rice, soybean, lotus; they have limited specific uses.

Foie Gras

Essentially, this name refers to the fat goose liver from specially fed French geese. Qualities vary considerably and many other preparations, containing only a percentage of goose liver or none, capitalize on the name; for example, Parfait de foie gras, foie gras d'oie, mousse de foie gras, pâté de foie gras. The genuine foie gras generally comes in tunnel tins (this, too, is imitated) in a solid block with a percentage of truffles. The label of any can should be carefully examined to determine exactly how much real foie gras the preparation contains. Remember that ingredients are listed in order of quantity.

Gelatin

Gelatin belongs to that category of ingredients which is too often ignored in writing recipes. As the quality of gelatin varies from brand to brand, no recipe can be exact. The home cook should choose a brand that has firm gel, no wateriness, and minimal clouding, learn about its setting time and the quantities necessary for liquids, and stick to it. In powder form it should be flavorless and odorless and light in color, rather than dark.

Mushrooms

Ordinary mushrooms are available in cans and in several dried forms. While these are generally good and of good appearance, their flavor is inferior to whole fresh mushrooms of good quality.

Wild mushrooms, canned or dried, are often used in cuisine because they are not available fresh in this country.

The *cèpe* is widely used as a garnish for game and as a vegetable. The cap is light or dark brown with a thick stalk. Generally these are sautéed with garlic and shallots. Some authorities advocate long cooking, braising in brown, red wine sauces or cream, but this seems unnecessary as cèpes are heat-processed in canning.

The morels, or morilles, are generally black but may be as light as beige. The cap is irregular. They are used widely as a garnish for salpicons and as a vegetable.

The chanterelle and girolle are small, frilled, orange-yellow mushrooms, widely used in France sautéed with veal.

Olives (Olives)

Olives are available as ripe, green (Queen or Spanish), Sicilian-style green, salt-cured, oil-coated (Greek).

Ripe olives are mature olives, generally of the small Mission variety, which are exposed to the air to darken during processing. The larger ripe olives (which are not Mission) are not as desirable. Ripe olives may be either black or a green-yellow mottled with brown. The latter are softer (and more ripe) than the black ripe olive.

Green olives are firmer and more bitter than ripe olives. They are generally packed in glass because of their action on metal, while ripe olives are packed in specially lined tins.

The Sicilian green olives are a more bitter variety.

Salt-cured, oil-coated olives are black (but not ripe), shriveled because of the salt cure.

Sizes of commercially sold olives vary from the peewee (181–220 per pound) to the supercolossal (fewer than 32 per pound).

Many green olives are imported. Olives may be pitted, or pitted and stuffed with pimento, onion, almonds, or compound stuffings.

Pickles (Cornichon)

The French pickle which is small, crisp, and well flavored has a minor place in cuisine, but it cannot be replaced by any domestic pickle in the sauces (cold, piquante, mayonnaise) which require it. Our pickles are either of the wrong type of cucumber or too sweet.

Pimentos (Piments Doux)

Good quality imported pimentos (a type of very red sweet pepper). Best brands are bright scarlet whole, with no seed core or stem.

Spirits (Eau de Vie)

A number of spirits are widely used in the kitchen: dry red wines, dry white wines, dry Vermouth, dry Madeira, dry Marsala, kirsch, cognac, sweet liqueurs (Cointreau, clear fruit liqueurs, etc.). There is one essential rule: if it cannot be drunk with comfort, it cannot be used in cooking.

This is not to say that the very best spirits must be used in cooking; rather they should be decent, solid, medium priced.

Sugar (Sucre)

While the origin of the sugar is not important in cooking, the fineness is. Granulated sugar is used for table use, and for ordinary sweetening. Sugars designated by an X, from one X to ten X (the most fine), is ground sugar rather than crystallized sugar. For example, XXXX is used in baking and icing, XX is used for drinks, and the finest sugar is used for coating. The other grades are for use in confections.

Berry or fruit sugars which are not derived from cane or beets are available and may be used in fruit mixtures.

Truffles (Truffes)

Truffles, an underground fungus, are important in some dishes, although in many more their purpose is decorative. Some are available fresh or fresh frozen, but most are canned. The best are French and black, although some white truffles come from Italy.

Whole brushed truffles are the most expensive. Whole peeled are second, while pieces, peelings and paste are also available.

Vanilla (Vanille)

Considering the minute quantities of this flavoring used, the best quality beans (Mexican) should be bought. Only pure vanilla extracts should be used.

Vegetable Coloring

Vegetable colors offer a measure of control in the preparation of red, green, and yellow preparations. Moderately used, they contribute to the appeal of dishes like tomato soup, pea soup, cakes, egg dishes, etc. Caramel, or blackjack, which contributes the rich color to most commercial sauce enhancers, is used in brown sauces.

Vinegar (Vinaigre)
(*See* Salads)

Wine vinegar, generally from red wine, is the preferred salad vinegar. Malt vinegar, cider vinegar, and white vinegar do have limited uses. It is important to purchase good brands; price is generally a reflection of quality.

Yeast (Levure)

Yeast for leavening is available dried and compressed. Dried yeast is a more stable form; compressed yeast will mold and deteriorate rapidly. One package of dry is equal to one cake of compressed.

▪▪

Glossary*

à la: in the style of, used in French with feminine endings
abaisser: to roll a dough flat
abatis: variety meats
abricoter: to coat a pastry preparation with a covering of apricot glaze
accolade, en accolade: the presentation of preparations back to back on the same platter
acidifier: to make a sauce or preparation slightly acid by adding lemon juice or vinegar
acidulated water: water made slightly acid, see *acidifier* above
acrid: having a sharp, sour, puckery tart taste in the mouth
adoucier: to reduce the bitterness or spiciness of a preparation by cooking or dilution
affriander: to make tempting, to tempt
age: to allow the natural enzymes of meat to work on the tissues for a protracted period
aiguiser: to spice heavily, to season highly
al dente: said of macaroni that retains its firm character after cooking
allumette: a fashion of cutting, in matchstick
amidon: a simple starch
anglaise: to cook à l'anglaise is either to cook in water or to bread in egg yolks and crumbs
aplatir: to flatten

* NOTE: the following list includes those basic technical terms in French and English that are encountered in cooking literature and may not be adequately defined in standard dictionaries. Comment on specific preparations (godiveau, mousse, etc.) may be found through the index.

appareil: a preparation which is an element, usually the major element of a dish; for example, an appareil for soufflé would consist of the soufflé mixture

aromates: a class of seasoning that includes sage, basil, rosemary, marjoram, thyme, bay, cinnamon, ginger, juniper berries, nutmeg, cloves, mace, vanilla beans, parsley, chervil, tarragon, pimpernel, savory, zests of lemon and oranges

aromatiser: to render a preparation fragrant, to perfume a dish with scented seasonings

arroser: to sprinkle

assaisoner: to season with salt and pepper

aspic: the presentation of cold dishes in a molded jelly

attelet: a skewer used for decorative purposes

attendrir: to tenderize

au gratin: refers to those sauce preparations which have been prepared with a browned crust

au jus: a roast dish served with its natural juices

baba: a pastry preparation, and the mold to make it

bain marie: a vessel containing hot water used either to keep food (mostly sauces) warm or for double boiler type cooking

bake: to cook by dry heat, usually in an oven. When applied to meat it is generally called roasting

ballotine: see *galantine*

barbecue: to roast meat on a spit, or over coals, basting it with a special highly seasoned sauce

barder: to cover a piece of meat with a sheet of bacon to protect it from the heat and to keep it moist while cooking

baron: the name given to the nether part of an animal cooked as a roast

barquettes: small boat-shaped pastry shells used for hors d'oeuvre and pastry preparations

baste: to moisten meat while cooking, to prevent drying and to flavor

batter: a relatively liquid flour mixture

Baumé: refers to the system of measuring the density of a sugar solution. Densities are expressed in degrees Baumé

beard: to remove the trailing appendages of mollusks

beat: to mix vigorously with a constant rhythm

beignet: a pastry preparation that is deep-fried

beurre manié: a mixture of butter and flour, worked together to a smooth paste, used for thickening certain dishes

bind: to thicken, generally with egg yolks, to hold together a sauce

blanc: a broth of flour, water and vinegar used for the cooking of certain
  vegetables to keep them from turning black
blanch: to cook in boiling salted water, with the purpose of hardening
  the protein in certain meats like brains, or removing the bitterness
  from vegetables like chicory, or to facilitate the peeling of thin-
  skinned fruits, or to entirely cook green vegetables like peas
blanchir: to blanch
blanquette: a white stew seasoned with cloves and thickened with egg
  yolks and beurre maníe
blend: to mix thoroughly or to process in a liquefier
blet: the point of ripeness bordering on rottenness in fruit
bleu: term describing the condition of red meat which has been cooked
  and removed from the heat before the coagulation of the blood elements, at this point it would be termed rare. Also refers to the cooking
  of small fish in acidulated water to develop an azure color
blond: can be considered as synonymous with fond ordinaire or fond de
  volaille
blondier: to fry in butter, proceeding as for browning but removing the
  article when a light gold color is achieved
boil: to cook in bubbling water, at sea level in water at 212°
bombe: refers to a mold and an ice cream preparation made in it
bone: to completely remove or partially remove the skeletal structure
  from a food
bordure: a form of decoration, generally consisting of some farinaceous
  preparation encircling the main element. The border of noodle paste
  is most often employed
boucanage: a term more or less synonymous with smoking, implying,
  however, a rather thorough drying
bouchées: a small pastry case
bouquet garni: the seasoning of stock and soups fashioned into a small
  bundle
braise: to cook a food by moist heat in a closed vessel
braisage: the cooking in a closed vessel by moist heat
brandade: a preparation of cod, pounded, strongly seasoned with garlic
  and mounted like a mayonnaise
bread: to cause bread crumbs to adhere to a food item
brew: to soak to extract the soluble material
brider: a method of trussing a fowl by passing the string through the
  thighs with a specially designed needle
broche: a spit

brochettes: various meats or other ingredients impaled on a metal rod (small spit) and grilled or roasted

broth: a liquid that has been flavored by the cooking of a foodstuff

brown: to cause to color by exposing a food to high heat or hot fat

brunoise: a fashion of cutting vegetables into small thin squares or rectangles

brush: to daub the surface of a food with a liquid element, for example breads with milk, or beaten egg

buisson, en buisson: a decorative form appearing as a short broad cone, a bush

candy: to coat with sugar

canapé: a toast on which either an hors d'oeuvre preparation or a cooked roast is placed

caramel: sugar which has been cooked until brown, moistened with water and cooked into a thick syrup. Blackjack. Used to color stews, etc.

cardinaliser: to redden the shells of a lobster by plunging it in boiling liquid

carré: the rib section of veal, lamb, mutton, or pork

chapelure: bread crumbs

charcuterie: equivalent to delicatessen

chaud-froid: a stew, generally of game or fowl, that has been cooked in its sauce and is served glazed with gelatin. By extension, chaud-froid is applied to almost any piece decorated and covered with gelatin, to the gelatin-based sauce used for coating

chemiser: to line the inner walls of a mold or terrine

chicken fried: said of food which has been mechanically tenderized, seasoned, floured, and fried

chiffonade: a fashion of cutting, usually of leaf vegetables to produce threadlike pieces

chiqueter: to lightly score the surface of a pastry

chop: cut into small pieces with a knife or a chopping device

ciseler: to score meat to facilitate cooking without curling

citronner: to sprinkle a preparation with lemon juice either to make it slightly acid or to prevent blackening

civet: a type of stew in which the liaison is made with blood

clarification: the removal of suspended particles from a liquid

clarified butter: the oil of butter, having been separated from the milk and solid parts by melting and decantation

cloche: a glass cover, bell-shaped, used with some enamelware or earthenware base

266

clouter: to stud a meat with some appropriate substance

coat: to cover a preparation with another element for purposes of flavoring, cooking, decoration, etc.

cocotte: a small cooking vessel, traditionally three-legged

color: to add vegetable coloring to a preparation, generally a liquid. Also, to brown slightly

compote: a cooked preparation of fruits

concasser: chop in coarse pieces

condiment: a nonherbal seasoning

consommé: a clarified broth

contiser: to stud a meat with some appropriate substance in half-moon slices

corned: said of meats cured by soaking in brine and seasonings

cornet: a cone, refers either to a fashion of presenting slices of meats or to a piece of paper fashioned in a pastry tube

corriger: to compensate for the unfortunate domination of a dish by one element or seasoning by adding proportionate amounts of the others

côtoyer: to rotate a preparation in the oven so it cooks evenly

coulis: a soup made from a purée of a substance, thickened with egg yolks; a bisque is a coulis made from shellfish

coupe: an ice cream preparation in a glass

court bouillon: a seasoned broth used for cooking fish

cracklings: the remains of fatty tissue after the fat has been rendered

cream: to render smooth and viscous like cream by rubbing with a spoon

crumb: the inner portion of bread or cake

crust: the outer surface of baked goods

cube: to cut in even cubic pieces. Also, to score a thin slice

curdle: to cause the precipitation of the solid portion of a sauce or soup, usually accidentally

cut in: to combine flour and shortening by chopping together with a knife

darioles: small round molds

darne: a slice of fish before cooking

decant: to separate a liquid from its sediment by pouring into another vessel

deglaçage: the process of washing the pan in which a meat has been cooked to dissolve the material adhering to it to form the basis of a sauce

dégorger: to soak in water in an effort to purify

dégraisser: to remove the grease from the surface of a liquid *déguiser:* to disguise, to mask the contents of a preparation sufficiently as to render it unrecognizable

délayer: to moisten with the thinning or rendering liquid in mind

dénerver: to remove the nerves and tendons

dépouiller: to remove the material which surfaces during the boiling of a stock or sauce, to remove the skin of an animal

déosser: to bone

dessécher: to dry a substance over the fire, like rice

détendre: to thin by adding liquid

détrempe: name given to the flour and water mixture in the preparation of a dough

devil: to treat with mustard and other spicy seasoning

dice: to cut into small cubes

disjoint: to separate the parts of animals at the joints, generally at the ball and socket joints

dorer: to make golden, either by direct exposure to heat, or by coating with beaten egg

dot: to cover with small bits of a substance, generally butter

doubler: to fold over on itself

dredge: to coat evenly with flour. Also, to coat a roast in the last stages of cooking with some element which will froth when moistened with clarified butter

dress: to season with a sauce, or dressing. Salads and vegetables are dressed

dresser: to arrange a preparation attractively

drippings: fats and juices rendered from broiling or roasting meats

dust: to sprinkle with a finely powdered substance

ébarber: to remove the gills of a fish, or the beard of a mussel

échauder: to scald

écorcher: to remove the skin

écraser: to crush

écumer: to scum

édulcorer: to render sweet

egg wash: refers to the egg or egg-milk mixture used in treating foods with bread crumbs

émincer: to cut into very thin slices

emulsion: a suspension of a liquid in a liquid, a solid in a liquid; a sauce like mayonnaise is an emulsion, so is milk or egg yolk

entrée: nowadays, refers to the main course of a meal

entremets: nowadays, refers to a sweet course

éplucher: to peel

essence: the soluble elements of food reduced to a thick paste

étoffer: to stuff

étouffee: to smother. The cooking of a substance slowly with little or no moistening

étuver: to stew

faggot: see bouquet garni

farce: a stuffing

farinaceous: having flour elements, related to flour

fécule: a simple starch, often extracted from potatoes

fell: the skin on a cut of lamb

fermentation: the growth process of microorganisms that produce water, alcohol, and carbon dioxide gas

flake: to divide a substance into small thin morsels

flamber: to flame with a liqueur

flan: a dessert confection. The mold it is made in

fleuron: a small pastry of puff paste used for decoration of soup

flour: to treat with flour

folding: to mix two ingredients by turning one into the other with a "folding motion"

fonds: stocks (*fond ordinaire,* veal stock, *fond de volaille,* fowl stock, *fond brun,* brown stock)

fouetter: to whip

fraisage: the process of thoroughly mixing dough by breaking it up and combining it with the palm of the hand

frapper: to chill

forcemeat: farce

frémissement: agitation of water before it comes to a boil

frire: to fry

frizzle: to cook a food in hot fat until the edges curl

frost: to coat with sugar or icing

fumet: a strong broth of a substance in wine or stock which is used for strengthening a weak sauce or moistening another preparation. Also a game consommé

garnish: an auxiliary element in a dish

garniture: a complementary preparation to some major element. Some formal garnitures in French cuisine imply a sauce

glaze: to give a shiny look to substances with sauce, sugar, aspic

gluten: the protein of flour

gratiner: to create a crust on a food

grate: to particulate a substance into a coarse powder

grind: to particulate a substance into a medium-fine powder *grease:* to treat the inside of a mold, a baking dish, or grill with a fatty substance

hacher: to chop

heel: to baste a roast in the final stages of cooking with some spirit, often the "heel" or remainder of a bottle of wine is used

hors d'oeuvre: a preliminary course to the main dish

hull: to remove the outer skin, or husk, or shell from a food

icing: a sugar-based coating for cakes and confections

inciser: to make shallow slits in a fish to be grilled

jagger: the pastry wheel used for cutting piecrusts

julienne: a fashion of cutting in matchsticks

knead: to mix a dough thoroughly with the hands to develop the gluten

lard: the rendered fat of pork

larder: to insert pieces of fat in meat by means of a special needle

lardon: strips of fat fashioned to be inserted with a larding needle

leavening: an agent that will cause a dough to rise during baking

liaison: a thickening agent

lights: variety meats

losange: a fashion of cutting, in a diamond shape

macédoine: a mixture of fruits or vegetables trimmed and shaped similarly

macérer: to soak in spirits or liqueurs, to effect tenderization, or flavoring

malaxer: to knead

mandoline: a device to facilitate the cutting of vegetables into regular shapes

marbled: said of meats having veins of internal fat

marinade: a seasoned liquid in which a meat is subject to maceration

marmite: a large pot

matignon: a mirepoix with ham

mask: to coat with a sauce, or aspic for decoration

mijoter: to simmer

milt: the male reproductive glands in fish, or their secretion

mince: to chop into fine pieces

mirepoix: a preparation of carrots, onions, celery, which is cooked in butter and added to stocks and sauces to increase their flavor

monter: to whip egg whites into a foam

mortify: see age

mouiller: to moisten

mousseline: a very fine strainer

napper: to coat with a sauce

panade: the farinaceous element in a stuffing
pan-broil: a cookery process by which meats are dry-cooked in a heavy pan
panure: breading
parer: to trim
pasta: macaronis and the like
pâte: dough
pâté: a preparation encased in a cooked dough
pâtes alimentaires: macaronis and the like
paupiette: a small stuffed roll of meat
paysanne: a fashion of cutting in asymetrical but regular shapes
peler: to peel
pilaf: a preparation of rice and a method of rice cookery
piler: to pound in a mortar
pinch: a small quantity of seasoning, that which can be held between the thumb and index finger
pipe: to decorate with icing forced through a narrow pastry tube
plank: to cook on a seasoned wooden plank by baking
poach: to cook in liquid at the point of simmering
pocher: to poach
poêler: a process between roasting and braising best described as roasting in butter
preheat: refers to the necessity of heating the oven to the desired baking temperature before introducing the food to be baked
proof: the period in dough making when the yeast is allowed to develop
purée: a substance made into a semisolid state by passing it through a strainer
râble: the saddle of a rabbit or hare
rack: the rib section of lamb, pork or mutton
ragout: the category of preparations which includes all stews
ramekin: a small vessel used for baked preparations
raper: to grate
réchaud: a chafing dish
reduction: the process of boiling down a liquid to intensify its flavor
render: to extract the fat from fatty tissues
ribbon: refers to the process of combining sugar and egg by beating with a spoon until "ribbons" trail from the uplifted spoon
rice: to pass through a device (ricer) to form ricelike grains of purée
rissolver: to brown in fat in the oven
roast: to bake a meat in an oven
roe: the eggs of a fish

271

roll out: to force a dough between a rolling pin and the surface of a pastry board, to assume a desired flat shape

royal: an unsweetened custard preparation used for soups

rousser: to brown in fat

roux: the thickening agent made by the conbination of flour and fat

saddle: the double section of back between the ribs and the haunches in meat animals

sauter: to fry quickly in a small amount of fat

scale: to remove the scales of a fish. Also, to measure all the ingredients in baking before preparation begins

scallop: fashion of cutting into serrated pieces

score: to mark regularly with a knife or hot grill

sear: to seal the outer surface of meat

seize: to sear

shirr: refers to the cooking of eggs in the oven in a shallow dish

shred: to reduce to thin long strips

shuck: to remove the shells of mollusks and the husks of corn

sift: to pass a dry powdered ingredient through a fine strainer to eliminate lumps

simple starch: a starch on the order of cornstarch, arrowroot

singe: to remove visible hairs and feathers from a plucked fowl by exposure to a live flame

singer: to sprinkle flour on a preparation (generally on a substance which has been fried and is still in the frying fat), to form a roux

skewer: a metal rod on which meats can be grilled and roasted

skim: to remove the material from the surface of a cooking liquid

sliver: to cut in thin segments

smother: to cook in a quantity of fat, covered, over a low heat

spit: the iron rod on which meats were fixed before an open fire in traditional roasting (spit cookery)

steam: to cook in the vapor of boiling liquid

steep: to soak to extract soluble elements

stew: to cook by moist cookery, over a low heat

stir: to mix with the aid of a spoon or paddle, generally while cooking

stock: a liquid in which the soluble elements of meats and vegetables have been dissolved

suer: to sweat

suprême: the boned breast section of a fowl

sweat: to cook in fat over a low heat

tamis: a strainer

272

tenderize: to soften the tissues (especially the connective tissues) of meat by mechanical or chemical means

terrines: a preparation of meat and seasoning cooked to a homogeneous loaf in a sealed container

timbale: a pastry case that has been prepared by deep frying in a mold

tomalley: the liver of lobster used to thicken lobster based sauces

toss: to butter vegetables by manipulating them with butter in a sauté pan away from the heat after cooking. Also, to mix salad and dressing

tourner: to trim vegetables into even shapes

travailler: to stir (a sauce); to thoroughly mix (a stuffing); to knead (a dough)

truss: to tie a meat or fowl for cooking

try out: to render fat

vanner: to stir a sauce, especially while cooking to prevent the formation of a skin on the surface

vol-au-vent: a pastry shell used for sauce dishes with a pastry cover

whip: to beat with a wire whisk

work: the action of fermentation in a yeast dough

zest: the outer skin of a citrus fruit

Selected Bibliography

Ali-Bab
  "Gastronomie Practique," 8th ed., Flammarion, Paris, 1928
American Meat Institute
  "Science of Meat and Meat Products," W. H. Freeman, San Francisco, 1960
American Spice Trade Assoc.
  "Spices," New York, 1956
Avery, Madelyn
  "Household Physics," Macmillan, New York, 1938
Bachmann, W.
  "Professional Knowledge," MacLaren & Sons, London, 1951
Baker, J. S. Mize, M. D.
  "The Relations of Fats to Texture, Crumb, and Volume of Bread," *Cereal Chemistry*, Vol. 19, 1943
Beauvilliers, A.
  "L'Art du Cuisinier," Vol. I & II, Polnet, Paris, 1824
Bernadi
  "L'Ecuyer Tranchant," Gustave Barba, Paris, 1845
Boyer, P. D. et al
  "Enzymes," 2nd rev. ed., Academic Press, New York, 1958
Burnet
  "Dictionnaire de Cuisine," Librairie Usuelle, 1836
Carême, A.
  "Cuisinier Parisien," J. Renouard, Paris, 1842
Carême, A.
  "Le Maitre d'Hotel," no pub., Paris, 1822
Carême, A.
  "Le Patissier Royal," I & II, J. G. Dentu, Paris, 1815
Cruess, W. V.
  "Commercial Fruit and Vegetable Products," 4th ed., McGraw-Hill, New York, 1958
Déliée, F. J.
  "Franco-American Cookery Book," Putnam's, 1888
Dubois, Urbain
  "Cuisine Artistique," E. Dentu, Paris, 1872

Dubois, Urbain
"La Cuisine Classique," E. Dentu, Paris, 1886
Dumas, Alexandre
"Grand Dictionnaire de Cuisine," Alphonse Lemerre, Paris, 1873
Easton, Alice
"Dictionary of Sea Food," Hospitality Guild, Stamford, Conn., 1935
Escoffier, A.
"Ma Cuisine," Flammarion, Paris, 1934
Etienne
"Traite de l'Office," Mlle. Laignier, Paris, 1845
Farmer, F. M.
"All New Fannie Farmer Cooking School Cookbook," 10th ed., Little, Brown, 1959
Fowler, et al
"Food for Fifty," Wiley, New York, 1941
Fox, S. J., Foster, J. F.
"Introduction to Protein Chemistry," Wiley, New York, 1957
Frandsen, J. & Arbuckle, W. S.
"Ice Cream and Related Products," Avi, Westport, 1961
Garrett, T. F.
"Encyclopaedia of Practical Cookery," L. Upcott Gill, London, n. d.
Gogue, A.
"Secrets de la Cuisine Francaise," Hachette, Paris, 1956
Gouffe, Jules
"Royal Cookery Book," Sampson Low, London, 1883
Gunstone, F. D.
"An Introduction to the Chemistry of Fats and Fatty Acids," Wiley, New York 1958
Halliday, E. G., Noble, I. T.
"Food Chemistry and Cookery," Univ. Chicago Press, Chicago, 1941
Halliday, E. G., Noble, I. T.
"Hows and Whys of Cookery," Univ. Chicago Press, Chicago, 1933
Harden, P.
"Traditional Dishes of Britain," Bodley Head, London, 1953
Hill, R. G.
"Fruit and Vegetable Buying Guide," USDA, Washington, 1955
Institute of Shortening and Edible Oils
"Chemistry of Food, Fats and Oils," Washington, 1957
Jacobs, M. B.
"Chemistry and Technology of Food and Food Products," Interscience Pub., N.Y. 1951
Justin, M. M. et al
"Foods," Houghton Mifflin, Boston, 2nd. ed., 1940
Kettner
"Book of the Table," Kettners Ltd., London, 1877
Kirkland, John
"Bakers A B C," Gresham, London, 1927
Kitchiner, Wm.
"Cook's Oracle," Simpkin and Marshall, London, 1829
Von Loescecke, H. W.
"Drying and Dehydration of Foods," Reinhold, New York, 1943

Selected Bibliography

Lowe, Belle
"Experimental Cookery," Wiley, New York, 1943
Macleod, A. L. & Nason, E. H.
"Chemistry and Cookery," 2nd ed., McGraw-Hill, New York, 1937
Packaging Catalog Corp.
"Modern Packaging Encyclopedia," New York, 1955
Montagne, P., Salles, P.
"Le Grand Livre de la Cuisine," Flammarion, 1929
Morgan, A. F., Hall, I. S.
"Experimental Food Study," Farrar and Rinehart, New York, 1938
Nord, F. F.
"Advances in Enzymology," Interscience Publisher, N.Y., 1961
Paul, P. et al
"Changes in Histological Structure and Palatability of Beef During Storage,"
Food Research, 221 (9), 1944
Pigman, W.
"Carbohydrates: Chemistry, Biochemistry, and Physiology," Academic, New York,
1957
Ranhofer, Charles
"Epicurean," Hotel Monthly Press, 1920
Richards, Paul
"Cakes for Bakers," Bakers' Helper Co., 4th ed., 1932
Rivers, Frank
"Hotel Butcher, Garde Manger and Carver," Hotel Monthly Press, Chicago, 1935
Rombauer, I. S.
"Joy of Cooking," Bobbs-Merrill Co., Indianapolis, 1962
Simon, A. L.
"Concise Encyclopedia of Gastronomy," Farrar, Strauss & Co., New York, 1948
Swanson, C. O.
"Physical Properties of Dough," Burgess, Minneapolis, 1943
Swettman, M. D.
"Food Preparation," Wiley, New York, 1943
Tanner, F. W.
"Microbiology of Foods," 2nd ed., Garrad Press, Champaign, Ill., 1944
Tiedjens, V. A.
"The Vegetable Encyclopedia and Gardener's Guide," New Home Library, New
York, 1943
Ude, L. E.
"French Cook," no pub., 1814
Ward, Artemas
"The Encyclopedia of Food," Baker and Taylor Co., New York, 1929
Zim, H. S., Ingle, L.
"Seashores: A Guide to Animals and Plants Along the Beaches," Golden, New
York, 1955

Index

Index

Index

Index